# Professional Bone

CHRIS WARNER

*Wagon Publishing*
*Fairhope, Alabama*

©2009 Wagon Publishing. All rights reserved.

No part of this book may be reproduced, stored in a retrieval system, or transmitted by any means without the written permission of the author.

First published on: 09/25/2009

Printed in the United States of America
Bloomington, Indiana

This book is printed on acid-free paper.

<u>Disclaimer</u>

This art-imitating-life story is inspired by actual events. However, certain characters may be loose composites consisting of traits from sometimes multiple, real people; or, are entirely, and singularly, fictitious. In some cases, incidents, characters and timelines have been liberally altered for obvious dramatic purposes. Any uncanny similarity to any person living or dead could be coincidental, and if not, is merely for entertainment value and bears no malicious intent whatsoever. Nevertheless, the plot, storyline, timeline, named characters and events depicted in this novel are purely and utterly fictitious and are meant chiefly to titillate the conscience and to inspire real change among humankind.

# Acknowledgments

Many people have supported me in this effort. However, Aaron Beam has been most instrumental in this regard. Thanks Aaron. Also, thanks to my friends, like Paul F. Ripp of Fairhope, and family, for they are always supportive of my endeavors.

# 1

Dr. Ron Barton admired the soft firmness and scent of Amanda Lucci's naked back and the tender way a small tuft of brown hair fell on the nape of her neck. He firmly placed a hand on each shoulder and drew himself closer. "Does it hurt?" he asked, as he gently massaged her upper back and neck with his thumbs and forefingers.

Amanda had sprained her upper back and neck a few days earlier playing polo when her horse stopped abruptly and threw her headlong from the saddle.

"I'm still sore," she faintly replied, seeming to enjoy his professional touch. "Although it's not bothering me as much as it was at first."

"Still using the whirlpool?"

"Yes, every night."

"Good. You still taking the pain medication I prescribed?"

"No, they give me an upset stomach. But it's not hurting like it was. I think I'm okay."

He removed his hands from her shoulders and grabbed a nearby clipboard and began scribbling.

"You should be fine soon--back in the saddle in just a few more days. You're healing nicely; just don't do anything strenuous—and no riding—for the next two weeks. I'll see you again then and by that time you should be ready for release." He paused.

"Okay?" he asked, raising the intonation of his voice.

She turned to him, squaring her shoulders. She looked up to him and smiled, clutching the hospital gown to her heaving bosom, its deep crease more than noticeable.

"Okay, Dr. Barton."

He returned the smile and made direct eye contact with her. Blushing, his gaze quickly shifted from her perfectly symmetrical face, to her cleavage, to the glistening 32-carat diamond on her left hand, which reminded him of her unavailability.

"I'll see you in a couple of weeks, alright?"

"You will." She coyly smiled.

"Go ahead and get dressed."

He exited the room, closing the door behind him. She shifted her gaze, following his every move until he was no longer with her.

*\*\*\**

Dr. Ron Barton was one of Birmingham's most eligible bachelors. A former standout pitcher and outfielder for Auburn University, he attended the University of Alabama at Birmingham Medical School on academic scholarship after being named a Rhodes Scholar in his third year at Auburn.

Although he'd had several girlfriends during his college and graduate school days, none had captured his focus as much as his studies had, and therefore he never married. Many had tried, however; and somewhat unbeknownst to him, many were still trying. When he first moved to Birmingham after medical school he met a young Harvard Medical School graduate, Dr. Leah Thompson, a general surgeon, at a cocktail party for the opening of a new surgery wing. Initially Ron found Leah as pretty as she was smart. A former National Merit Scholar from Rhode Island, she was extremely intelligent. Ron dated her steady for a couple of years, and even lived with her for six months, but ended the relationship when she pressured him to marry. While Ron certainly thought she was a likely candidate, his dedication to his profession and the fact that he was not completely "sold" on the concept of a lifetime of Leah, returned him to the freedom and fun associated with bachelor life. Despite the breakup, he and Leah remained friends, as they had much in common. They regularly had lunch since their offices were nearby one another.

Born in Fairhope, Alabama in 1960, Ron Barton was a hometown hero. The son of a pediatrician and housewife, the former young polo player, high school quarterback and pitcher was named "Most Athletic" and "Most Likely to Succeed" by his classmates, as he was as well-rounded as he was an academic, boasting a 4.0 grade point average as well as holding the office of Class President. It turned out his classmates were correct in their prediction, as Barton became one of Birmingham's most promising young orthopedic surgeons with a thriving practice, a beautiful home, a shiny black *Porsche 911* and an equally impressive polo game.

It was during one of his many competitive polo matches that Ron Barton previously spotted Amanda Lucci's glaring beauty. She had finished her ladies' match and was intently watching—in particular, Dr. Barton aggressively attack the field on his gorgeous black stallion. At the time, in which they traded several glances over the course of the match, he'd asked a fellow teammate and colleague who Amanda was, only to discover that she was the much younger wife of Philip Lucci, the profligate CEO and Founder of Dixie Rehab, one of Birmingham's biggest and most successful businesses. In short—she was taken—big time. Nevertheless, during their second meeting in his medical office in as many weeks, he felt a definite attraction between them.

\*\*\*

Amanda Bishop was born into abject poverty in Pelham, Alabama in 1959. The daughter of an alcoholic father who barely worked between drinking binges and a mother crippled badly by Multiple Sclerosis, she vowed early to find a way out of the paycheck-to-paycheck misery that was her troubled matchbox home family life. A high school cheerleader and beauty pageant queen five times over, she was the kind of girl that made heads quickly turn. With dark brown hair, piercing blue eyes and a sultry, olive complexion, she was strikingly good-looking, and possessed a busty, athletic figure that made her a shoe-in during University of Alabama Cheerleader tryouts. During her senior year she was crowned Miss Alabama. Because of her ravaging looks, everything always seemed to fall into place for Amanda. After graduating from the Capstone with a marketing degree, she landed a lucrative position selling pharmaceuticals to doctors in Birmingham's burgeoning medical complex. Although she often dated wealthy doctors, she somehow managed to stay single, until a fateful day in 1989.

During a hospital visit in downtown Birmingham to see one of the doctors she regularly called on, Amanda was introduced to Philip Lucci, the recently divorced, multi-millionaire entrepreneur who had taken Birmingham and the medical industry by storm with his innovative Dixie Rehab Corporation. Although she did not find Lucci particularly physically handsome, she was nonetheless more than intrigued by his overflowing confidence, enormous wealth and growing social status and power. Lucci subsequently courted her relentlessly, lavishing her with bouquets of flowers, exorbitant shopping sprees, jaunts to Vegas, Paris and Belize, and of course, jewelry. After dating for three months Philip proposed on one knee at the popularly exclusive *Highlands* restaurant. When Amanda opened the box the ring came in and saw the scintillating 32-carat rock, she was speechless. Although she secretly had reservations about Philip's dubious character, she said yes, as she knew as Philip's wife that she would never have to work again, and that she would always enjoy the finer things in life. It was her dream fulfilled. A few weeks later they were married in Palm Beach, Florida in the backyard of Philip's newly purchased, 10,000 square-foot pastel mansion, before 500 family, friends and subservient employees of Dixie Rehab.

***

Philip Darin Lucci was born in Phoenix City, Alabama in 1950. A former high school dropout and pot dealer, Lucci spent his early years chasing good times, loose women and an insatiable pipe dream of becoming a country and western star. A series of failed garage bands were his mainstay during those early years, barely enabling him to manage a single-wide trailer park existence. When his fifth band failed to make it big like he planned, his 21$^{st}$ birthday arrived and he finally realized it was time to try something else. A litany of odd jobs, ranging from gas station attendant to used car washer to brick layer barely paid the bills for him and his wife and son born out of wedlock. Soon a second child came, and the bills only mounted further.

Upon losing his trailer to a tornado spun off from the eye of a category five hurricane, Lucci turned to higher education as an answer to his financial troubles, enrolling at Jefferson State Community College, where he later earned an associate's degree. From there he enrolled in the University of Alabama-Birmingham's Physical Therapy program, where he graduated within three years as a full-fledged physical therapist—with honors.

Nearly broke, Lucci began working immediately as a physical therapist. The money he made was more than he'd ever had, but the newfound privilege only fueled his want for more. He worked nights at UAB teaching physical therapy classes and within two years of his graduation—at the age of 26—he was offered a corporate position at Southern Rehabilitation Services, a health care company that managed rehabilitation clinics within larger hospitals. Soon after taking the much higher paying position of Vice President for Rehab Services, Lucci learned that he had an uncanny business knack. He realized that he was as smart, or smarter than his competitors, and more importantly—that he easily outworked them all, putting in on average an 80-hour work week.

In due time, Lucci was Southern Rehab's brightest star—responsible for over 200 reporting employees in over a dozen hospitals across the Deep South. With a generous salary and bonus package he was bringing in six figures during the late 1970's, a more than respectable amount for the times; that is, until Wall Street came calling.

In early 1980, at the beginning of what can only be typified as the Post-Modern Health Care Bubble, Southern Rehab was bought out by Blue Shield Health for millions. Blue Shield's management chose not to hire Lucci, and after the acquisition he found himself out of work and seemingly out of luck. However, Lucci learned much at Southern Rehab. Specifically, he saw that the United States Federal Government was paying big bucks for rehabilitative care; and he knew that if he could provide the service at a much lower cost than competing firms, he'd reap not only great profits, but more importantly—he'd spawn a business model that was so attractive to investors that it would be nearly impossible to keep it from going public. Moreover, Lucci knew that if it went public, he'd soon be a millionaire many times over. As it turned out, he was absolutely right on both counts.

After meeting with venture capitalists in the wake of Southern Rehab's buyout, Lucci formed Dixie Rehab with his former controller at Southern, Baron Screem, and two other physical therapists from Southern, with Philip serving as the CEO and Baron being the CFO. Within six months Dixie had acquired two small facilities and outfitted them to provide what they termed "World-class out-patient rehabilitative care." Within a year the fledgling company was deemed profitable with revenues approaching ten million. Riding the rising health care industry trend Lucci aggressively sold his novel concept to any and every investment banker that would listen to his lofty pitch.

Apparently for Lucci, the timing was right, because getting the capital necessary to go public wasn't a problem. Moreover, the initial public offering went equally well. In a matter of months Lucci's dream of becoming a millionaire was realized—almost five times over. But for Lucci, it was only the beginning. As he saw it, he was on his way to becoming even richer.

***

Ron Barton wasn't a successful medical doctor because of his looks; although, they certainly didn't hurt, especially with his female clientele. Barton was sought after as a physician because he was innovative and thorough in his approach to treating patients. Specifically, his methods countered in many ways the prevailing orthopedic standards forged and practiced by his competing Birmingham colleagues. Barton believed in prehabbing, rather than rehabbing his patients. This unique practice, born from his experience as a conditioned athlete, entailed putting each surgery candidate through a rigorous pre-surgery training regimen that he felt strengthened the body to the point that it gave it the best possible chance for post-surgery success. Of course, he prescribed rehabilitative care like his colleagues regularly did, but less of it. Nevertheless, it was his progressive patient prehab exercise routine that set his practice apart from that of other local and national orthopedic surgeons.

Barton's unorthodox methods proved fruitful as patient after patient reported by word of mouth that they bounced back from surgery quicker and their range of motion reverted almost always as it was before the surgery. Within five years Barton's practice boomed and his name was regularly mentioned among the city's other elite sports injury physicians.

# 2

Amanda Lucci entered the four-digit code that opened the heavy, beautifully-adorned, automatic, black wrought iron gate that controlled access to her sprawling 40-acre Vestavia Hills estate. After the gates slowly moved inward, creating an adequate opening, she pressed the accelerator on her cardinal red *BMW* convertible and zoomed up her half-mile long, winding driveway leading to a 7,000-square foot Tudor-style home that her husband Philip built for her shortly after they were married.

The marmalade autumn sun began its slow descent into the western horizon, casting a long, tree line shadow over their property. Her husband, Philip, was shooting skeet with his bodyguard, Jim Boudreaux, in the vast designated recreation area to the right of their home. In the distance four horses grazed. She opened the automatic garage door with the clicker button attached to her sun visor, parked the vehicle and closed the door with a second click.

Upon entering her home through the garage entrance Amanda was greeted in the kitchen by her maid, Isadora, a Spanish immigrant who had been working for them for almost five years since the home was built in 1991.

"Good evening Miss Amanda."

"Hello Isadora."

"How is your neck and back? Are you feeling better?"

"Yes, I am. Thank you. I just left the doctor and he says I'll be riding again soon."

"That is excellent. I am glad to hear it. I have cooked dinner for you and Mr. Philip and Mr. Jim. I will be setting the table in a few minutes. Should I open a bottle of wine?"

"Jim's having dinner with us?"

"That's what Mr. Philip said."

Amanda grimaced and said nothing.

"No wine for me. Thanks Isadora. I'm going to shower and change. When do you expect dinner to be ready?"

Isadora looked at her watch.

"It's 5:45 now. I guess in about 45 minutes or so. I told Mr. Philip 6:30."

"Okay. I'll see you then."

Amanda went upstairs and turned on the water to her sunken Jacuzzi tub for two. She walked into her thirty-yard long closet, picked out a dress that she had never worn, and laid it over her vanity bench. She stripped naked. She turned on the television with a nearby remote control and put in on the local *Fox News* affiliate. With a hand on the towel rack she tested the water temperature. It was above tepid, just like she preferred. She stepped into the tub and slowly eased her torso below the water line, assuming a supine position on the angled tub bed. She pressed the button to turn on the whirlpool and slowly decompressed as the dual jets worked her neck and upper back.

The portrait of business, the evening news anchor was a handsome young thirty-something in a dark suit, white collared shirt and bright red tie.

"Dixie Rehab CEO Philip Lucci announced today plans to build a world-class digital hospital off of Interstate 280 within two city blocks of its corporate offices," he began. "Lucci said that the $50 million state-of-the-art, standard-setting building will take nearly two years to complete and will create more than 10,000 construction jobs and 4,500 permanent health care positions once it's completed."

The television image switched to a head shot of Lucci in a $5,000 Armani suit. His receding, dyed hairline was made less noticeable by his seemingly sketched, pencil-thin moustache. Behind him was Dixie

Rehab's logo—a large "D/R" emblazoned onto a glistening shield fleeced with gold paint. As he spoke, he gesticulated emphatically with his right hand.

"The digital hospital is something we at Dixie Rehab have envisioned for some time now. It's just the next logical step toward bringing unparalleled rehabilitative sports medicine to Birmingham, Alabama. It will be a facility that the community will be proud of—one that houses the world's best health care providers in an unprecedented, completely digitally-wired, health care environment."

The news anchor reappeared instantaneously.

"Lucci said that Dixie Rehab will immediately begin recruiting qualified health care professionals from around the world to staff his newest health care venture, and of course, that special consideration will be given to area providers. In other news today in Birmingham…"

Amanda was shocked at the news. Philip had told her nothing of his latest grand plan to revolutionize Birmingham health care, but it was not surprising, since he had told her little regarding his business dealings since they had been married six years earlier. It seemed that Philip wanted Amanda only as a trophy wife—for her to be there when he needed her—at social and media events, and of course in the evenings, when he wanted action. She was expected to be there and be square at these appropriate times and to do what was necessary to please him. In return she received an allowance of $20,000 every four weeks—deposited automatically into her personal account on the last day of each calendar month. While she certainly enjoyed the money, the worldly stuff and the opulent, upscale lifestyle, she had become increasingly miserable over time, as her relationship with Philip was like any other of his—strictly business.

During the time that they had been married Amanda had begun to not only question why she had married Philip simply for money, she began to question herself. At 36 she was no longer naïve. She now wondered about her future, her long-term happiness, and whether or not she would ever have a loving family life. Philip had two children from his first marriage—a boy and a girl. He spoiled them rotten and as a result Amanda's relationship with them was tolerable, at best. Philip had repeatedly urged her to become pregnant, but she had so grown to loathe him and his narcissistic, controlling ways that she continued taking the pill.

The timer on the whirlpool finished and the water and bubbles began to settle. Lost in her thoughts, Amanda was no longer watching the television, so she turned it off. She rose and stepped out of the tub. She grabbed a thick cotton towel and buried her face in its softness. She held the soothing comfort of the towel to her face for an extended several seconds, letting her pores dry as they cooled in the chilly, conditioned air. Her nipples stood fully erect on her natural, still perky breasts.

"Looking good, kid!" yelled Philip from behind her.

Startled, she quickly removed the towel from her face and wrapped her torso, folding over the towel in front to secure it.

"You know I hate it when you do that!" she said. "Why do you do that?"

Philip quickly moved into her bubble. He put his arms around her and nestled his chin at the base of her neck, making kissing noises as he pretended to smooch her up and down her shoulder.

"My neck! Stop! You are going to hurt my neck! I'm still sore!" she yelled.

Philip quickly pulled away.

"I'm sorry sweetheart. I forgot. I didn't mean to hurt you."

He appeared genuinely sympathetic, as he was secretly fearful she might not give him sex that evening if he had hurt her.

"Leave me be. I need to get ready for dinner."

"Sure darling. I'll leave you alone. I see you are wearing this pretty dress," he said, pointing to the one she had selected.

"Yes."

"It is new, isn't it?"

"Yes Philip, it's new! Please let me get ready!"

"Yes darling. I'll see you downstairs in a few minutes. Jim is here, you know?"

"Yes, I know, Isadora told me. Please let me get ready! I'll be down soon."

"Alright then," he said, closing the French bathroom doors behind him.

# PROFESSIONAL BONE

Philip asked Amanda if her dress was new because he refused to allow her to wear any piece of clothing—underwear, stockings, blouses, dresses, pants, suits, or anything else—more than once. As ridiculous as the rule was, he never let his wife wear the same thing twice. He did not make her throw the clothes away, however; although she could for all he cared. He allowed her to donate the clothes to the *Salvation Army* or the *Goodwill*, to local churches or for charitable fundraisers. Amanda was at first appalled at being forced into the unfathomable, wasteful practice, but in time it became customary, and just another routinely peculiar aspect of her life with the uncompromising "King Philip" of Birmingham.

Amanda checked her look in the mirror. The new dress fit her well, accentuating her hourglass figure in more ways than one. It was revealing on top and snug around her narrow midriff. She checked her magnificent look in the mirror, sprayed perfume on her wrists, rubbed them together and then misted her neck before beginning her descent down the winding, alabaster staircase to join Philip and Jim for dinner.

Amanda grimaced earlier when she realized Jim Boudreaux was having dinner with them because she disliked him. The head of Philip's ridiculous security detail, he was a shifty character, with equally sinister looks. He had a long, narrow face. His black wavy hair was long and worn in a ponytail; and his bushy, black eyebrows grew together in the middle of his short forehead. Moreover, he was a tall fellow—a good head taller than Philip, who was only 5'8". As his name would indicate, Boudreaux was from South Louisiana—Lafayette to be exact. A former Louisiana State Policeman and Baton Rouge city beat cop, he met Philip at the dog track in Mobile, Alabama a year earlier while Philip was winning big. Philip bought drinks for everyone that night, and Jim, who knew a good thing when he saw it, introduced himself. After several rounds of complimentary drinks and conversation regarding Jim's security expertise, Philip was convinced he needed his protection. By the end of the night Philip told Boudreaux he wanted to hire him to form and run Dixie Rehab's new security force. Since that time Jim's presence had become more and more commonplace around the house, as Philip insisted he follow him home to ward off what he curiously labeled "bad business."

Amanda had a difficult time understanding why Philip needed a security detail for a rehabilitative health care company. In addition to Boudreaux, Philip hired six other "bodyguards" to assist him in securing the Dixie Rehab headquarters and maintaining protective confidence when Philip traveled. After his hire, Boudreaux implemented an incredibly expensive security system at the company headquarters that included over two dozen closed circuit television cameras and multiple layers of fingerprint and identification card recognition throughout the multi-story building. Dixie Rehab employees joked that it was more secure than Fort Knox. Furthermore, in order to enter Philip's penthouse on the top floor required special permission. Once upstairs after clearing a litany of checkpoint hurdles with the help of downstairs security, any visitor had to stand before a video camera and await an official "buzz-in" from King Philip himself—not his secretary. To Amanda, it was all too hokey, and she blamed it squarely on Jim Boudreaux.

"Good evening, Amanda!" said Jim Boudreaux once he noticed her at the base of the staircase. Jim stood next to Philip. Both men wore dinner jackets without ties. Both held cocktails, as they stood at the full bar, looking up at her as she descended. Nearby, the dinner table was set, replete with silver candelabra and candlelight. The living room was a massive, luxurious space with large sofas, extravagant pillows, sitting chairs, Afghan rugs, nineteenth century European tapestries and rare artwork. The space was so overdone with showmanship that it appeared gaudy.

"Hello, Jim," she smugly replied.

"You look lovely this evening," he added.

"Doesn't she though?" chimed Philip.

"Thank you gentlemen," she relented.

"Can I fix you a drink?" asked Jim.

"Certainly. Vodka Collins—thank you much," said Amanda, thinking she needed one to put up with his shit.

Jim jumped at the chance to serve her. He scurried around behind the bar and began concocting her libation.

"How was your day today darling?" asked Philip.

"Fine. I went to the doctor's office again and he said that I'll be back riding in a couple of weeks if I continue to rest."

"Really? That's good news."

There was a pause. Jim handed Amanda her drink. She thanked him.

"Who were you seeing again? I forgot," said Philip.

"I told you last time," said Amanda. "Dr. Barton. I'm seeing Dr. Ron Barton, at the Sports Med Clinic."

Philip was embarrassed. He remembered she had mentioned the doctor's name before. It was a name he had also heard repeatedly recently from other doctors and health care administrators. Barton's reputation was good—the buzz was that he was young and smart—and especially handsome.

"Oh, yes. I'm sorry darling. I forgot. I understand that he is a reputable physician."

Lucci paused for effect.

"Do you like him?" he asked.

Amanda cautioned her response.

"I think he's a good doctor. He is pleasant, and he seems to care."

"I've heard about this young doctor. He is really building a practice from what I hear."

"You may want to contact him about joining Dixie," interjected Boudreaux.

"That's exactly what I was thinking!" exclaimed Philip. "Our new digital hospital will have an entire wing dedicated to sports medicine. Dr. Barton could be a tremendous draw for us. I think it's definitely time we look into the possibility of having him join our team. A horse like Barton could really help us pull the Dixie Rehab wagon," said Philip, winking at Boudreaux after he spoke.

Jim beamed.

Amanda cringed at the thought of Barton too being used.

Isadora walked into the living room.

"Dinner is served."

\*\*\*

Ron Barton finished the last five-minute interval of a sixty-minute workout on the elliptical machine at the Birmingham YMCA. Sweating profusely, he was in a zone that he knew resulted only from continuous exercise. A firm believer in the famous Greek adage that, "When the body's in motion the mind is at ease," he was a gym regular in the early morning hours, as it was his therapy. He worked out daily before reporting to his office at 8:30 a.m., alternating between cardiovascular and free weights.

Having come to the end of his programmed workout, Ron Barton stepped down from the machine's foot holds and used a hand towel that had been resting on the handrail to dry the dripping sweat from his body. The LED display blinked that he had burned 560 calories.

"Hey Ron! What's up man?" asked a familiar voice.

"Pete! Good mornin'!" They shook hands.

Dr. Pete Goldman, from Houston, was an osteopath near the same age as Ron, who worked with him in the Birmingham Sports Med Clinic. While they shared the same workplace, rarely did they ever see each other, except at the Y, since they were both avid exercisers. Pete had just finished running, and like Ron, was drenched in sweat and feeling the rushing endorphin fruits of his labors.

"Ron, I'm glad I ran into you! It seems like we hardly ever see each other anymore."

"No kidding. I've been slammed. New patients all the time it seems."

"I hear you, man. No problem. I understand."

"It's been crazy."

"Look, I wanted to tell you—I'm leaving the clinic."

Ron was surprised. He couldn't imagine Pete leaving their group.

"What? Why? What's going on?"

"I got an offer from Philip Lucci at Dixie Rehab. I'm going to be a part of their group that moves into the new digital hospital when it's built. In the meantime, I'm going to work at their Mountain Brook satellite office."

Ron wondered about the digital hospital—he had not heard of it, and why Pete would leave. He telegraphed his thoughts with an incredulous look.

Pete picked up on it immediately.

"They're nearly doubling my salary, Ron. I've got to take it. Besides, when the hospital's finished my office is going to be incredible—state of the art—a fantastic tower view, digitized records, the whole nine yards. It's a no-brainer, really."

Ron thought it sounded too good to be true, and he remembered what his dad had always told him about such things.

Nevertheless, he pushed his rational thoughts aside, given the circumstances.

"I'm happy for you, Pete! Congrats! Good luck, and you know I'll still refer clients to you."

"Thanks Ron! Hey, let's stay in touch! Although, I'm sure I'll be seeing you here in the mornings."

"Absolutely!" replied Ron.

"Good enough, then. I'll check you later!"

"Have a good one, Pete!"

Ron's conversation with Pete Goldman was unsettling. He thought about this larger-than-life, multimillionaire character Philip Lucci he'd only read and heard about and his boastful concept of a state-of-the-art digital hospital, him doubling Pete's salary, and the possibility of his losing clients to this obviously growing and potentially formidable medical group. Pete Goldman was a respected doctor. More than that, he was a good guy who was popular. His joining ranks with Dixie Rehab meant that other good doctors were surely going to follow him. Ron's thoughts drifted back to the other Lucci—Amanda, and how beautiful she appeared the day before, and how she flirted with him. "Philip Lucci," he thought. "Who the hell *is* this guy and how does he pull all this shit off?" As he headed to the showers and eventually to work, he was perplexed.

Later that day Ron met Dr. Leah Thompson, his old flame, for lunch at *Surin West* at Five Points South near the burgeoning, hive-like downtown medical complex. He enjoyed ice water and lemon and a fantastic bowl of spicy soup while he waited for her to show. As usual, she was running late. It was 12:40 and they were supposed to meet ten minutes earlier. He simply couldn't wait to nourish. He had eaten a light breakfast of toast and juice and had already burned those calories during the workout. He needed fuel. A couple minutes later Leah walked through the vestibule and spotted him in the first table to her left. Ron was drinking the tasty soup from the bowl.

"Thanks for waiting for me. I see I am still highly regarded."

Ron gave her a contrite "That's unfair" look, as if they were still dating.

"I was starving. I worked out this morning before work. I've had nothing since breakfast!"

"And you couldn't wait ten minutes?"

He looked at his watch. It was 12:42 p.m. He pointed to his watch face.

"*Twelve* minutes to be exact."

"Whatever." She smiled. "What's going on Doc?" she implored in her Northeastern accent, in a much more feminine, higher-pitched tone that got his attention and indicated that everything was still fine between them.

Ron thought she looked good. She did most of the time. But today she glowed particularly in her navy business attire. They both had left their white coats at the office.

"Are you ovulating?" he asked.

She nearly spit her water.

"What?" Leah asked, incredulous to the lofted grenade. "Are you serious?"

"Yes. Are you ovulating? It's science-related…seriously…"

Her expression shifted. She blushed.

"I am, as a matter of fact." She cracked a timid smile. "Why?"

"I read that women appear to glow when they are ovulating…sort of a nature's makeup, you know?"

"Really?"

"Yeah. *New England Journal of Medicine*—last month. You look great, by the way."

Leah was taken aback by his odd approach to flattery, but she liked it.

"Thanks Ron."

The waiter arrived, took their orders, their menus, and left.

"What do you know about Philip Lucci?" asked Ron.

Leah was the kind that was well-read. She wasn't an exercise freak; she didn't play polo, and she wasn't consumed with her job. Some might say she had a life. She religiously read the papers and the local society magazines, like *Black & White*. She gossiped. As a result, she was firmly "in the loop."

"Well, other than the fact that he's definitely creepy, I know he's a former gas station attendant turned health care CEO, probably a narcissist, and on his second wife, a former Alabama cheerleader and beauty queen. Why do you ask?"

"He offered Pete Goldman a position at his new digital hospital making nearly twice his salary. Pete took it. He says that Lucci promised him an office with a spectacular view, state-of-the-art trappings, everything except the moon. How can he afford to do all of that? And what do you mean he's 'definitely creepy'?"

"First off—he can afford to do 'all of that' because he has created with Dixie Rehab what is the equivalent of the *McDonald's* of rehabilitative care. He operates rehab clinics in all fifty states, Puerto Rico and Guam, employs over 100,000 people and is either a principal or equity investor in over a dozen different health care companies. He's a darling of Wall Street. Dixie Rehab's stock has met Street expectations for almost a decade. He's an unreal success story. He's got his name on everything around here—the Philip Lucci Day Care Center, Philip Lucci Field, the Philip Lucci Library in Vestavia. I'm sure I'm missing something. He's all over the place."

Ron was duly impressed. "But creepy?"

"Oh, yeah. I was at a cocktail party one night for a friend who is friends with Amanda Lucci, Philip's brunette *Barbie Doll* wife. It was my friend's birthday out at her house in Vestavia Hills. Phil and Amanda were invited. She's got this obnoxious ring she wears. It's absurd. It must be fifty carats! Anyway, Amanda and my friend were on the other side of the room admiring her designer dress when Lucci made his way over to where I was. He introduced himself and we made small talk, but I swear it was like he was mentally undressing me. It gave me the willies. I felt like I needed to shower afterward. He's gross. I don't see how she sleeps with him."

Ron thought, "Because he's filthy rich."

"So Dixie Rehab is that big now?" he asked.

"And getting bigger. Didn't you read the paper this morning?"

Ron shook his head. He was busy working out at the YMCA.

"Lucci announced yesterday that he's building a $50 million digital hospital. It's another great idea. I hate chasing paper records for patients, and Lucci's plan, according to one of my colleagues that knows him, is to completely change the way patient information is entered, stored, retrieved and shared by health care providers. Creep or no creep, he's brilliant. Somebody should have done this a long time ago. The technology has been available for a decade."

"Your colleague you mentioned, is she going to work for Lucci too?"

"You know, I bet she does. She mentioned before that she felt she would get an offer to work for him, and it said in the paper this morning that Lucci is going to be recruiting local doctors to fill the hospital. His plan is likely to get all the doctors to refer their clients for rehab and physical therapy with his clinics inside the building. The Feds are paying big bucks for rehab through Medicare and Medicaid."

Ron was starting to see it all for what it was.

"How much do you think he is worth?" He asked.

"Who? Lucci?"

"Yeah."

"Hmmm…that's a really good question. I read in *Forbes* that he's one of the highest-paid CEO's in the country—that with his salary, generous bonuses and outrageous stock options for his many companies that he pulls down about $100 million annually. But, he spends nearly as much as he makes from what I hear. He has several homes and cars—and jet airplanes. I'd say he is worth somewhere in the neighborhood of a half billion when you consider his equity in Dixie and his other companies, with at least fifty million in cash and other movables."

"That's a pretty upscale neighborhood."

"You think?" she teased.

Ron thought of his own net worth, and how it paled in juxtaposition. While he made nearly $300,000 per year, malpractice insurance and taxes killed him. He was lucky to see half that as disposable income. It was actually much closer to 45%.

Leah saw Ron's wheels turning fast.

"Do I sense a little jealousy of Mr. Lucci?" she probed.

Ron snapped out of his funk. He felt her question was rude. She knew him well enough to know better.

"There's more to life than money, Leah. I have all the money I need. I know it sounds trite, but I work to make a difference in people—my patients—I work to help them, by being the best doctor that I can."

Leah felt smaller than before the question.

"I wasn't being serious, Ron. You know I think you're a good doctor. I also think you're a good person."

Ron saw she was genuinely sorry and upset that she said what she did. He shouldn't have been so quick to castigate her.

"I'm sorry I snapped Leah. It's no big deal, it's just that I'm a little concerned about this Lucci guy. I have a feeling he's trouble."

The waiter returned with their food.

"Barbecue Chicken and Sushi…" he reported.

# 3

Philip Lucci, CFO Baron Screem and CAO Mack Dawkins, along with the company controller, Will Bowens, and a handful of other reporting vice-presidents, met in the Dixie Rehab Headquarters' posh meeting room. In the center of the long meeting table was a large ice bucket containing diet drinks and bottled water. Near the doorway, situated on each side of the entranceway, was one of Jim Boudreaux's husky, intimidating bodyguards. Each was dressed in a black suit, white shirt and black tie. Each wore an earpiece, a hanging microphone and dark sunglasses.

"All of you know that we are now moving forward with our plans to build the digital hospital. We have approval from the Certificate of Need Board, our financing is done, and we should be breaking ground on the site within the next few days. The construction company says that it will take eighteen months to complete the building, but I have told them they'll get a ten percent bonus if they finish in twelve—that's a ten million dollar bonus—so I suspect it *will* be done in a year like I prefer—if the foreman has any business sense that is." Philip said, laughing heartily.

Will Bowens raised his hand and spoke, "Ten percent of fifty million is five million, boss."

Philip Lucci trained his gaze directly toward Will Bowens, an overweight, balding, pear-shaped accountant from Troy State who had been with the company since just after it went public. Prior to that, he had worked for the *Ernst & Young* accounting firm.

Lucci's eyes darkened. His brow furrowed. His countenance, like Jekkyl and Hyde, altogether changed. The right side of Philip's face twitched nervously three or four times like he'd been hit with small electrical shock treatments. Bowens should have known better. If anyone knew Philip, he did.

"Shut the fuck up Will! You stupid, fat bastard! Who the fuck do you think you are, talking to me like that?"

Will cowered in his seat and looked down at his blank yellow legal pad. The room went deathly silent after the outburst.

"Answer me! Who the fuck do you think you are?"

"I'm sorry Philip."

"You better be sorry you sorry obese sack of shit! Keep that up and you'll be doing taxes from your car!"

In a quick shrug Philip adjusted his tie and took a long sip from his condensation-soaked *Diet Dr. Pepper*. Everyone else around the table pensively waited for him to collect himself and resume the meeting. Strangely, as quickly as he had morphed into a monster, he reverted to the persuasive, charismatic, reassuring salesman that had made him a most unlikely millionaire.

"So, if the building is completed like we want it in a year, we are going to need professionals to staff it. I've already talked to Baron and his accountants and we've created a professional salary schedule and budgeted for it. Our plan is to bring these new professionals into the fold and set them up in our existing metro area clinics until the construction is finished, which we feel should work fine, since it will give them time to learn the Dixie Rehab referral system, and how we do business. Mack has been working on a list of area professionals we are going to aggressively recruit, with a special emphasis on sports medicine, due to its high-profile nature. We feel that we can tailor our marketing efforts toward sports medicine and the celebrity clientele we plan to bring in to be treated. We think this will give us a tremendous edge as we move forward and finally open the new hospital. This is going to require substantial work on our part, but it's doable, according to Baron and Mack—right guys?"

Baron Screem sat up in his chair. He cleared his throat.

Mack spoke up immediately.

"Like Philip said, we're targeting some of the area's hottest sports medicine physicians—orthopedics, osteopaths, and chiropractors, along with their physical therapists and support staffs. We want to build a world-class team, right here in Birmingham—a dream team of physicians that will far surpass the level of care offered amongst our current competitors. In fact, that's our intent—to steal the competent competition across the board to the point where we are the only reputable sports and rehabilitative game in town. We will reduce our competitors to inadequacy. In essence, it will be a monopoly--but it will all be legal, of course."

Mack looked to Philip, who was smiling proudly.

"Of course it's legal!" interjected Philip. "It's pure competition—it's the American way...the Dixie Rehab way!"

Philip laughed out loud. Mack followed, along with the other well-paid sycophants. To all of Philip's subordinates, business was super, their people were terrific, and life was wonderful--except for Baron Screem. Baron bit his tongue. There was nothing more he could add. Mack and Phil had pretty much covered everything. He took another large *Prilosec* pill and washed it down with a gulp of cold, bottled Artesian water.

***

Just after daybreak on a Saturday, Ron Barton drove his two-ton *Ford F-150* pickup truck in front of the empty, covered dual horse carriage he was pulling to Fairhope, Alabama to the horse farm where his mother and father lived. Fairhope was a small retirement community of barely 10,000 people on the Eastern Shore of Mobile Bay near the coast of the Gulf of Mexico. His father had recently retired after thirty years of practice and had been busy breeding polo horses as a way to fill his extra time. His dad had two fillies that were ready to be trained. Ron intended to pick them up and return to Birmingham, where he'd bring them to their new home--the Birmingham Polo Club stables, the place where they would also learn to help Ron play the game he loved almost as much as his profession.

Ron began playing polo when he was in elementary school. His mother and father both played at the field off of Alabama State Highways 98 & 32 in Fairhope, just a mile and a half from his house. Ron really didn't play when he was a youngster, he just tried to—since there wasn't any type of organized league for kids. However, as time passed and he grew, he gradually became proficient with riding and the rules to the point that he was allowed to participate in practice matches with the men, who often welcomed him as it was sometimes difficult to find available players. As did his love for baseball and football, Ron's love of polo grew as quickly as he did on the Eastern Shore of Mobile Bay.

Ron drove into his family's estate at about 10:30 a.m. The Barton's had a four-bedroom, two-story brick home that sat on 25 beautifully landscaped and manicured rolling acres. Live oak and pecan trees dotted the undulating, verdant turf, along with evergreen pines, silver birches and cypress chestnut oaks. Azaleas, Crape Myrtles and Indian Hawthorns added vibrant color. It was the only home he'd ever known.

His dad was busy working in the nearby corral with four horses. Two of them were fillies. The other two were their mothers. Ron's dad noticed him. He settled the horses and exited the corral, walking straight to Ron and his mom, who had already run out to greet him.

"How are you honey?" Ron's mother asked, hugging him tightly. She hadn't seen him in months. She stepped away from her only child and took a good look at him.

"I'm fine, Mom. You doin' okay?"

"I'm good, baby. Daddy and I have been taking it easy. It's been pleasant."

She hugged him again.

"You look so good...so handsome."

"Thanks, Mom. Hey Dad!"

Ron peeled himself away from his mother's clutches and shook hands with his dad. The two hugged afterward.

"How's it goin' son?"

"Fine, Dad. Looking forward to seeing these two new horses run. That's them over there, huh?" Ron pointed to the two younger horses frolicking in the pen.

"That's them," he replied. The fillies pranced around with seemingly boundless energy, their coats shining in the early sunlight. "I think you're going to like them. They come from good stock."

"I can't wait to get them up to Birmingham. I already have a potential buyer for one of them," said Ron.

"Let's go inside. I have brunch ready for us." Ron's mom said.

They moved into the air-conditioned house.

Ron's mother had prepared cut cantaloupe, pimento cheese sandwiches, tomato basil soup, potato chips and fresh iced tea with lemon. Ron loved his mother's pimento cheese sandwiches. It was certainly good to be home. Hungry from his long ride, he finished two sandwiches before he even touched the soup and cut fruit. After devouring the sandwiches, he decided to ask his father questions he'd formulated during the morning drive.

"Dad, have you ever heard of Philip Lucci?"

His father finished chewing his bite of sandwich and swallowed. His expression changed from relaxed contentment to seriousness. He straightened in his chair.

"Yes, I have."

"What do you know about him?"

"He has a house on Ono Island four doors down from ours. He bought it two years ago and completely renovated it. He added two stories. Then, he caused a huge uproar amongst the neighborhood association when he tried to put a 1,000-gallon gas tank in the ground next to the water to fuel all of his boats and jet skis. The association board stopped him and he sued. The association won. He's a real piece of work. I saw him last year at the power boat races driving a cigarette boat about 90 miles per hour after he'd been drinking on the award stage. He's reckless."

Ron's family had maintained a home on Ono Island since he was a young boy. They bought the lot and built their beach home when the parcels sold for only $7,000 apiece because most of the owners thought the land was useless. Their reasoning was that you couldn't grow anything there because of all of the sand. The house was built for $20,000 in 1970. In 1995 the property was appraised by the Baldwin County Tax Assessor's office as having a value of $850,000, as Ono Island no longer had any available lots for development, and was home to many local celebrities, including former Alabama Football quarterback Kenny "The Snake" Stabler.

"Why do you ask?" his father continued.

"Lucci's a big player in the Birmingham health care scene. Actually, he's a huge player. He's building a digital hospital and snatching up good doctors from all over town to work in it. I think he's trying to completely control the market by getting all of the best doctors under one roof and demanding that they refer their patient's rehab care to his company, Dixie Rehab. This past week he got one of my colleagues, Pete Goldman, to sign with his group, after he offered him twice what he was making with us. I'm concerned that his approach will corrupt the system and that if he gets his way he could possibly ruin provision—all for the almighty dollar."

The older Dr. Barton listened while he swallowed two spoonfuls of soup. He wiped his face with a napkin and let his food settle with his thoughts.

"I think you're right. Lucci is definitely all about money. His excess is sickening. He has a heliport behind his house at Ono. He's ridiculously loud and obnoxious. His country band even plays at that beach bar *Live Bait* when he's down here. They put his name on the marquis outside and he even does some silly radio show from there. He's a weirdo if you ask me. Stay clear of him. Let him run his own course. If he makes you an offer, tell him no thanks. Build your practice. You're doing fine, son. Remember what I told you about things that sound too good to be true."

Ron took it all in. He sipped his tea, biting into his lemon peel. "He has a country band? How strange." he thought.

"I remember, dad. I remember." Ron said. He smiled at his father. His dad beamed in appreciation. He was proud of his son.

On his way home to Birmingham that afternoon, Ron's concerns of Philip Lucci and his grandiose plans were somewhat diminished. After talking to his father, he felt that Lucci was the kind of guy that if given enough rope, would ultimately hang himself. He felt his dad was right—he needed to simply stay out of Lucci's way and everything would be okay.

Ron pulled the two new young fillies into the parking lot of the Birmingham Polo Club's stable area. There he met Hector Romero, the trainer who maintained his horses. In all, Ron had three horses stabled at the club, but with the two new arrivals, it raised his total to five. Hector was waiting for Ron outside the stable area. Just as Ron had been in Fairhope, Hector was anxious to see the young creatures he would soon get to care for and train. Both men equally respected the awesome beauty and power the mammals possessed.

"Here they are, Hector. Aren't they pretty?"

Hector walked straight to the trailer and petted the animals through the length-long side opening.

"That they are! Gorgeous my friend! Absolutely gorgeous!"

The two men shook hands. Hector took the first horse out and walked her to her new home inside the stable area.

Ron remained behind and softly stroked the mane of the remaining animal.

"Hey girl," he said. "You're at you're new home. Everything's gonna be alright. Yeah, that's it sweetheart…everything's gonna be just fine…Hector's gonna take good care of you."

"You certainly have a way with the ladies, don't you?" the familiar feminine voice asked. It startled Ron. He turned toward the sound. A few feet away stood Amanda Lucci, wearing skin tight navy blue jeans, smoke gray snakeskin cowboy boots and a pullover sweatshirt that read "Crimson Tide" in bold white block letters. She wore her hair different from a few days earlier in his office. It hung to her shoulder blades and appeared to have been curled. She was walking a beautiful, bridled paint stallion.

"Miss Lucci--well, hello." He blushed, and continued petting the horse through the trailer, although he turned the top of his torso toward her, in amazement.

"You must be feeling better. How are you?" He asked.

"She looks fabulous," he thought, staring at her curvaceous hips and long, muscular legs.

"I am—much better—thanks to you." She smiled, flashing her pearly whites and sky blue eyes behind long, curly eyelashes.

"Now, I don't know about all that…nature is simply taking its course."

She tied off her horse to a nearby post and walked toward him. He continued petting but turned even more toward her approach. When she drew near he offered his hand. She took it.

"Good afternoon," he said. She lightly squeezed and released.

"A new filly? How exciting!" she interjected. She placed her left hand on the new horse's neck and lightly patted and stroked her. Ron noticed her wedding ring was gone from her ring finger.

"Yes, how about it…there is another one, too. Hector just took her away. I think this one is going to be mine. I'm selling the other one."

"She's beautiful!" cooed Amanda. "So sweet."

The young horse appeared to stare out of the side of her head, directly at Amanda.

"You haven't been riding, have you?" Ron asked, the doctor in him coming out.

"No." she said, petting the young animal. "My doctor advised against it, so I'm just walking my horse today, instead of riding. I'll have to wait until he releases me, to ride."

Ron played along.

"Oh, I see."

Butterflies filled his stomach. It was something he had not experienced since Leah.

They made eye contact and held it. Their hands that were petting the horse, spontaneously touched.

Ron pulled away.

"I'm sorry," he said.

She lightly laughed.

"Where's your ring?" he asked, making the necessary move.

Her smile dissipated. Nevertheless, she too seized the opportunity.

"My marriage is one of convenience, *Ron*," she answered. "But lately, it's been wholly inconvenient."

"I see," he managed.

The butterflies again fluttered.

"And you—how have *you* managed to remain single? I cannot see how that's possible," she said.

"Let's just say I'm still looking for 'the one.'"

"Oh, I see. So you're still shopping?"

"Exactly," he answered with a big smile.

"Do you want me to bring the other one inside?" Hector asked, interrupting. "Excuse me."

"Oh, yes, please, Hector. Hector, this is Amanda. Amanda, this is Hector Romero, my trainer."

"Nice to meet you M'am."

"Likewise."

Hector opened the trailer and led the second horse into the depth of the stable, leaving them alone once again.

"What the hell," Ron thought, "I might as well go for it."

"When do *you* plan on *shopping* again?" He asked.

Amanda giggled and replied, "I'm shopping *right now*."

"Oh, really?" he asked, smiling.

"Yeah, really," she said. She was dead serious, looking straight into his eyes. For the first time he saw her vulnerability. Deep in her eyes he saw a little girl.

"I'm scheduled to see you on Tuesday morning at 10:30 a.m. Maybe we could have lunch afterward…what do you think?" She asked.

Staring at her pouting, puffy red lips, he countered.

"Sure, we could have lunch." He thought briefly of Philip Lucci. "There's nothing wrong with that, is there?"

"Hardly," she answered, downplaying the scenario.

"Okay, then. Be thinking of where you would like to go."

"I will. I've got to walk Albert," she said, pulling away. "I'll see you on Tuesday, okay?"

"You will." He said, watching her every move as she sashayed to her horse, untied him, and walked away. After she traveled a few yards she looked over her shoulder and saw that Ron was still watching her. She waved. He returned the wave.

"What the hell am I doing?" he thought. "I'm losing my fucking mind."

As he later drove home he thought about the fact that his superego was disallowing him to "stay out of Lucci's way," like his father advised.

# 4

On Monday morning Ron was walking on the treadmill watching the morning news, when to his surprise, Philip Lucci was again the news focus. The morning anchor said that the State of Alabama was renaming Highway 280 in Birmingham "The Philip Lucci Parkway" later that day in a ceremony involving a local high school band, the Alabama State Department of Transportation and Governor Dan Siegel. The news report only heightened his concerns of Lucci's growing power, as it seemed he was becoming an iconic local figure. "Unreal," he thought.

Later that day Ron had lunch with Dr. Frank Quitman. Frank was a chiropractor friend who worked near the Birmingham Sports Med Clinic with a respected chiropractic group. They were both hurried, so they walked to a nearby Mediterranean café just a block from Ron's office. Ron asked Frank to have lunch with him because Frank was from Phoenix City, Philip Lucci's hometown, and he and Lucci were about the same age. He hoped Frank would be able to tell him something about Lucci's past. He also wanted to talk to him about Lucci's plans for a digital hospital and if it was successful, what it could potentially mean to Birmingham health care.

After they ordered and received their gyro sandwiches, Ron and Frank found a two-top table in the corner, away from the hustle of the lunchtime crowd. Frank's salt and pepper hair was parted to the left. Unlike Ron, Frank was hardly athletic, and his 47-year old body looked more like that of a 55-year old due to lack of exercise. Nevertheless, Frank by all accounts was a capable chiropractor, and was liked by everyone for his bubbly personality and quick wit.

"Frank, you grew up in Phoenix City, right?" Ron asked.

"I did. I call it God's country—it's where God sends the less fortunate."

Ron chuckled.

"Did you know Philip Lucci growing up? He's from there."

Frank was in the middle of chewing a bite of his sandwich. He lost his jovial look as he swallowed.

"I knew Philip, but not well. He wasn't the type your mom wanted you hanging around with, if you know what I mean. Besides, I am a couple of years older than he is."

"What was he like back then? Why wouldn't your mom want you to hang out with him?"

"He was a hippie. I'm pretty sure he dealt drugs. He definitely did drugs. He was pretty psychedelic—and he looked it. He always had a band, but he wasn't a very good country singer."

"He was a country singer?"

"He tried. His act was pretty bad, too. I heard him one time at the county fair. He couldn't carry a tune if it was in a bucket, and the whole performance thing seemed unnatural for him. His hair was really long back then. Darin was one of the first to popularize the mullet—you know—business in the front and party in the back."

They both laughed. Frank continued.

"Darin was his middle name—and everybody called him by his middle name. He never went by Phil or Philip back then. It was always Darin."

"So he went to your high school?" Ron asked.

"He did for a while—until he was expelled for smoking pot in the school restroom. I was a senior when it happened. He was a sophomore. We went to the parochial school together and he had to finish high school at the local public school with the blacks. He may have only gotten a GED, but I am not sure."

Ron had a hard time believing Lucci, despite his sordid past, was on his way to becoming a billionaire.

"He made a real turnaround, wouldn't you say?" Ron asked.

"I would say. It's pretty amazing what he's become, although Darin will probably screw it all up somehow. I wouldn't be surprised if he winds up in prison. He's crazier than a shithouse rat. Believe me."

Ron had no reason to doubt it, after all he had heard.

"Can you believe they're renaming 280 'Philip Lucci Parkway'?" Frank asked.

"I know. I saw that this morning on the news. It's like he's an icon." Ron said.

"I was listening to the Butch Bierbaum show yesterday afternoon and Darin was on with him, announcing that he is now the show's premier sponsor, and that he'll be on twice a week to comment on Alabama Football and Dixie Rehab. I wonder how much that costs? Bierbaum has one of top radio shows in the country. He's all over the Deep South."

Butch Bierbaum was a radio god within the State of Alabama. While he was the talk show host everyone loved to hate—they all listened to him—even when they said they didn't. The quintessential "shit stirrer," he used divisive commentary to daily pit Bama and Auburn fans against one another on nearly every issue. As a result, it made for great radio—and more importantly—great ratings and ad sales. There was always a wait to call in and get on the air with him. Moreover, when anything news worthy happened in the State of Alabama, the national networks always interviewed Bierbaum, as his rolodex of mainstream media contacts was extensive.

"He sits in with Bierbaum during the week, too?" Ron asked.

"Yeah, on Tuesdays and Thursdays."

"Man, he's everywhere."

"Ubiquitous," added Frank. "The way I see it, if he's not part of the solution, he's part of the problem. The guy's a freak. I hear he never sleeps and has no social life. His quest to become a billionaire is all-consuming."

Frank finished his last bite and gobbled a couple of last potato chips.

"Hey, Ron, I'd love to talk about Phil's insanity some more, but I really need to get back to the office. Let's head back."

"Sure thing."

As they walked back to the office, Ron asked a final question of Frank.

"Frank, do you think Lucci will pull off his digital hospital plans?"

"Only if we let him, Ron. Only if we let him. I gotta run, buddy. I'll talk to you soon--and thanks for lunch."

"Sure thing Frank," said Ron, wondering exactly what he meant as he went to his section of the building.

***

Amanda Lucci removed her blouse and placed it on the back of the chair inside the small patient room in Dr. Ron Barton's office. Braless, she donned the multicolor hospital gown provided on a coat hanger that hung on a wall hook. After pushing each of her arms through their respective sleeves, she did not bother to tie the gown behind her neck. It was cold as she waited, as the air conditioning vent briskly blew chilled air into the small workspace that contained a patient table, two metal chairs, a sink, and a mirror. She checked her makeup and decided to freshen up. She reapplied her rouge and combed her hair with a thick brush from her purse. She sat and waited for her doctor in the antiseptic room.

Dr. Ron Barton anticipated his meeting with his most important patient on Tuesday. He checked his watch. It was 10:25, and he had another patient before he saw Amanda Lucci—a ten-year-old boy who had cracked his elbow playing youth football. The X-rays showed that the injury required surgery, and he needed to explain this important fact to the boy and his mother. It was going to take longer than five minutes. He hated to make Amanda wait. He decided to check in on her and let her know he had another patient, but that he'd be right with her. He wondered about where they would have lunch, as planned. He knocked on the door to the room where she waited inside.

"Yes?" she replied. He recognized her lovely high-pitched voice and Southern drawl.

The butterflies again came in a rush. He slowly opened the door and stuck his head through the crease. A seated Amanda looked like packaged dynamite in the hospital gown.

"Good morning!" he said.

"Hey!" she said, sounding nearly two syllables as she spoke.

"I've got to meet with a little boy and his mama. He needs surgery. I'll be right with you, okay?"

"That's fine. I'll see you after that. No rush."

He left her momentarily and went directly to tend to the boy with the cracked elbow.

***

Philip Lucci and Mack Dawkins met in Philip's penthouse suite at the top of the Dixie Rehab headquarters.

"Wanna bump?" asked Lucci, as he spilled two grams of high-grade Columbian cocaine on to the glass-topped area on his mahogany desk.

"Sure, why not?" replied Mack. He was Jonesing for a line. "Make it a rat tail," he added.

Lucci laughed.

"Don't you worry about that."

Lucci pulled out his wallet and removed a hundred dollar bill and his *Platinum Visa* card. He threw the C-Note to Mack.

"Roll this up while I cut the lines," said Philip.

"Not a problem," said Mack.

Philip arranged two long, fat lines of cocaine—one about six and another about nine inches long.

When he was done he asked Mack for the rolled bill. Once he had it in hand he placed it into his right nostril and descended on the line like a hound on a June Bug. Amazingly, like a *Hoover* vacuum, he took the entire line in one slow pull across the glass.

"Damn Philip! You're an animal!" cheered Mack.

Philip stood erect with the bill still in his nose, tilted his head and snorted the remaining powder in the makeshift cylinder. He tilted his head back down and handed the bill to Mack. He stepped aside and walked over to the wet bar. He poured two fingers of triple malt scotch over a short crystal highball glass topped with crushed ice. He turned on the water in the bar's sink, ran the fingers on his right hand through it and placed them underneath his right nostril. He sucked the moisture from his fingers straight into his sinuses, facilitating the drip he so loved and craved. Mack repeated the sequence on his own. After the two were done settling in, they got down to business.

"Phil, Dr. Ron Barton is giving a speech on Friday in St. Louis at the United States Orthopedic Association's annual convention. He's being recognized as one of the nation's top orthopedists, and will be given some type of award while he's there. We really need this guy. If we get him along with Drs. Muster and Appleton we'll be well on our way to where we need to be. Those three are arguably the top orthopedic guys in town."

Philip listened intently. He gave no appearance of being high. The coke was the best money could buy, and he was more than used to its wildly narcotic effects.

"What's your plan for reeling him in?"

Mack smiled, and moved to the edge of his seat. Unlike Philip, he looked antsy.

"I'm going to attend the convention. I'm going to listen to his speech, and then I'm going to approach him and introduce myself as a representative of Dixie Rehab, tell him how impressed we are with him and tell him that we want to meet when he gets back to Birmingham. Once we get the meeting set, I'll leave the rest up to you."

Philip's countenance went from expressionless to a broad smile. He loved it.

"Very clever, Mack—very clever! Introducing yourself at the convention is a great angle. From a professional standpoint, I think he'll be impressed. He should be, anyway. He'll at the very least give us a sit down. Good job. Do it!"

"I plan on it. I fly out Thursday afternoon."

"Want another bump?" asked Philip.

"Absolutely!" Mack said.

\*\*\*

Dr. Ron Barton knocked on his most important patient's door.

"It's Dr. Barton," he called.

"Come in," was the melodic reply.

He entered and closed the door behind him. While he thought of lunch, he knew there was other professional business to handle.

Amanda Lucci sat before him on the examining table. Her legs were crossed at the ankles.

"How are you today?" he asked.

"I'm fine. I feel great. I no longer have any pain in my back and neck. I think I'm all better now."

"Really? That's great. I'm sorry you had to wait."

"It's no bother."

"Okay, let's have you sit here in the chair and we'll take a look and see if you're 'all better.'"

Amanda stepped down, crossing her arms over her chest, holding the gown to her bosom. She took a seat and Ron stepped behind her. He noticed the gown was not tied, completely baring the previously injured area. Her open back was before him. He placed his thumbs and forefingers on her upper back and neck, rubbing her gently.

"Are you feeling any remaining soreness?" he asked.

"Not a bit. Like I said, I feel great."

He pressed harder, kneading her flesh with his digits.

"It seems like you are indeed better. I think you will definitely get a release."

He stepped from behind her and walked to his clipboard on the work counter, turning his back to her.

Amanda uncrossed her arms. The gown fell into a wrinkled pile at her waist, revealing her D-cup cleavage. The air was still cold, and her nipples were completely erect. Goosebumps riddled both breasts. She felt a slight chill.

Dr. Barton scribbled on the clipboard and began talking, his back still turned.

"It's official now," he said.

"What is?" she asked.

He turned and saw her dark brown, silver-dollar-sized areolas staring at him. He saw no tan lines.

"Your release," he stammered.

Amanda smiled seductively.

"I have a suite reserved at the *Wynfrey*. What do you say we order room service for lunch?" she asked.

Ron's head was spinning. He never expected this.

"I'd say you're on," he replied. "Get dressed. I'll be downstairs in the parking lot in ten minutes. I drive a black *Nine-Eleven*."

"I'll be in the red convertible *Beamer*. Follow me." She said.

Ron cancelled his afternoon appointments before he left, citing a family emergency. It was something he'd never done before, as was Mrs. Lucci.

The couple arrived at the *Wynfrey Hotel* at 11:30 a.m. They parked in the covered area underneath the adjoining *Galleria Mall*. Once inside the suite Ron and Amanda quickly shed their clothing. Amanda gave herself completely to Ron, as it had been years since she felt such a physical attraction to a man. During the last several months she and Philip had sex sparingly, if ever.

Ron became lost in Amanda's voluptuous sex appeal. She was the most beautiful woman he'd ever made love to. Physically she was a near perfect ten. "Movie star looks," he thought in his excited state. He loved the way she looked, felt and smelled. He couldn't get enough of her.

Ron finally relented to his growing hunger. At 2:30 p.m. he called room service and ordered breakfast food. After a third round of lovemaking the food arrived and they devoured it, in bed.

"You seem like you haven't had a thing to eat all day."

"Nothing nourishing, anyway," he quipped.

She punched him lightly in his washboard stomach. He pretended that it hurt, laughing.

"Just kidding!" he insisted. "I haven't eaten *any food* since breakfast, and I lifted this morning!"

"Well, you've worked up quite an appetite, then." She admitted.

Ron finished the Eggs Benedict and took a bite of the bagel and cream cheese. After he finished chewing, he stared at Amanda. She wore only her panties and brassiere.

"How is this going to work?" he asked, full of wonder. It was all so surreal. He was as excited as he was scared.

"However we want it to." She replied.

"You sound like you've got it all figured out."

# PROFESSIONAL BONE

"Hardly, but I'm confident we can."

"I like your attitude." He said with a grin.

Ron imagined waking up to her everyday, and what a prize Lucci was losing. Despite the titillating fear, all he could think about was how incredibly sexy Amanda Lucci was. Amanda grabbed the remote control and turned on the television. The tube lit to live coverage of the renaming of Highway 280 the "Philip Lucci Parkway." Footage of Lucci's $25 million *Sikorsky* helicopter landing was displayed. Awaiting his arrival was a host of dignitaries standing next to a symbolic, extremely large red ribbon and bow wrapped over a green road sign with white glittery letters that read "Philip Lucci Parkway." The Governor of the State of Alabama stood nearby with a ridiculously large pair of scissors.

"I can't believe this shit. Can you believe this?" Amanda asked motioning toward the TV. She was on her knees in the middle of the king-sized bed.

"The governor probably drove a pickup all the way from Montgomery to the ribbon cutting. Philip took a helicopter from two miles across town! What a fucking asshole!"

Ron stared in horror. All of this was hitting way too close to home now.

He thought again of what his father had told him.

"I need to get back to the office," he said, putting on his pants and shirt. "I have to fly to St. Louis later this week to give a speech. I need to work on it because I have patients all day long tomorrow."

Amanda was surprised. She didn't want him to go.

"When will I see you again?" she asked, moving closer to him on the bed.

He could smell her lingering sex. He wanted to stay.

"Call the office and make an appointment for early next week," he said, before leaving.

\*\*\*

On Thursday afternoon Dr. Ron Barton boarded the American Airlines Flight 4598 to St. Louis. He took his first-class window seat on row six and began reviewing his speech on "Prehabbing for Surgical Success" he'd penned after being asked to present at the convention.

Unlike many of his colleagues, Ron was a true scholar, and was a trained researcher who was used to writing academic-style papers. Earlier in the year he'd submitted a paper of the same title to the *Journal of Orthopedic Surgery* and it was immediately accepted for publishing. After its appearance in the journal his phone rang off the hook from doctors across the country wanting copies of his instructive material given to patients prior to surgery and other information related to his pioneering approach to surgery and recovery.

As he waited for takeoff, the young blonde-haired stewardess introduced herself and asked if he needed anything. He declined and focused instead on his speech, which he'd tailored to a conversational, layman's tone. The stewardess continued greeting the rest of the first-class passengers. Two rows behind Ron Barton she introduced herself to a sniffling Mack Dawkins and asked him if he needed anything.

"Double *Pinch* and water, please," he replied.

"We have only *Glenlivet*," she said. "Is that okay?"

"Sure," he relented. "Cheap bastards," he thought.

As he waited for his stiff drink he cracked and read the latest issue of *High Times*.

*\*\*\**

On Thursday evening Amanda Lucci met Philip at the *Highlands* for dinner. As it was for many in Birmingham, it was their favorite restaurant—not only for the unbelievable Southern cuisine, but also because it was where Philip had proposed to her six years earlier. Given her intimate activities with Dr. Ron Barton two days prior, Amanda was somewhat preoccupied. Moreover, she knew Ron was boarding a plane for St. Louis, and that it would take him even farther away from her. Philip had been out of town on Tuesday and Wednesday looking at a prospective rehab clinic for purchase in Little Rock, Arkansas and had returned earlier that day. He'd called her from his jet and asked if she would meet him for dinner.

"How did your doctor's appointment go on Tuesday, darling?" Philip asked.

"It went well," said Amanda. "Dr. Barton released me."

"Really? That's great! So you can ride now?"

"Yes! And I can't wait! I'm going to the club on Saturday. The weather is supposed to be perfect."

"And you aren't feeling any more pain?" he asked.

"None. I'm one hundred percent."

"Excellent."

The waiter, dressed in a white shirt, vest and black tie, brought their appetizers of raw oysters and grits. They both worked on the grits, as they were the signature appetizer.

"I'm heading to the camp at Lake Martin this weekend." Philip said. "Jim and I want to do some fishing. He's got some new buzz baits he wants to try out and I'd been promising him we'd go for a while now."

"That's okay with me," said Amanda. "I'm going to go riding on Saturday and on Sunday after church I'll probably go shopping at the *Galleria*."

\*\*\*

The next day just after lunch Philip Lucci and Jim Boudreaux flew in Philip's seaplane toward Lake Martin, just outside town where Philip had a 6,000 square foot home that he called a "weekend getaway." A registered pilot to fly all of his prop planes and jets, Philip was at the controls. The posh lake house was one of 18 homes he owned across the country. However, given its proximity to Dixie Rehab, it was where he most often "got away" to play with his many watercrafts, toys and other "play" things. At the palatial home he had two high powered cigarette speedboats, 14 different wave runners and jet skis, a pontoon party boat and his own parasail rig and sport pleasure craft. His neighbors of the Italian Renaissance architecture home and boat house with automatic garage doors hated him for his penchant for creating a huge, disturbing wake every time he drove one of his power boats on the normally placid water body. Many of them jeered loudly and threw beer bottles toward him as he sped by. Philip of course, never cared. He usually just flipped them off and sped ahead.

As they made their approach to the lake, Philip, wearing his pilot sunglasses and a black baseball cap that read "Dixie Rehab" in gold cursive lettering, asked a favor of Jim.

"Jim, I want you to follow my wife."

Jim had noticed that lately they had not been getting along. He immediately thought of a possible affair. There was a pause before he answered.

"Do you suspect she's seeing someone?" he asked.

Philip's face reddened. He was deeply embarrassed.

"I don't know. I'm not sure. All I know is she's not having sex with me—which makes me wonder if she's having any at all."

Boudreaux said nothing. He let Philip continue.

"I'm so busy with the company that I haven't paid her much attention lately. I don't even know what she does during the day anymore. I do know she's been spending a lot of time at the polo fields. Send one of your newer guys that she won't recognize to check her out. Watch her routine. Let me know what she's up to, okay?"

Boudreaux felt somewhat sorry for him. Even though he didn't particularly care for Amanda, because he knew she didn't like him, he still thought she was gorgeous. Every heterosexual man with a pulse did. He saw how losing a hot piece like that could severely hurt a man's ego.

"Sure thing, boss. I'll handle it. Don't worry about it. We'll take care of it. That's what we're here for, remember?"

Philip didn't answer for a few seconds. He was lost in deep thought. The craft tilted and began a quick descent.

"Buckle up—we're coming in," he said, as the plane's altitude meter bounced on the dash.

Boudreaux tightened his belt and held on to his seat. Moment's later the plane's pontoons touched down lightly on the surface of the lake, creating large ripples on the previously tranquil reservoir. One of Boudreaux's security captains, Pepe' Alvarez, a former U.S. Border Patrol agent, waited with a rope on top of a wave runner at the dock, ready to tie the plane off once it cut its engine. He'd driven up earlier in the day. As Philip hit the prop's kill switch, he asked Jim, "When you spoke to Pepe' earlier did he say whether or not he got in touch with those Mexican whores?"

"They're already here," he replied. "And they brought their own Tequila!"

Philip smiled.

"Perfect!" he said. "Just perfect!"

# 5

Dr. Ron Barton wore a dark gray wool suit, a light gray shirt and a navy blue tie with a spiffy Windsor knot. After being introduced to the crowd of about 250 physicians and health care professionals, he began his speech on the inherent benefits of pre-habbing patients. The speech was good. It possessed brevity, levity and repetition. After opening with a line about promising to be brief, and another about Alabama being the second-fattest state in the Union, he thanked the overweight doctors from Mississippi for a quick laugh and proceeded to preview the content of his discussion, reminding them as he spoke the most important aspects of his unique approach to orthopedic surgery and rehabilitation. His speech lasted only 22 minutes, and was met with rousing applause and a standing ovation from the diverse crowd.

After the speech, Mack Dawkins, also wearing a coat and tie, approached the staged area and walked up to the podium where Dr. Ron Barton had spoken moments earlier. As expected, Ron was rushed by a number of physicians—most of them women—wanting to know more about his learned insight into orthopedic surgery and care. After ten minutes, and several doctors later, Dawkins was able to finally meet and greet the young doctor.

"Dr. Barton, how are you?" he said, offering his hand.

Ron shook his hand.

"I'm fine, thanks."

"I'm Mack Dawkins."

"How are you Mack?" he asked. Ron looked for a nametag like the other physicians and attendees wore, but he saw none.

"Fine, just fine, thanks. I was really impressed with what you had to say. You are an amazing doctor, but you are also a good speaker. That was thoroughly entertaining. The time really flew by, and you were interesting."

Ron was genuinely flattered.

"Thanks Mack," he said. "Are you a physician?"

"No, I'm not," he said. "But I recruit them—and the growing health care company I represent is extremely interested in your services."

Ron was taken aback.

"Really?" he asked. "Who would that be?"

"Dixie Rehab in Birmingham," Mack proudly stated, puffing out his chest as he spoke. "We're building a state-of-the-art digital hospital and we're bringing in some of the best sports medicine and orthopedic physicians from around the globe to staff it. It's an unprecedented health care model and we would love to sit down and talk to you about it once you're back in Birmingham."

"This guy flew out here to pitch me," he thought.

"Who is 'we'?" asked Ron.

"Philip Lucci and me—I'm the CAO and Philip is the CEO. You've surely heard of him, no?" He asked with a condescending smirk.

"I have indeed. I've read about him in the newspapers."

"Well, let's get together then. I'll call you early next week and we'll set up a meeting with the three of us. Whattayousay?"

"Hell no," he thought; but his curiosity got the best of his better judgment.

"Sure. Give me a call at my office and talk to my secretary. You guys might have to come out to the office, however. I'm really busy lately—I've got a slough of new clients."

"Hey—no problem, Ron. It's okay if I call you Ron, huh?"

"Sure thing, Mack."

"Good enough. I'll call your secretary early next week. Thanks for your time. I see I'm holding up your fan session here. I'll look forward to our meeting with Philip. Have a safe flight home."

"Likewise, Mack."

Ron watched the back of Mack's head bob up and down as he strutted away through the thinning crowd.

"These guys are professionals," he thought.

***

Amanda Lucci rode her horse at full stride at the Birmingham Polo Grounds. She wore her hair up in a bun and had it neatly tucked underneath a black riding helmet. She wore a long-sleeved red shirt and tan riding pants and black riding boots. It was a beautiful fall Saturday morning. Spans of thin cirrus clouds lingered overhead, filtering brilliant white sunlight on the verdant, groomed pasture. The humidity in the air was low, providing for wonderful outdoor conditions.

Amanda thought of Ron, and whether or not he would be out at the club, as she badly wanted to see him. She planned on calling his office on Monday like he asked, but she couldn't keep him out of her thoughts. Philip was out of town for the weekend at Lake Martin, and as long as he was out of town, she felt comfortable doing as she pleased.

Fred Foster sipped a cherry coke inside the clubhouse at the polo grounds. A former FBI agent of thirty years, the 57-year old retiree stood near the large, panoramic windows that provided a grand view of the polo fields. Wearing traditional riding garb, he intently watched Amanda Lucci. A part-time private detective, Fred had received a call the previous evening from his business associate, Jim Boudreaux, with instructions to tail the beautiful wife of Philip Lucci, and to watch and report daily her routine. Fred had learned from Jim that Amanda planned to ride at the Polo Club on Saturday.

Fred watched Amanda ride and practice her shots for about forty-five minutes. When she rode back to the stable area, he left the clubhouse. Amanda dismounted her horse in front of the stable areas and was met by her horse trainer, Armando Ricos. Armando took her horse, helmet and riding crop and disappeared into the stable area. Amanda removed her gloves and released the bobby pins that held her long brown hair up on her head and shook her locks to her shoulders. She sauntered into the women's dressing room. Fred, now wearing dark

*Ray-Ban* sunglasses, watched her enter the building from his vantage point under a small oak tree nearby.

Ron Barton parked his gleaming *Porsche* and strolled right past Fred Foster toward the men's dressing area. As he approached the entrance to the men's dressing room Amanda Lucci exited the women's dressing room, wearing a bright pink and white flower print dress, a large-brimmed white straw hat and white-rimmed designer sunglasses. Ron nearly walked directly into her, but he stopped in stride before doing so. He was surprised as he was excited to see her.

"Hello Amanda," he said.

"Hello Dr. Barton," she answered, thrilled to see him.

He wanted to kiss her, but realized it was inappropriate. He noticed her lovely scent, and that she was wearing her massive wedding ring.

"Did you ride today?" he asked.

"Yes, I just finished. It was wonderful. It's such a beautiful day. Are you going to ride?"

"Later on I will. I came to see the fillies. I'm showing one later today to a prospective buyer. I think he's going to take her."

Ron wore khaki *Polo* pants and a collared gold *Tommy Bahama* fishing shirt and shades with Auburn-labeled eyewear retention. Amanda thought he looked cute.

"I'm hungry. Would you like to have lunch with me here at the club?" she asked.

Ron had eaten breakfast and had gone for a long walk near his Highland Park home. He wasn't really hungry, but he knew he would be later.

"Sure. Give me a minute. I've got to talk to Hector and let him know I'm here. I'll meet you inside in about five minutes or so."

"Okay," she said. She walked toward the clubhouse. Ron disappeared into the stable.

Fred walked toward the direction where Ron vanished. He had heard their entire conversation. He removed his sunglasses as he entered the shade. He walked into the stable area and saw Ron talking to Hector. He continued toward them. He approached them and stopped a few feet away.

"Excuse me?" Fred asked.

"Yes?" Replied Ron. Hector looked on.

"I'm sorry, gentlemen," Fred said. "I'm from out of town. I'm trying to find the clubhouse so I can get a bite to eat."

"I'm headed that way in just a minute. You can walk with me." Ron answered. "Hector, I'll be back here after lunch and we'll run the fillies together."

"Sure thing, Doc."

"Okay my friend, the club house is right this way." Ron said. They walked side-by-side back in the direction Fred had come from.

"I'm Dr. Ron Barton, by the way."

"I'm Dr. Ted Thompson," Fred replied, playing the part. "I'm down here from Columbia, South Carolina for a family wedding. I have a horse farm up there and I just love horses. It's in my blood. My cousin, who's getting married for the third time—can you believe it? She told me about this place. It's great."

"It's over here," said Ron, leading him in a different direction.

"So you have a horse farm, huh?" Ron asked.

"Yes. I have sixteen head, mainly paints."

"I see. My folks have been breeding lately. I'm showing a filly later this afternoon." Ron said.

They approached the clubhouse double doors.

Ron stopped at the front entrance and decided to take advantage of the opportunity before him.

"I'm meeting someone for lunch, but if you want to come by the stable area later—where we just were—I'll show you the two new fillies I have. One may still be for sale. I have an interested buyer, but I have nothing finalized. Are you in the market for another animal? She's a real beauty."

"I would love to come back by after lunch. I'll come back around in an hour or so. Thanks for the directions, Dr. Barton."

"You're welcome, but please, just call me Ron. But do come by if you can. I'd love to show her to you."

"I will, Ron. See you later. Enjoy your lunch." Fred said.

"Thanks Ted. See you in a bit."

Ron entered the clubhouse and saw Amanda seated at a table near the large window area. They made eye contact and smiled. He joined her.

"So you're hungry, huh?"

"Famished," she replied.

"The riding worked up my appetite…"

There was a pause. "For you," she added.

Ron blushed. He nervously scanned the room. There were two other couples in the dining area, much older, but they appeared to be occupied with conversation. He saw Dr. Thompson at the bar looking over a menu, enjoying a beer and pretzels.

"Watch it now," he said gently. "You never know who might be watching and listening."

"I don't really care if anyone's watching."

"What do you mean—you don't care?" Ron asked.

"I'm done with Philip. I'm ready to divorce him. Sometimes I wish he would just initiate it."

A concerned Ron listened. She saw he wanted more.

"I grew up destitute, Ron. My dad was a drunk and my mom was nearly an invalid. It was terrible. My looks allowed me to make it out of an awful home life but I vowed I would never live like that. When Philip came along I saw a way to ensure that I'd never have to worry about money. I was stupid."

Ron listened intently. She noticed and continued.

"We are no longer intimate. We're like two ships passing in the night. There's nothing there, Ron. It's over. Philip will end it when he realizes there's nothing else left in it for him."

Ron realized the difficulty of her predicament and was reminded of the fact that he was indeed involved with a married woman.

"So, he doesn't yet realize it?"

"No, not yet, but I'm sure he has an inkling. We haven't had sex in nearly five months."

Ron wondered what Philip would do to him if he knew he was seeing his wife.

"Where is he today?" Ron asked.

"He's at our Lake Martin home. He said he was going fishing. Who knows? He took his seaplane. He could be anywhere for all I know."

"Do you trust him?"

"Are you kidding?" she answered. "*Never* trust Philip Lucci! Believe me—I know him well. He's not trustworthy. He's a manipulator. It's how he gets what he wants."

Ron again recognized the beauty in her vulnerability. She seemed distraught.

"What are you doing tonight?" he asked.

She smiled. "I don't have plans, why?"

"I thought maybe we could have dinner and drinks—at my place."

"At *your* place?"

"Yeah," he answered, cautiously managing a smile. He was so nervous about the entire affair, yet he couldn't resist her.

"Where do you live and what time do you want me there?"

"Near Five Points South—156 Highland Avenue, near the public golf course. I guess you could come over around 8:00 p.m."

"Sounds great," she said.

"When you drive up, come around to the back of the house through the garbage alley and park in back."

After lunch Ron walked back into the stable area and waited for Dr. Thompson, who walked up a few minutes later. Ron was busy brushing the young filly he had for sale.

"She's a real beaut," said Fred, posing as Dr. Ted Thompson.

"Oh hey Ted, thanks. I've got a guy coming by at 2:00 to take a look at her. I think he's going to buy her."

"How much are you asking for her?" Fred asked.

"Twenty," Ron replied, meaning twenty thousand dollars.

"That's reasonable," said Fred.

"I think so," said Ron. "She has great bloodlines."

"I'll tell you what, Ron. I have to get ready for the wedding. I've got to get back to my cousin's place. I know you want to run the horses, too. Do you have a number I can call to get in touch with you? I'd like to follow up and see if you sell her."

"Sure," said Ron. He reached into his wallet and retrieved a business card with his office and cell phone numbers and handed it to Ted. "Here's my info. Get in touch with me if you are still interested. Even if I sell this one, my dad's a breeder."

"Thanks Ron."

"No problem, Ted. Enjoy the wedding."

"I will, thanks."

Fred walked away from the stables happy with his morning's work. However, it had not yet ended. As he walked back near the entrance to the clubhouse, he noticed Amanda getting into her red *BMW*. He quickly entered his dark blue *Crown Victoria* and followed her home.

Later that evening, at about 7:20, Fred napped in his car on the shoulder of the rustic mountain road outside the gates to the Lucci Estate. In the fading early evening light his car was concealed under the branches of thick birch trees lining the road's edge. He was awakened by the sound of the automatic gate doors opening. He quickly started his engine and put his car in gear. He watched the gates open and Amanda ride out in a hurry. He let her pull away a few hundred feet before he began tailing her. He ironically followed her on the Philip Lucci Parkway down toward Birmingham's South Side, to Dr. Ron Barton's home, the old Berger Phillips House.

Berger Phillips was a popular Birmingham department store in the early 1900's. The owners of the department store, a prominent Jewish family bearing the same name, had built Dr. Barton's home in 1911. Through the years it had three different other owners, until Ron bought it in 1990. The two-story home overlooking the public golf course was a classic Frank Lloyd Wright design, with a garage apartment in the back that Ron rented to a UAB graduate student.

Amanda drove around to the garbage alley until she came to the small garden-style sign that read "156." She saw Ron's Porsche, which was covered with a gray tarp, and parked next to it. She exited her vehicle, locked the doors with her automatic locking mechanism attached to her keys and walked down the dark orange cobblestone stairs and path leading to Ron's side door. She saw light emanating past curtains from what appeared to be the living room or den area. She then saw Ron through the window—walking toward the door. She went to knock but he opened the door before she got there.

"You're right on time!" he said. "You look great! Come on in!"

Ron was dressed in jeans, a knit Polo shirt and sandals.

Amanda, wearing jeans and a pink cotton pullover, stepped into the house and he closed the door behind her.

"I love your house," Amanda said. "It's really neat."

"It was built in 1911. It's the old Berger Phillips house. They were downtown merchants way back in the day."

Amanda looked around his place. It was neat and comfortable, with a large leather sectional and a big screen television in the living area. In front of the TV she noticed a buff cocker spaniel.

"Oh, look how cute! A puppy!"

"Well, he's not a puppy anymore. His name is Scooter. He's five years old. I got him right when I bought this place."

Amanda walked over to the spaniel and crouched and petted him. He rolled over onto his back, encouraging her to pet his stomach.

"Oh what a sweet dog." She petted his tummy and his right leg shook madly. "Hey Scooter! That's a sweet boy…"

"You're spoiling him!" Ron said. "Hey, I need to empty the garbage out back. I'll be right back, okay."

"Sure. I'll be here petting Scooter."

Scooter continued enjoying the attention. He remained on his back, leg shaking.

Ron removed the overflowing garbage bag and headed out the side door to place it in garbage can adjacent to the garage near the alley outside. He walked the bag to the can, removed the lid and tossed it inside. When he did he noticed a dark blue vehicle making its way down the alley toward him. As Ron placed the lid back on top of the can he looked at the driver, who accelerated, allowing only a quick glance. Ron thought he looked familiar.

"Was that Dr. Thompson, the guy I saw at the polo stables today?" he asked himself. "It looked just like him," he thought, although he wasn't sure, as Fred was wearing shades, and it was dark with the only light being a mercury vapor street lamp several yards down the alley. Nevertheless, he downplayed it. There was a beautiful woman waiting for him, and he had no reason to believe that he was being followed.

Fred Foster removed his cigarette lighter and plugged his mobile phone into the power jack. He dialed Jim Boudreaux's cell number and waited.

Jim and Philip were busy. After spending the day fishing on Lake Martin, they started drinking frozen margaritas with the Mexican whores. Things quickly got interesting. Jim was naked, in bed with his second prostitute of the evening, when his phone rang. He was almost finished, so he let it ring. Fred left a message.

"Jim, this is Fred. Call me. I have some news." He hung up.

About five minutes later a satisfied Jim freshened his margarita and checked his phone. He listened to his message and returned Fred's call.

"Yeah Fred, this is Jim. What's up?"

"Amanda Lucci has a friend."

"Really? Who?"

"Dr. Ron Barton."

"You sure?"

"Positive."

"Okay, but stay on her. Keep her in your sights. We need to make sure."

"She's at his house right now."

"Well, call me in the morning and let me know what happens tonight."

Ron cooked roasted duck for Amanda that evening. They enjoyed a bottle of French merlot before dinner and another afterward. Amanda stayed over and they made love into the early morning hours.

Before daybreak Fred's vehicle crept along the garbage alley until it came to where Amanda's *BMW* was still parked. Amanda woke a few minutes later and left before the exercisers emerged and jogged the walkways and sidewalks that transected the hilly, older area of town. Jim hooked up his mobile phone in his car and dialed Jim's number. It was 5:45 a.m.

Jim was sleeping hard with the third Mexican whore—a "hat trick" as he and Philip had earlier put it, when his cell phone rang. He heard it on the third ring. He reached over her bare shoulder and grabbed it on the nightstand. He looked at the display and recognized the number.

"Yeah, Fred?"

"She slept over."

"She never left?"

"No. She spent the night with him."

"Alright then, I guess that's it. I'll tell Philip. Stay on her, though, okay?"

"Sure thing Jim."
The Mexican prostitute woke and disappeared beneath the sheets.
"I've gotta go. I'll talk to you later, okay, Fred?"
"Later."

# 6

On Monday morning Philip Lucci's secretary called Dr. Ron Barton's office at 8:30 a.m. Ron's secretary, Amelia, answered. Lucci's secretary explained that Mack Dawkins had spoken to Dr. Barton about a meeting, and that he and Philip Lucci wanted to come to their offices later that afternoon. Amelia explained that Dr. Barton had just arrived, and had not yet started seeing patients.

"Let me check and see if he can meet with them. His last appointment is at 3:30 p.m." She put Lucci's secretary on hold and walked and found Dr. Barton.

"Dr. Barton?"

"Yes Amelia?"

"Good morning."

"Good morning—what's up?"

"I have Philip Lucci's secretary on the phone and he and a Mr. Mack Dawkins would like to come to the office and meet with you at 4:00 p.m. Can you meet with them?"

Ron thought, "These guys are coming at me hard." Philip Lucci greatly intrigued him. Although he was nervous, he couldn't help but relent.

"Sure, I can meet with them. Tell them to come at four. My last patient is at 3:30."

"Will do Dr. Barton."

Ron pensively approached meeting his first patient, knowing that the end of his workday would bring a most interesting experience.

\*\*\*

Dr. Leah Thompson was eating lunch with two of her colleagues at South Points Grill when she saw the breaking news story on the mid-day local news. The twenty-something blonde, blue-eyed anchorwoman spoke with an enthusiasm that was reserved only for big news stories.

"News Five has just learned through a press release from Dixie Rehab that two of Birmingham's most successful orthopedic surgeons, Dr. Andrew Muster and Dr. James Appleton have signed contracts with Dixie Rehab and will be a part of the new digital hospital being built off of the Philip Lucci Parkway. Muster and Appleton and their Birmingham Orthopedic Clinic are well-known throughout the Deep South and the country for their expertise in sports medicine, with both doctors having a client list that reads like a *Who's Who of Professional Sports*. Athletes like Michael Jordan, Roger Clemens, Flo Thompson, Dennis Rodman, and Shaquille O'Neal have been patients of B.O.C. in the past. However, their respective signings with Dixie Rehab means that they will soon close their doors and move into one of Dixie Rehab's many Birmingham offices until the digital hospital is completed. Dixie Rehab CEO Philip Lucci said the signing of Drs. Muster and Appleton is 'just the beginning' of bringing world-class rehabilitative health care to Birmingham, Alabama."

Leah immediately thought of Ron, and their lunch conversation from the previous week. Drs. Muster and Appleton were considered two of Birmingham's best doctors and were nationally-respected for their expertise. She knew that this was a watershed event—one that would surely precipitate the signing of many more area doctors. She needed to call Ron.

"Excuse me ladies," said Leah to her friends. "I have to make a phone call."

Leah left the table and sought the lone pay phone at the rear of the restaurant. She dropped 35 cents and dialed Ron's office. Because it was lunchtime, his answering service picked up.

"Hello, Dr. Barton's answering service. What is the message you would like to leave for Dr. Barton?"

"Hi, this is Dr. Leah Thompson. Please tell Dr. Barton that Dr. Muster and Dr. Appleton have signed with Dixie Rehab."

"Is that all?"

"Yes, that's it." Leah said.

"Okay. I will get him the message."

"Thanks."

"Thank *you*, Dr. Thompson."

***

Dr. Ron Barton returned from lunch and checked his message bin on his desk. He picked up the three pink slips and glanced at the one on top—it read something about one of his patients—a Mrs. Long, wanting to schedule an urgent appointment that afternoon at 3:45 after his last patient. He shuffled the message to the bottom and looked at the next one. It was a message from Dr. Ted Thompson calling to inquire about a horse. The message left no return number and it said he would call back. The third was the message from the other Dr. Thompson—Leah. It simply read, "Muster and Appleton signed with Dixie Rehab, from Dr. Leah Thompson."

Ron couldn't believe the message. Muster and Appleton were his main competition. They were the most respected orthopedic surgeons in the area and held the professional position and status that he wanted to eventually achieve. It was a huge development. It meant that many more doctors would follow these two. Moreover, Lucci's vision of creating a monopoly was much closer to being realized as a result. Ron felt that things were quickly turning against him.

"And they're coming for me at four o'clock," he thought.

***

Philip flew back to Birmingham alone Sunday afternoon, leaving Jim Boudreaux to drive back to Birmingham with Pepe Alvarez on Monday morning. Philip asked him to stay and help secure the lake house with Pepe and to make sure the three Mexican whores were sent off "safely and happy." Heeding his boss, on Sunday evening Jim called the girls a cab after he screwed them each one more time and gave them an extra five dollar bill to make sure they were "happy."

Jim decided he would wait to tell Philip about his wife seeing Dr. Barton until after he got back to town. Sunday afternoon was spent fishing with Pepe in Philip's bass boat. They caught several large Florida strain bass over four pounds. Pepe filleted the bass and put them in plastic *Ziploc* bags on ice in a large *Igloo* ice chest before they locked down the compound, shutting off all the lights and securing all the entranceways before leaving early Monday.

When Jim made it back to the Dixie Rehab headquarters on Monday afternoon he asked Philip's secretary where he was. She told him that Philip and Mack had left for lunch, had two afternoon appointments and would not be back to the office until Tuesday morning. Jim wondered if he should call Philip on his cell phone and tell him about Amanda. Although he knew it was important, he also knew it would be best to tell him such a thing in person, away from someone like Mack. He remembered the embarrassment on Philip's face when he asked him to follow her, and he realized that it would be a difficult moment when the axe finally fell.

"I'll wait until tomorrow morning," he told himself.

***

At 3:55 p.m. Dixie Rehab's largest and most ostentatious, shiny black stretch limousine pulled under the awning to the front entrance of the Birmingham Sports Medicine Clinic where Dr. Ron Barton practiced. The driver, a tall, well-built white man with broad shoulders and blonde hair, exited the driver's side door and walked to the opposite side's middle door facing the clinic's façade. The driver, wearing a black driving cap and dark sunglasses, opened the door, allowing Philip Lucci to step out onto the concrete. Wearing dark aviator sunglasses and a black dress suit with a designer shirt and sky-blue, single-knot tie, Philip appeared the consummate CEO. After standing and adjusting his coat, Philip stepped aside and cleared a path for Mack to exit the limo. Like Lucci, Mack wore dark glasses and a dark suit, although not nearly as expensive. The driver shut the door and the two men strolled confidently into the building.

Early in the day the receptionist was informed by Dr. Barton's secretary that Philip Lucci would be arriving to meet with Dr. Barton. It was all she could do to only tell her best friend in the workplace, but that was enough to start a predictable chain reaction of interest in "King Philip's" arrival. The vestibule and lobby area at 3:55 was full of onlookers hoping to gain a glimpse of Birmingham's most notorious multi-millionaire benefactor.

Mack and Philip walked to the receptionist bubble and Mack spoke for the two of them.

"Good afternoon, M'am. My name is Mack Dawkins and I'm here with Mr. Philip Lucci to see Dr. Ron Barton. We have an appointment."

The receptionist's face became flush red and her breathing quickened. What was normally routine, became extraordinary, in the presence of the health care icon, Philip Lucci.

She managed into her headset microphone, "Amelia, Philip Lucci is here to see Dr. Barton."

Amelia was on watch, waiting for their arrival.

"Send them in," she answered.

Amelia hung up the phone and walked to the lobby area.

"Hello Mr. Lucci. My name is Amelia Brown, Dr. Barton's secretary."

They shook hands.

"Good afternoon Amelia. This is Mack Dawkins, CAO of Dixie Rehab."

Amelia shook hands with Mack.

Philip looked at his $50,000 diamond-studded *Rolex* watch face.

"We're a couple of minutes early. Is Dr. Barton available to see us now? We know he's awfully busy."

"Dr. Barton will be with you shortly. He's finishing up with his last patient of the day. He had a late emergency call in. Can I get either of you anything to drink—a soda or coffee?"

"Thank you, Amelia. I'll take a *Diet Dr. Pepper* if you have one."

"I'll have one too, if you've got it." Mack added.

"I do. Come with me this way to the meeting room."

Dr. Ron Barton met with his last patient of the day, Mrs. Long, who two weeks earlier had surgery on a torn knee ligament. Mrs.

Long was overweight and he knew that she had not taken her prehab exercise routine as seriously as she had the maintenance of her high-fat, high-cholesterol diet. She said she was experiencing pain after surgery and wanted him to prescribe more pills, her initial prescription having already been depleted. He encouraged her to do her walking and wrote another small script for Hydrocodone, emphasizing the need for her to move to regain her health and range of motion through steady exercise.

After he was done with Mrs. Long, Dr. Barton went to his office. Amelia came in shortly after.

"Mr. Lucci and Mr. Dawkins are waiting in the meeting room." Amelia said.

Word about Dixie Rehab signing Drs. Muster and Appleton had made its way through the clinic. That fact, coupled with the presence of Philip Lucci in their workplace, had the place buzzing like a beehive. Many workers wondered openly in break room conversations whether or not Dr. Barton would also sign with Dixie, as their jobs hung ultimately in the balance of his decision.

"Thanks Amelia," he said. "I'll be there in a minute."

"I'll let them know," she replied.

"Thanks."

Dr. Ron Barton took a deep breath and contemplated fully what was about to transpire. He'd gone through the meeting in his head a dozen or more times. He knew what it was all about. He knew what he was going to do and say. He looked at his reflection in his office bathroom mirror. He remembered who he was and what he was about. He thought of his education, all that he had worked for, and his mother and father. He walked down the hallway in his long white coat, tan slacks, button-down blue shirt and gray silk tie. He quickly entered the meeting room without knocking, closing the door behind him.

"Good afternoon gentlemen," said Dr. Barton in an authoritative tone.

Philip and Mack were seated next to each other on his right. Both men stood after he entered.

"Good afternoon Doc," said Mack.

Mack shook his hand.

"Dr. Barton, this is Philip Lucci, CEO and Chairman of the Board of Dixie Rehab," said Mack, introducing the two.

"Nice to meet you, Sir," said Dr. Barton, shaking hands with Lucci.

"It's all my pleasure, Dr. Barton. I've heard great things about you from my wife."

Ron swallowed hard. He was at a loss for words. He froze, but managed a polite smile and a slight nod in recognition.

"Others have said that you're one of Birmingham's brightest young doctors."

"I try my best to be a professional."

"As do we—as do we," replied Lucci, smiling in the direction of Mack Dawkins, who listened intently. Mack returned the smile.

Philip took control.

"Dr. Barton, I don't know if you've seen the news today, but Dixie Rehab just signed Drs. Andrew Muster and James Appleton to be a part of our forthcoming world-class digital hospital sports medicine group."

"I heard about it earlier today. People in the office were talking about it. I've been with patients most of the day, so I didn't hear the report."

"What do you think about joining them—about being a part of the Dixie Rehab team—about making nearly twice what you currently make here?"

Ron was ready for the question. Mack had told him as much in St. Louis.

Mack pulled a readied contract from a nearby opened briefcase. In large text "DRAFT" was superimposed horizontally in gray over the document. Ron scanned it momentarily and saw that it was an agreement outlining patient referrals and other obligations.

"A draft? Why would I sign a 'DRAFT'?" He asked himself.

"Mr. Lucci, Mr. Dawkins told me that you were interested in having me work with your company," said Ron, pausing for effect. "I appreciate your offer, Mr. Lucci. The money is certainly attractive; but money is not what motivates me. I know this sounds scripted, but I am more concerned with the medicine I practice and the patients I benefit. Furthermore, my approach to orthopedics is altogether different. Given the nature of your business—which is rehabilitative care—you try and get patients to work their muscles post-surgery. Contrarily, my way involves prehabbing the patient—putting them through a rigorous exercise regimen prior to surgery so that they can achieve better post-surgery results that require less rehabilitation and hopefully achieve a shorter down time. Overall, I feel my approach offers many long-term health-related benefits as patients tend to realize the inherent need for regular exercise—and not just in the post-surgery phase. My overall intent is to help people become healthier and to stay that way, improving their overall quality of life."

Philip Lucci was used to the tough sale. He'd cut his teeth selling, and it was his salesmanship that had earned him hundreds of millions.

"Dr. Barton, I don't think your approach is so different from ours that it would prevent us from working together. After all, you readily admit that you too prescribe rehabilitative care for your surgery patients. I think that without question we could work together. Furthermore, in addition to the generous salary increase, we offer another serious upside in terms of insurance provision and office setting. You will find that our insurance premium rates for malpractice per doctor are much better because we are larger, and the digital hospital, once finished in a year or so, will be equipped with all of the latest, state-of-the art trappings and professional accoutrements a medical professional of your stature would ever need. Furthermore, our digital records capacity will be a standard setter. Imagine, Dr. Barton—paper records will be a thing of the past—every time you and your staff log information into the patient database, it will be seamless—patient records will be available to you and to other medical professionals in a mere keystroke. Picture a pristine, professional medical environment unlike any other on the planet—here in Birmingham, Alabama—with you being one of its biggest rock star physicians."

Dr. Barton didn't appreciate the "rock star" tag. Unlike Lucci, he had never thought of himself in such a narcissistic light. He'd heard enough. His answer was still an emphatic no. He was quickly losing his patience for Mr. Lucci's pitch. Besides, he was fucking his wife. It was time for him to go.

"Mr. Lucci, I appreciate the offer, but I want to do it my way. I'm flattered that you would want me, but I'm going to build my own practice."

There was a moment of silence.

Mack Dawkins attempted to speak, but Dr. Barton cut him off before he could answer the objection.

"Dr. Barton I think…"

"My answer is final, gentlemen. Thank you for coming by."

Philip Lucci wasn't fazed. He continued his pitch.

"Dr. Barton, in addition to your salary you'll receive a special Medical Director's fee for overseeing one of our orthopedic groups. Also, you'll have access to Dixie Rehab's corporate jet for Auburn sporting events."

Dr. Barton stared in amazement at Lucci. He was relentless.

"He's offering me the world," he thought.

Lucci didn't stop.

"Also, I understand you're big into polo, and that you annually organize and co-sponsor a charitable polo event. Dixie Rehab would be greatly interested in sponsoring such a worthwhile function."

"He's getting desperate," Barton thought.

"I'm sorry Mr. Lucci, but I must decline. Thank you though."

Dr. Barton stood and pushed his chair back underneath the table. Lucci and Dawkins both followed his lead. Lucci was noticeably uncomfortable. He was not used to being told no.

"Thanks for your time Dr. Barton," said Lucci, offering his hand. Dr. Barton shook it and when he did Lucci squeezed it unnecessarily, and held it—without letting go.

"If for any reason you would like to reconsider, let me know. I really feel you would be perfect for our new concept."

"Mr. Lucci, I assure you I will not reconsider—but thanks again. Mr. Dawkins, thank you."

Dr. Barton pulled his hand away from Lucci's clutches and shook hands with Mack.

"Good day gentlemen," said Dr. Barton, as he opened the meeting room door. Lucci and Dawkins left and headed straight for the front door. Dr. Barton returned to his office, thinking the entire way that he didn't like the way Lucci clung to him. He also wondered if Lucci knew about him and his wife.

After Dawkins and Lucci left the building, Amelia went to Dr. Barton's office to discover the verdict.

"What did you decide? Are you leaving for Dixie Rehab?" she asked.

Dr. Barton, seated behind his desk, only stared.

She was full of wonder. He could tell she was hanging on the moment.

"I told them no." He said.

She smiled.

"I told them I want to do it my way." He added.

"I knew you wouldn't go. It's not your style," she said. "They're all glam and glitz. I wonder about them to tell you the truth."

"You're not the only one. You're not the only one, Amelia."

***

Philip Lucci pushed the automatic partition button inside his limousine. A solid black divider automatically rose from the back of the driver's seat, providing privacy for him and Mack. Once the partition had finished raising Philip removed a small dark brown vial with a black screw cap from his left coat pocket. He removed the cap and dumped half of the vial's white powder contents on the dark glass table in the middle of the vehicle. He removed his wallet and retrieved a credit card and a crisp one hundred dollar bill. He handed the bill to Mack and began cutting long, chalky white lines.

"Can you believe that little prick?" Lucci asked. "That cocky sonofabitch! He was almost defiant!"

Mack rolled the note into a tight straw-like tube. Philip continued his rant.

"Fuck him! Once all of his noteworthy colleagues are with us he'll change his tune and we'll be able to get him for much less." Philip remarked.

He grabbed the bill from Mack and went down on the line with the same enthusiasm he'd shown earlier in Dr. Barton's office. He cut another line and snorted it and handed the bill to Mack. Before Mack snorted his smaller lines he spoke obsequiously.

"I think the guy is overrated myself. He's too young to be taken seriously."

***

That evening Leah Thompson called Ron at his house. She had to talk to him about Drs. Muster and Appleton signing with Dixie. When Ron answered the phone she couldn't contain her enthusiasm.

"Did you get my message?"

"Yeah, I got it."

"Can you believe it? Muster and Appleton are considered the best. This is big for Lucci, don't you think?"

"I do. Lucci came to my office today and pitched me on Dixie."

"What?"

"Yeah, he was at my office today—him and his CAO Mack Dawkins, the guy he sent to St. Louis last week to pitch me."

"Lucci sent a guy to St. Louis to talk to you about going with Dixie?"

"Yeah, and you're right about him—he's definitely creepy. He wouldn't let go of my hand when we shook hands before he left. He squeezed it and held it."

"Really?"

"Yeah."

"What did he say?"

"He offered me money, use of the corporate jet for Auburn sporting events, said he'd sponsor the Polo Tournament—he was relentless—even after I told him I wasn't interested."

"So you told him no?"

"Of course I told him no! Wouldn't you be surprised if I went to work for that bastard?"

"Well yeah—what did you tell him? How did you say it?"

"I told him what I told you—that money isn't everything and that I care more about my practice and my patients. I added that we were different in our care philosophies, and that I was into prehabbing patients while he was into rehabbing them. He discounted that and just kept on offering me everything. I just said thanks but no thanks and after I stood up he finally realized I was serious."

"Well, good for you Ron Barton! I'm proud of you!"

"Thanks Leah."

He meant it. It was important to him that she said that.

"Well I am. Not many people would be able to do what you did. It shows that you have principles."

"Well, yes, but I don't know how all of this is going to pan out. In a year or so the new hospital will be built and it's going to be an entirely different story. I don't know if I'll be able to retain all of my patients. Lucci is going to create a medical *Disneyland* I'm afraid."

"You'll be fine, Ron. Don't worry. You shouldn't worry about anything.

Ron disagreed. He felt he had everything to worry about.

"I hope so, Leah. I hope you're right."

# 7

On Tuesday morning Philip Lucci arrived at work as usual at 7:00 a.m. At around 8:00 a.m. his secretary phoned and told him Jim Boudreaux needed to see him.

"Tell him to call me," Philip said. "I'm busy right now."

Philip finished the last of what were two extremely large cocaine lines and the phone rang. He put the rolled bill into his desk drawer and answered the phone.

"Jim is on line one Mr. Lucci," said his secretary.

"Patch him through please."

The line was connected. Philip used the speakerphone, as his hands were busy.

"Hey Jim, what's up?"

"Philip, I need to come up and talk to you. I'm in the building."

"I'm sorta busy right now. What's going on?"

"It's about Amanda. I've got some news."

Philip knew by the sound of his voice it was not good.

"Get up here," he said.

Five minutes later Philip buzzed Jim into his office. In the interim period it took Jim to get to the penthouse, after yet another healthy line of Peruvian flake, Philip made himself a *Diet Dr. Pepper* with crushed ice. He was flying high by the time Jim arrived. Jim's face was sullen. Philip saw he was all business.

"Who is it? Who is she seeing?" Philip demanded.

Jim didn't hesitate. He'd waited long enough already.

"Dr. Ron Barton, the orthopedic surgeon—he was treating Amanda's neck injury. He works for the Birmingham Sports Clinic. I made sure that it was legitimate. I have confirmation that she slept at his house on Saturday night."

"Son of a bitch!" Lucci yelled. "You've got to be fucking kidding me!"

Jim was startled. He knew Philip would be upset, but he didn't expect such an outburst.

"What?" Jim asked.

"I just met with that little prick yesterday! Mack and I tried to recruit him. He refused. He said, 'money isn't everything' and that he'd 'do it his way.'"

"Sonofabitch!" Lucci yelled. He threw his gold-plated *Cross* pen at the wall behind Jim, shattering the glass of a framed certificate of recognition from the local Boys' Club given to Lucci for a prior charitable donation. Jim instinctively ducked, but the pen was never close to hitting him.

"I'm sorry boss."

Philip hung his head. With both hands on his desk in front of him he rocked back and forth in a fit of anger.

"That bitch! That fucking little bitch! She's gonna pay for this! She'll get nothing in the divorce! Nothing! I'm gonna ruin her—and him! Barton will wish he was never born!"

Philip plopped himself down into his padded leather chair and rocked slowly backward, running both hands across his face and through his badly thinning, dyed hair; holding his head as if it were about to burst.

He remained in that position—lost in deep thought—for several seconds.

"What are you going to do?" Jim finally asked.

Philip said nothing.

"How can I help?" He added.

Philip rocked back into an upright position. His countenance shifted completely from anger to happiness.

"Wait a second…this could be a good thing, Jim." Philip said enthusiastically.

Jim was confused.

"What do you mean?"

Philip smiled.

"Because, Amanda wasn't giving me any to begin with, and now I have clear grounds for a divorce—she was cheating on me. Also, now I have a way to fix that little prick Barton! I'll leak this to Bierbaum and he'll have a fucking field day with it! I'll give him an exclusive! After that it will be statewide news and I'll come across looking like the unfortunate husband, with Amanda being the complete gold-digging whore turned bad! I'll get big-time sympathy out of this—I'll come out smelling like a rose!"

Jim laughed halfheartedly. He was still somewhat confused. Philip's reaction wasn't what he thought it was going to be. Moreover, he wondered if going public with a scandal like this was good for business.

Philip interjected, "I wonder how well Barton's reputation handles a highly-publicized, scandalous affair with a married woman who is also a former patient?"

Jim was beginning to get the picture.

"Not too well, I would assume. He'll be the bad guy," said Jim.

"Exactly—how does the Bible say it? Thou shall not covet thy neighbor's wife…"

"Ooh, now that's really bad." Jim answered, "So bad that you should be able to get any of the other reputable doctors in his office to sign, because they won't want anything to do with him. They'll have no choice—they'll have to sign with you!"

Lucci's smile was bigger.

"Like I said, this is a good thing, Jim."

Lucci picked up his phone and buzzed his secretary.

"Get Butch Bierbaum on the phone for me Helen."

***

Later that morning Philip Lucci used his cell phone and called his wife. Amanda was leaving the gym when she took his call.

"Hey Philip."

"No wonder you don't have sex with me anymore," he said angrily.

Amanda panicked. Her heart skipped a beat.

"What do you mean?" she asked.

"I know about you and Barton you little slut!" he yelled into the bulky phone. "And don't you even think about a divorce settlement! You'll take what I damn well give you!"

Amanda's emotions were mixed. Although she was scared to death of Philip, she was also glad it was finally going to be over. She wondered how he discovered their relationship and then quickly remembered he had Jim Boudreaux and a security force. She knew there was nothing she could say. She was busted.

"Look Philip—I don't want anything. I'm sorry, but it was over anyway. I just want out. That's it. Just let me go."

Philip hoped she would put up more of a fight. The fact that she was willing to leave him without trying to take his money hurt him—it also rendered him, for the first time since they were married, powerless over her.

"You're already gone as far as I'm concerned. Go home and pack your bags. I'll give you until Friday to get your shit moved. After that I'll have it moved to the dump. I'll stay out of your way at the house until then."

Amanda thought briefly of where she would go, and where she would put her things.

"Okay Philip. I'll get everything out by Friday."

"Damn right you will! And you'll be hearing from my attorney later today."

Philip abruptly ended the call.

Although she was somewhat relieved, Amanda couldn't help but cry. Her immediate future was uncertain.

***

Amanda Lucci arrived at Dr. Ron Barton's office at 10:25 a.m. for a 10:30 a.m. appointment. She had made it after he suggested she do so after their Wynfrey hotel encounter. Still wearing her sunglasses, she reported to the receptionist and took a seat. A couple of minutes later her name was called and she was led to one of the many small patient rooms. Five minutes later Dr. Ron Barton knocked.

"It's Dr. Barton."

"Come in," Amanda said.

Ron noticed a dull ring to her voice. Something was noticeably wrong. He entered the room and closed the door. Amanda obviously was upset. Her runny makeup and red, puffy eyes indicated she had been crying.

"What's the matter?" he asked.

She sniffled, and began to cry before she spoke.

"Philip found out about us," she managed. "He just called me a little while ago. He told me his lawyer is calling me later today."

Ron's heartbeat quickened. He was incredulous. "Jesus," he thought.

"What do you mean he found out? How the hell would he know?"

Amanda quit sniffling. She glared.

"He has a paid security detail! He has eyes and ears everywhere!"

Ron thought about what she had told him earlier at the polo grounds—that "she didn't care" if Philip found out about them.

"You asked for this," he thought. "Dad told you to stay clear of Philip Lucci."

He experienced a cold, sinking feeling as he pondered the inevitable repercussions—more specifically—what Lucci might do in retaliation for him rebuffing his employment offer *and* screwing his wife.

"He's rich and seemingly omnipotent," he thought. "I'm likely in trouble."

In a minute his life had changed irreparably.

"What are you going to do?" Ron asked. He handed her a *Kleenex*.

She wiped her nose and used the back of her right hand to wipe the tears from her eyes.

"I guess I have until Friday to move out. He said he'd give me until Friday and then he was bringing all of my stuff to the dump."

"He said that?" he asked.

"Yeah. And he said he wasn't going to give me a settlement, either. I guess I'll need to start looking for a job."

Ron couldn't believe it.

"He can't just cut you loose without taking care of you. You need to get an attorney. He has a responsibility to take care of you. You're still his wife."

"Ron, I cheated on him—he has grounds for divorce. I'll likely get something from him, but it won't be what I'm used to. I'll figure it out."

She looked to him with incredibly sad eyes.

He couldn't help but feel for her, as he was almost as scared as she was.

"Philip came here to my office yesterday with this guy Mack Dawkins and pitched me on working for Dixie."

"Philip came here?" she asked.

"Yeah. He wanted to double my salary and give me access to his corporate jet—he offered me the moon like he has everyone else. I told him no thanks. He didn't take no for answer easily, either."

"That's Philip," she said.

Ron was in a haze. He wondered what would happen next. He had a hunch Philip would do something in retaliation.

"What do you think he'll try to do to me for this?" Ron asked.

"What can he do?" she asked.

"I don't know, but I've got a feeling it could be a lot."

\*\*\*

Amanda left Ron to his afternoon patients. He was devastated. He felt trapped—almost like he had been trapped; but he knew otherwise. It was his fault—no one else's. Lacking an appetite, he skipped lunch and stayed in his office to catch up on paperwork. However, his mind was so scrambled in thought, that he couldn't muster the necessary focus. His phone rang. He picked it up.

"Yeah Amelia. Who is it?"

"It's a Dr. Thompson. He's apparently interested in a horse."

This was a call he definitely wanted to take.

"Put him through please."

"Sure."

"This is Dr. Ron Barton," said Ron, after he heard the connection go through.

"Dr. Barton!"

"Yes?"

"This is Dr. Ted Thompson—I met you at the stables at the Birmingham Polo Grounds." Fred Foster said, posing as Dr. Thompson.

"Yes Dr. Thompson, how are you?"

"Fine, I was calling about the horse. Did you sell her?"

"I did."

"Oh well, I just wanted to call and check. She's beautiful, and I would have loved to have had her."

"Dr. Thompson?" Ron interjected.

"Yes?"

"Why were you in my garbage alley on Saturday night?"

There was a moment of silence. Ron noticed his hesitation. He continued.

"Do you work security for Philip Lucci?"

Fred Foster was compromised. His cover was no longer effective. Made, he hung up the phone.

"Bastard!" Ron yelled inside the solitude of his office. Holding his forehead in his hands, he realized further the kind of real trouble he was in.

# 8

"So Philip, why don't you share with our listening audience what's new with Dixie Rehab these days," said Butch Bierbaum live on the air.

"Well, Butch, things have been going really well with Dixie. Since we signed Drs. Muster and Appleton last week our stock is up considerably to an all-time high and we are continuing to build a world-class medical team that will serve the Birmingham area well once the new digital hospital is built. Furthermore, nationally we continue to open and acquire new rehab clinics, as our concept is understood and embraced. We're really moving right now, Butch. Everything is falling into place. The hospital's groundbreaking is scheduled for next week and for Dixie Rehab, things really couldn't be any better. We're on a monster roll."

"For those of you just joining us, we're talking with Philip Lucci, CEO of Dixie Rehab, who *Forbes* Magazine recently listed as one of the country's highest-paid CEO's. Philip, you're an amazing guy--a multi-millionaire businessman, chairman of the board, accomplished country and western singer, philanthropist, airplane and jet pilot, cigarette boat racer…the list is a mile long. You are certainly a man of action. You're almost like a chameleon. Tell us--which new title could we possibly use to describe you lately?"

"Single," replied Philip.

There was a two-second interval of purposeful silence.

"Excuse me?" Bierbaum asked.

"Single. I'm single again. I'm not happy about it, but my wife and I are going through a separation."

"Whoa Philip—this is somewhat of a bombshell. Philip Lucci—CEO of Dixie Rehab—is now available to all of you single ladies out there. Now, let's see, Amanda—your current wife, is wife number two, correct?"

"That's right."

"Well, you certainly don't have to say it on the air, but any particular reason why number two didn't work out?"

"Now Butch, you know I don't like to kiss and tell, but in this case, it's not like that, so I don't mind at all. I caught her cheating on me."

"Whoa Philip—check that—double whoa—you're listening to the Butch Bierbaum show and we're chatting with Philip Lucci, CEO of Dixie Rehab, one of the richest men in America—who is now single, going through a break-up and what I can logically assume will eventually be a divorce—because his wife has been…"

Bierbaum enacted a long pause for dramatic effect.

"…cheating on him."

There was another emphatic pause.

"Do I assume correctly, Philip? Are you getting a divorce?"

"Yes Butch. I am."

"1-866-786-3345 is the number to get involved. Talk with Philip Lucci right now. Single ladies, you may want to call in. This guy has more cash than *Scarface*."

"Come on now, Butch," laughed Philip. "That's a bit much."

"Oh, I see our phone lines are lighting up for Philip Lucci—but before we take a few of these calls—I have to ask—Phil, who was your wife cheating with? Is it anyone we know?"

"I don't want to embarrass that person by saying any names, but I will say that he is her doctor—an orthopedic surgeon here in town—who likes to play polo."

"Whoa! You are listening to the Butch Bierbaum show, folks—the *only* place where you will get breaking news of this kind! Well, that pretty much narrows it down. I'm sure many of you out there have

PROFESSIONAL BONE

a pretty good idea of who the culprit is. Give us a call at 1-866-786-3345 to discuss it."

"Now Butch, I don't want to bring harm to this person. I mean that, too." Philip laughed.

"Yeah—I bet," said Butch. "Let's take a call from Fairhope, Alabama. Bill—you're on the Butch Bierbaum Show."

"Thanks for taking my call, Butch. Long-time listener, first-time caller."

"Thanks for the call, Bill." Butch answered.

"No problem. I wanted to say I'm sorry for Mr. Lucci. I know what he's going through. My wife cheated on me last year with a co-worker of mine. It was awful. It's a terrible feeling. I'm sorry Mr. Lucci."

"Thanks Bill. I appreciate it. Thank you very much. I'm just going to pray and hope for the best."

"Well, you've got the right idea, Mr. Lucci. Put your faith in the Lord."

"That's my plan—and I'm sticking to it." Lucci said.

"Thanks again for the call Bill. On line two we have Thad from Birmingham. Thad, you're on the Butch Bierbaum Show."

"Thanks for taking my call, Butch."

"No problem Thad. What's your question for Philip Lucci, CEO of Dixie Rehab?"

"I think I know who your wife is screwing."

"Really?" Bierbaum asked.

"Yeah."

"Who do you think it is, Thad?" Bierbaum asked.

"I think it's this young guy, Dr. Ron Barton. I saw him on TV last year promoting a polo tournament for charity. I remember he said he was an orthopedic surgeon. He's pretty sharp, too--and studly-looking. I can see why Mrs. Lucci was interested. He's probably a lot better in the sack…"

"Thanks for the call, Thad," said Bierbaum, cutting the caller off before any further damage could be done to the psyche of his most favored and lucrative sponsor.

\*\*\*

Dr. Ron Barton finished seeing his last patient at 4:15 p.m. He returned to his office and found Amelia waiting for him in the doorway. Ron could tell by the look on her face that they needed to talk. She had worked for him for nearly six years. They knew each other well as she handled the business side of his practice.

"What's up?" he asked.

"Come into your office. We need to talk." She answered.

They entered his office and closed the door. He sat behind his desk and she took one of two padded sitting chairs.

"Ron, Philip Lucci was on Butch Bierbaum's show today and the focus of the program was you and his wife."

Ron Barton became nauseated. He was almost physically sick. He knew where the conversation was going.

"What did he say?" Ron asked.

"He said that his wife is screwing her orthopedist who plays polo."

Ron hung his head in shame. He hadn't made it through the day and the entire state knew about his mistake.

"This is not good, Doc." Amelia said. "A couple of the late patients heard it on the radio on their way in to the office. I don't know what it will do for your practice, but it can't help."

Ron looked up, his face flush with color.

"What can I do?" he asked.

"You may want to get an attorney. If Lucci keeps using his media stroke to run your name through the mud, no telling what may happen. But seriously, what can an attorney do—if what he says is true?"

There was silence.

"Is it—is it true?" she asked.

He looked her in the eyes.

"Yes, it is."

# 9

Fred Foster rang Jim Boudreaux on his cell phone.

"Jim Boudreaux."

"Jim, this is Fred."

"Yeah, Fred. What's shakin'?"

"Dr. Barton."

"What about him?"

"You told me to stay in touch with him and I did."

"And?" Boudreaux asked.

"Well, I introduced myself out at the polo fields to him as a Dr. Ted Thompson. I led him on to think I was interested in purchasing one of his horses. So, I called him up today to inquire about the horse. And it didn't go too well."

"What happened?"

"When I followed Amanda to his house on Saturday night I made a pass behind his house via the garbage alley and when I rode through he was putting out his garbage. He apparently saw me. I had tried to avoid him seeing me, but he did because when I called him today he asked me if I was behind his house Saturday night—and if I worked for Philip Lucci. What's going on?"

"Don't worry about Barton—in fact—screw him! Forget about it. It's not a big deal. You've done your job. It's over. I told Philip what he wanted to know. He's getting a divorce. We're going to take care of Barton. In fact, it's already in the works."

"You sure I'm done?"

"You're done. Lay low."

"Okay then, will do. Thanks. Call me when you have something else."

"We will."

***

When he got home Ron noticed the red light on his phone was blinking, indicating that he had messages.

"Lovely," he thought. "I'm sure mom and dad have even heard by now."

Butch Bierbaum's show was syndicated across the State of Alabama to over 40 radio stations on the Butch Bierbaum Radio Network.

Ron delayed listening to his messages. He dreaded what he'd find on the machine.

He went to his bar instead and made himself a Long Island Iced Tea in a large insulated cup he used when tailgating at Auburn Football games.

Ron wasn't a big drinker, but he needed something to soothe his nerves. He had too much on his mind. He sat on his leather sectional couch and knocked back a fourth of the drink in two gulps. The three liquors worked quickly. He felt the drink's effects within a couple of minutes. He wondered if Lucci would try to ruin him. He then wondered *how* he would ruin him.

"He got a good start today with Bierbaum's show," he told himself.

His thoughts were interrupted by a phone call. He checked caller I.D. It was Amanda. He'd asked her to call him after 6:00 p.m. They planned to have dinner.

His emotions were mixed. He was both happy and sad to see her call, as he was trying to pin some of the blame on her—on someone other than himself. Yet, he knew it wasn't her fault. His mind raced back and forth.

"Hello," he answered.

"Hey," she said.

"You want to come over?" he asked. "I'll order Chinese. I don't feel like going anywhere."

"Sounds great," she said. "Do you have any wine?"

"Plenty. But if you have your own, bring it. I'll order the food. See you in a few, okay?"

"I'll be there in twenty minutes," she said.

Ron called in for the food. When he was done he again saw the blinking red light. He played the messages by entering the proper code on his phone handset. The computerized voice said that he had four messages. The first was from his father. All his dad said was to please call him when he got a chance. He erased the message. The second message was the exterminator trying to set an appointment for the annual termite treatment. The third message was from Dr. Pete Goldman. The message read:

"Ron—Pete Goldman—hey man, I heard about what's going on and I just wanted to let you know I'm behind you 100 percent. Look—give me a ring and let's have lunch. I have some things I want to talk to you about anyway. Hang in there man. Talk to you later."

Ron thought it was nice of him to call. The final message was from Leah. It read:

"Ron, it's Leah. Call me."

"That will be awkward as hell," Ron thought.

He sank back into his couch and tried to finish his drink while he waited for Amanda.

\*\*\*

Philip Lucci and Mack Dawkins finished the last of what were several lines of primo cocaine before they got into Mack's Black Eddie Bauer Edition Ford Explorer and headed to Birmingham's South Side to a favorite haunt of Mack's. It was a bright fall Tuesday evening. Both men wore shades and each carried a drink in a plastic Solo cup that they'd made inside Philip's office. Mack drove.

"What's the name of this place?" Philip asked.

"Club South" he replied. "I've had luck there before. It's a good place to hang out. There's often a nice mix of hookers in there—anything from college-aged talent to premium MILF."

Philip liked it. He'd already removed his wedding band. He was officially single and off and running full speed as always.

Minutes later they walked in the wide-open front door to Club South. It was cool, damp and dark inside. The bar, which reeked cigarette smoke and stale draft beer, was virtually empty, except for the bartender and an early thirty-something petite blonde wearing heavy makeup and silver eye shadow. The blonde sat at the bar and unflinchingly smoked her cigarette. She seemed wholly preoccupied.

Philip and Mack sat at the bar in front of where the bartender stood and ordered a drink. Philip ordered a *Lite* beer and Mack ordered a *Pinch* and water. While the bartender worked they traded glances at the blonde at the opposite end of the bar.

"She's not that bad," said Philip.

"I'd do her," answered Mack.

"That ain't saying much," laughed Philip, reeling in his bottled brew.

The bartender interrupted their conversation with a basket of fresh-popped popcorn from a nearby old-fashioned popping machine.

Philip looked at the basket. It gave him an idea.

"Watch and learn," he said to Mack.

Philip stood, grabbed the basket and his beer and walked to the other end of the bar to where the girl was seated. She was just finishing her cigarette, stamping it out in the glass ashtray before her. When Philip was a couple of feet from where she sat he stopped.

"Want some popcorn?" he enthusiastically asked in his best sales voice, placing the popcorn just inches from her reach.

She turned to her right, squared her shoulders and looked him in the eyes, simultaneously clutching her purse with her left hand.

"You wanna fuck?" she replied.

Philip could tell she was serious. She was ready to go.

Twenty minutes later at a nearby roach motel Philip was engaged in doggy-style sex with the stranger from the bar while she performed oral sex on Mack Dawkins. The two men high-fived each other and laughed wildly. For the next two hours they took turns with the woman, drinking a twelve pack of *Busch Lite* beer they stopped and bought on the way as well as cutting up more lines of coke. They even smoked a little of the reefer the girl said she scored earlier that afternoon. After each of the men had had enough, they dressed and smoked another joint that Mack rolled. They passed it around like they had earlier her sex. She was still naked as a jaybird as she waited to get high.

"Where are you from?" Philip asked, toking on the fat joint.

"Gadsden." She said. "Don't Bogart that thing," she added.

She took the number and puffed hard. She exhaled and spoke simultaneously.

"I've been in the halfway house here in B'Ham for the last three months. I was discharged this morning. God I hated that fucking place!"

She passed it to Mack. He didn't hit it. He just held it, wearing a dumbfounded look. It continued to burn, sending smoke in a continuous, wavy vertical line toward the stained ceiling. The long ash on the end of the joint fell to the tethered carpet. Philip and Mack looked at each other. Mack registered the fear in Philip's face as marijuana smoke filtered a column of waning window night light across the dingy motel room.

***

Amanda arrived at Ron's house just after the food arrived. Ron heard a faint knock at the door. He answered it. Amanda stood in the doorway in a blue jean skirt, hot pink muscle shirt and matching sandals. A bottle of white wine riddled with condensation swung from her left hand. She cradled her designer purse slung over her shoulder with her right hand. Two-carat diamond pendant earrings hung from each ear. Her sunglasses served as a hair clip. As usual, she looked fabulous.

"Goodness you're beautiful," he said. He was sincere. He was immediately no longer upset with her. It was impossible.

"Come on in," he added, gesturing her into the house. "The food just got here."

Amanda sauntered in with a purpose. She placed the wine on the dinner table next to the aromatic, boxed food. She gravitated toward Ron and planted a huge, wet kiss on his liquor-filled lips. They finished the long kiss with a tight embrace before finally pulling apart.

"I heard about Bierbaum's show today." She squeezed his arm. "I'm sorry Ron. I'm really sorry. I didn't want it to turn out like this. I didn't. I never wanted to hurt you."

"I know Amanda. I know. It's not your fault."

"Ron, you're a good person. You don't deserve this. I just want you to know that whatever happens that I care for you, and that I really admire you. The last thing I wanted was for you to be hurt because of me and my problems. I'm so sorry." Tears like tiny clear bubbles welled in her eyelids.

He appreciated her words. She appeared even sexier when she cried.

"I found out who discovered us." He said.

"Who?" She demanded. She was suddenly no longer crying.

"When we were at the polo grounds on Saturday there was a guy in the stable area who asked me where the clubhouse was. I was just talking to Hector so I told him I would walk him to it, since I was heading that way to have lunch with you. As we walked he told me that he was a physician—a Dr. Thomas—who was also interested in horses, and was visiting to attend a relative's wedding. I told him I was showing the second filly and that it was for sale. He asked for my card, said he was interested, and I told him to call me in a couple of days and I'd let him know if it was still available. Well, on Saturday night, when you came over for dinner, I took out the garbage right after you got here, remember?"

"Yeah."

"Well, when I went out back to the can in the garbage alley there was a blue car driving through. It was dusk, but I saw the face of the driver, and it was this Dr. Thompson, but I don't really think that's his name. I think he's the guy Philip paid to follow you."

"What makes you think so?"

"He called my office today and asked if I had sold the filly. I told him I had. But while I had him on the phone, I asked him why he was lurking in my garbage alley on Saturday night. He didn't say a thing after I asked. I then asked him if he worked for Philip Lucci."

"What did he say?"

"Nothing. He hung up the phone."

"Oh my God!" she said. She placed her hand over her mouth and her eyes widened.

"Philip told me that I'd hear from his lawyer today, but he never called."

She sounded as distraught as she looked.

"Philip has almost infinite resources and power, Amanda. I'm afraid he's going to ruin my practice. After the episode on Beirbaum's show today I am sure many of my patients will never see me again. I've thought a lot about it. I have a feeling he's going to go after my other colleagues at the clinic and make them the same offer he made me. Most of them will take it—not only for the money, but to also get away from me. I'm tainted goods now."

"What do you mean?" she asked.

"I am an accessory to adultery. You are my patient. This is the Bible Belt. I did more than just covet my neighbor's wife."

Amanda looked at the ground and again started crying.

She threw herself onto his couch and assumed a fetal position. There, she loudly wept. Ron ran to her side and held her.

"Amanda, come here," he said, grabbing each shoulder and turning her into his chest. She nestled her head at the base of his neck and cried. He stroked her soft, shiny hair and engulfed her scent. He rocked her gently.

"It's going to be okay, Amanda. I'll make it."

There was silence for just a moment.

"*We'll* make it," he added.

She stopped crying. He continued stroking her hair. She lifted herself and they embraced in a passionate kiss.

\*\*\*

After encouraging her to dress herself, Philip and Mack drove away from the motel room with the strange, psychotic woman. The ride back to the bar was only five minutes. She rode in the backseat of the *Explorer*.

"Do you need a job?" Mack asked her. He looked into the rearview mirror at her. She smoked a cigarette next to the open window.

"I do. Do you have anything for me other than a blowjob?" she asked.

Philip laughed.

"As a matter of fact, I do," replied Mack. "We have an opening in the mail room at our company. Do you think you could sort mail eight hours a day?"

She shrugged her shoulders and finished her cigarette with a flick of the wrist.

"Sure, I could handle that."

"Well," Mack said, "Why don't you give me your contact information and we'll see if we can get you set up to start working with us."

Philip handed her a pen and paper.

"Do y'all own some company or something?" she asked.

"Sort of. We run Dixie Rehab, and we're always looking for an extra hand."

It was now dark. She instructed Mack where to go and they drove up to her car. Before she exited the vehicle through the backseat passenger door she handed the paper and pen back to Philip.

"Y'all call me. I could work for y'all, cuz I need a job. Okay?"

"I'll give you a call in a day or two. Be careful." Mack said.

She shut the door and got into her vehicle.

Philip looked at the paper and let out a yelp.

"What' so funny?" Mack asked.

"Chastity Jones," Philip squealed. "*Chastity*--her name is Chastity Jones."

They both laughed uncontrollably as they drove away.

# 10

The next morning at the gym Ron was in between bench press sets working his shoulders on the dip bar when the morning television newscaster read the headline story.

"Philip Lucci's long-awaited dream of a world-class digital hospital breaks ground tomorrow next to the Dixie Rehab headquarters just off of the Philip Lucci Parkway. However, all is apparently not perfect in the multi-millionaire's world. He announced this morning via a company press release that he and his wife of six years—Amanda—are divorcing. Lucci in the release cites 'irreconcilable differences' as the cause for the sudden breakup. However, Lucci appears unfazed by the latest bit of bad news, as the release also announced that his country and western band, "The Honky Tonkers" will play on an outdoor stage tomorrow after the ground-breaking ceremonies involving a number of Alabama dignitaries, celebrities and socialites, including former Auburn running back and pro baseball star Flo Thompson, Governor of Alabama Dan Siegel, Randy Owen, lead singer of Alabama and Winston Groom, Fairhope author of Forrest Gump, among others."

Ron looked around the gym. He saw three guys a few benches over standing and talking. One of them motioned toward him. The two others looked his way before they noticed Ron was watching. Ron knew they were talking about him. Bierbaum's show had quickly destroyed his reputation. Six years of practice and philanthropy was now effectively all for naught. He was embarrassed. He cut his workout short and hit the showers. "I'm royally screwed," he thought.

When Ron arrived early at his clinic a few minutes later, as he walked toward the building he saw a huge black limousine underneath the drop-off area near the front entrance. The license plate read "Dixie 1."

"Lucci," he thought. "He's back."

The tall white limo driver walked around the vehicle and opened the middle passenger side door. Out came Lucci and Dawkins, dressed in suits. Ron walked straight toward them. Philip exited first. He stood and straightened his dark tie. He scanned the area and immediately spotted Dr. Ron Barton walking in his direction. Mack came out and stood next to him.

"Check this one out, Mack," said Philip, nudging Mack and pointing toward Dr. Barton.

"Oh look," said Mack, pointing directly at Ron, "It's the thief of hearts."

"Good morning Dr. Barton," said Philip. He showed no signs of malice or ill will.

Ron stopped a few feet short of the entrance and turned to the two men.

"Good morning gentlemen. Here to see anyone special?"

"Three of your colleagues, to be exact," answered Mack.

"They're going to bleed me dry," he thought.

"Fabulous. Good luck with that, gentlemen." Ron answered. He turned and walked hurriedly into the clinic and into his office. He buzzed Amelia.

"Yeah?" she answered. He didn't like her tone.

"I need to see you. Please come here," he said.

Two minutes later Amelia appeared in his doorway wearing a disturbed look. Her voice started to crack when she spoke.

"Lucci's here to see Drs. Furman, Leach and Palifax. I've already heard that Leach and Palifax are goners. If Furman bolts we won't be able to make the lease payment Ron. When Pete left we took a hit in terms of overhead costs. We're going to have to shut this place down and you'll have to go solo."

A familiar, nauseous feeling overcame Ron. His biggest fears were coming to fruition. Drs. Leach and Palifax were both in their mid-forties and had significant client bases. Moreover, Ron sub-leased their space within the building, and therefore he was responsible for the monthly rent. His dad had encouraged and helped him lease the larger space and sub-let to the other doctors in order to reduce his overhead expenses. It had turned out to be a great move—until now.

"Leach and Palifax are leaving?" He asked.

"I heard it straight from their secretaries' mouths. They're outta here, and that leaves only Furman. He's older, so I don't know if he'll want to go, but it's sorta becoming the en vogue move after yesterday's media blitz against you. I don't know what to say other than it doesn't look good, Ron. To tell you the truth, I'm really worried."

Amelia started to cry. Ron reminded himself that she was a single mom with three boys in private school. Their father had been killed a year earlier in a motorcycle accident. She was alone. Ron stood. She put her hands over her face and the tears fell.

"Amelia, hey, look, everything's gonna work out. If I have to go solo, I will, but I'll take care of you and your boys. I promise. You've been too good to me."

He walked and stood before her. He put his hand on her shoulder.

"Amelia, I vow to you I will not let you suffer because of any of this. We'll get through it. Things may change, but we'll make it."

She wiped her eyes and face and rubbed her cheeks on her sleeves.

"I'm just scared."

"I am too. But we're going to make it! I'm a good doctor and surgeon—regardless of what Lucci and Bierbaum say!"

"Screw Lucci!" Amelia snapped. "He's a prick!"

"Wow!" Ron laughed. "Where did that come from?"

Amelia perked up. She cracked a brief smile.

"I have a friend that works at Dixie."

Ron looked at her seriously, as if to say tell me more.

"And?" he asked.

"She told me that Lucci has all this wild security—nobody can get to his office without going through multiple levels of security staff, but that once every two weeks this well-dressed black guy arrives and walks right through and goes straight up to Lucci's office and he buzzes the guy in. She and everyone else there are positive the guy's a drug dealer and that Lucci's a user."

"Really?" countered Ron.

"Uh huh."

Amelia was again composed.

"Yeah, the word is he's a coke head. Plus, I heard through a friend that he tells his hired help at his house not to look him in the eyes like a military general would expect and he makes them change the toilet paper rolls whenever they use the bathroom—he makes them change the entire roll if they use only part of it. The guy is a complete jerk. He thinks his shit doesn't stink, I'm sure."

Ron couldn't help but laugh.

"What?" she asked.

"I love your spunk."

"Thanks, but I really hate that S.O.B.—and I'm proud of you for not going with him. Most would have. You are a good guy Ron—and you're a great doctor."

"I appreciate that, Amelia."

"I mean it. And I want you to know that I don't blame you for falling for Amanda."

Ron blushed. He didn't have an answer.

"She's absolutely gorgeous, and I'm sure she was beyond miserable with Philip. I see exactly how it happened. Maybe under different circumstances none of this would have gone down like it did. It just so happens she's married to a narcissist sociopath."

Ron gritted his teeth.

"I'm down, but I'm not out Amelia. Don't write me off."

"I'm not, Ron. I'm still with you. You can count on me."

"That's my girl." He said.

***

At the digital hospital groundbreaking site Philip Lucci stood shoulder-to-shoulder with Mack Dawkins, Baron Screem, and several other members of Dixie Rehab's Board of Directors, along with Governor Dan Siegel and other prominent local politicians. Each man wore a white hard hat adorned with a Dixie Rehab logo and each had in

# PROFESSIONAL BONE

hand a brand new shovel, except for Philip, who clutched a gold-plated shovel and wore a gold hard hat. Everyone wore coats and ties. It was a brilliant fall day. The air was crisp with little wind. It was a great day for a groundbreaking. The ceremony went off as planned with all of the local media outlets attending. Dozens of still photos were taken and there were many video cameras. The event was thoroughly covered—just as Lucci had planned.

Shortly after the ceremony was over Philip disappeared. He reappeared moments later on an adjacent staged area wearing blue jeans, cowboy boots, a five-gallon, black Stetson cowboy hat, a blue denim western shirt with the sleeves cut off and an electric guitar slung over his shoulder. He walked to the microphone, waving to everyone in attendance. Strangely, in the moments after Philip left to change clothes the crowd grew exponentially, consisting entirely of over 350 lanyard and I.D.-wearing Dixie Rehab employees who walked over from the nearby headquarters. Some of the media stayed and trained their video cameras on the burgeoning spectacle. Philip addressed the well-paid throng.

"Good afternoon, everybody," he said in his best Alabama drawl. "I really appreciate y'all coming out to attend the groundbreaking ceremony for our new digital hospital. Our plans are to revolutionize health care not only here in Birmingham, Alabama, but across the country and the world. As many of you already know, we operate facilities in all fifty states and even overseas. However, we're just getting started. And speaking of getting started, I would like to introduce all of you to the members of my band, "The Honky Tonkers.""

Philip introduced the four members one-by-one. They consisted of former professional and semi-pro musicians from Nashville who had all at one time or another in their careers experienced at least a modicum of success. Moreover, just like the crowd of Dixie Rehab employees that had forcibly gathered to watch and listen, they were well-paid. Each of the band members took their respective spots on stage and audibly tweaked their instruments. The drummer gave Philip a nod, indicating that they were ready.

"Ladies and Gentlemen, we are "The Honky Tonkers" and this is our best-selling single, "Honk if you want to Honky Tonk.""

The song wasn't really a best-seller, but it had been played incessantly on the local country radio scene because Philip paid the station managements handsomely to get it air time.

Philip crooned, "When staying home has lost its fun…when you no longer feel she's the one…you have to go and do your thing…I say—Honk, if you want to honky tonk…"

The spectacle unfolded. The compensated crowd clapped and gyrated back and forth in what could only be described as a ridiculous Southern stereotype gone bad. Nevertheless, footage of the staged event held to purchased applause later aired on the evening Birmingham television news.

# 11

On Wednesday afternoon after work Ron went home and decided it was time for him to call his father. He and his dad had a great relationship, and it was wholly unlike him to not quickly return his calls. It was just that he was ashamed of what had happened. He knew his dad would not approve of him seeing a married woman, and he of course wanted the best for him professionally. It's just that it was difficult for him to broach such a topic as adultery with his father. Ron was raised Baptist and he knew that back in Fairhope his dad would be in a difficult position. He dialed his home number. It rang three times before there was an answer.

"Hello," Ron's mom said in a melodic tone.

"Hi Mom." Ron said, sounding like he did when the Fairhope High School football team lost to rival Daphne in overtime during his junior year.

"Hi Ron. How are you?" She said, trying to sound consoling.

"I'm okay, Mom. Is Dad there? He called."

Ron's mom knew he would rather talk to his dad at this point. She knew the story. She'd unfortunately heard about it during water aerobics at the city pool the day before. One of her good friends had pulled her aside in the locker room and explained the horror of the Bierbaum program revelation.

"Yes honey. He is home. He's in the backyard. Let me get him."

Moments later his father was on the line. He cleared his throat before he spoke.

"Hey Ron." He said in a hushed, fatigued tone.

"Hey Dad. You called?"

His dad wasted no time.

"Yes, I did. What's this I hear about your new girlfriend—Philip Lucci's wife?"

"Dad, I made a mistake."

"I'd say." He said with emphasis.

There was silence.

"I told you to stay clear of the guy. Shacking up with his wife isn't exactly that."

This was difficult for Ron. He respected his father.

"Dad, she wasn't happy with him."

"She's married, Ron."

"She's getting a divorce."

"Ron, son, this isn't good for you. The publicity is awful. How is your practice going to handle it?"

"Dad, I'm going to deal with it."

"Ron, you need to stay clear of her. I don't think any good can come of it. Lucci is powerful and vindictive. He'll hurt you."

"He already has."

"What has he done?"

"He's likely stole all four of my doctors in the clinic. Three signed with him and the last is likely gone too. They bought into his new digital hospital contract. They're working in Dixie Rehab-friendly clinics until the hospital is built."

"All four of them are likely gone?"

"Yeah. Lucci gave them a sweet deal. I am the only one who's said no."

"You're kidding?"

"No. I turned him down—he offered me money, Auburn football tickets, use of the corporate jet, sponsorship of the polo tournament, a new office—the whole nine yards. But the other guys couldn't. After the revelation on the Bierbaum show I think they had a hard time saying no to the money *and* having to stay with me."

Ron's dad didn't say anything about the Bierbaum show. He wasn't a fan of the program. He found out about it at Ken & Vernon's Barber Shop in downtown Fairhope. It was embarrassing.

"Is Amelia still with you?"

"Oh yeah. She's golden, as always. We're fine. We'll go solo if we have to."

"Well, hang in there, Ron. It seems like you have feelings for the woman."

"Dad—she's absolutely drop-dead gorgeous."

***

Ron and Amanda met on Wednesday evening at a restaurant in Homewood, Alabama, a nearby suburb. They nestled into the upscale bar & grill and ordered cocktails. While they waited for their appetizers they couldn't help but notice the evening news report on the widescreen television above the bar just a few feet away.

The black female newscaster was dressed sharply in a bright red dress. She was outdoors at the scene of the groundbreaking. In the background, Lucci and the other dignitaries could be seen pushing their shovels into the ground.

"One man's dream became a reality today when Dixie Rehab's CEO Philip Lucci and members of the board of directors, key employees, Governor Dan Siegel and local celebrities broke ground on a new standard-setting digital hospital that will eventually employ thousands of Birmingham residents. But the event turned out to be more than just a mundane groundbreaking…"

The television image and sound switched to Philip Lucci in a black cowboy hat playing his guitar and singing on stage. "I say—Honk, if you want to honky tonk…"

Images of the compensated crowd wearing Dixie Rehab lanyards were shown providing their purchased applause. The segment finished with a short shot of Philip smiling and waving to the crowd.

"He makes me sick!" Amanda said to Ron.

"He doesn't appear to be a good singer." He answered.

"He's horrible!" she said.

"Why does he do it, then? Certainly people have told him he sucks, huh?"

"I've told him he sucks. But that doesn't matter with Philip. He's a narcissist. He does things like that because it makes people look at him. Did you notice that everyone in the crowd was Dixie Rehab employees? He pulled them all out of their cubbyholes at Dixie to go outside and cheer his pathetic country act! What a joke!"

"It seems like he would think that being a country singer would make him look less serious as a business man. I don't know."

"Ron—you don't get it—he's crazy! He's concerned only with feeding his insatiable ego. I don't think he even realizes how wealthy he is. It's all about power and ego for him now."

Ron thought of Amanda's pending divorce and how she would fare given she'd committed adultery. He knew little about divorce law but he had heard that it would definitely give Philip the upper-hand in terms of a settlement toward alimony.

"How's moving going? Did you get a lot of your stuff moved today?" he asked.

"I moved a few things, mostly clothes and jewelry and other personal effects. I guess Philip will allow me to have some of the furniture that I want. I don't really know where I'll move to."

"I've got an extra bedroom," Ron answered with a smile.

Amanda returned the smile.

"You mean I could stay in your guest room?"

"No." Ron answered. "Your stuff could. You would stay with me."

They laughed.

"I met with a divorce attorney today," Amanda said.

"Really? How did that go?"

"Okay, I guess. Since I cheated on Philip it gives him grounds for divorce. The lawyer said that short-term until the finalization he has to continue to take care of me, but that long-term, he will be availed from having to do so. Basically, because I cheated on him I lose my meal ticket. In short, I need to start looking for a job; because once I'm divorced I won't have an income. Oh, and Philip asked for his ring back."

Ron had noticed earlier that she wasn't wearing her boulder.

"He's taking the ring back?"

"Well, it's worth $3.2 million."

Ron's eyes widened.

"Is he asking for all of 'his' jewelry back?"

"No, not yet. I'm sure he'll come up with a list of what I can keep. I have several bracelets and necklaces that are really valuable. I guess I'll just have to wait and see what he decides."

"Well, Philip's going to do what he wants to do, I guess."

"Now you're starting to understand him." She said. "That's how it works with him."

The waitress brought their food and drinks. Ron continued their conversation.

"Things aren't going too well for me at the clinic."

"What's wrong?"

"Philip was there this morning."

Amanda's face wore immediate concern.

"What for?"

"He stole two more doctors from my group. That makes three now, and it really hurts because I sublease the space to them and when they go I'm going to be in a real financial pinch. I'm likely going to have to go solo. Like you, I'll have to wait and see, but it doesn't look too good. I also have a sinking feeling a lot of my former patients will find other doctors. Philip is going to have his way with me here for a while. I'm going to have to claw my way back, but I'll do it."

"I have faith in you, Doc." Amanda said.

"Thanks."

There was a pause.

"And I'll eventually settle the score with Philip." Ron's tone was deadly serious.

While Amanda was attracted to Ron's bravado, it simultaneously scared her into a shiver. She knew how ruthless Philip could be.

# 12

Dixie Rehab CFO Baron Screem nervously perused the spreadsheets on his computer screen inside his posh Dixie Rehab Headquarters office. The tabulated figures were the actual cash reserves of Dixie Rehab. He kept these records completely separate of his office computer—on a laptop he kept locked in a lower desk drawer. They were altogether different from the numbers the company quarterly reported to Wall Street.

Dixie Rehab's cash was being rapidly depleted as a result of the new professional hires it had recently made, but mainly because of Philip's continued, brash excessiveness. Baron had been trying to tell Philip for many months that he had to slow down the discretionary spending, but to no apparent avail. A year earlier Philip had purchased the company's twelfth jet, a $35 million toy that Philip said was absolutely "necessary" to cut future hospital deals. Moreover, Philip had spent hundreds of thousands on "business" trips for him and the board of directors that were wholly avoidable. Baron felt he was going to bankrupt the company if Philip didn't stop spending what was essentially stockholder money.

Baron Screem was born in Blanchard, Louisiana near Shreveport in 1943. He attended Louisiana State University where he earned an economics degree. After taking additional accounting courses he took the CPA exam and passed. He worked for two small mom and pop companies as an accountant before landing the job of controller for Southern Rehab after an interview with their bright young Vice President, Philip Lucci.

Baron reported to Lucci at Southern Rehab and when the company was bought out Philip looked to him to invest in the founding of the new company and to serve as its CFO. Baron knew Philip's questionable tendencies well, but he also knew he was as brilliant as he was dubious—and a fantastic salesman. He had to give the new venture a chance, even though his wife was always leery of Lucci.

In addition to the spending, Dixie Rehab had less cash because it was proportionally taking in less money—even though it was still growing as a result of its latest acquisition spree. Baron's building consternation stemmed from the fact that predictably, as Dixie grew and succeeded, so did its emulating competitors. By late 1995 Dixie had serious competition in the rehabilitative care market. There were at least four viable national firms purporting to provide the same services as Dixie. Albeit they were smaller, but because of that they were offering their services at a cheaper rate. As a result, Dixie's market share was shrinking. However, Baron's repeated attempts to report to Wall Street this alarming revenue trend was repeatedly squelched by Philip, who insisted that he wouldn't, "let an accounting glitch kill his baby." The company had reported for 42 quarters revenue projections that met or exceeded Wall Street expectations, but for the last five and a half years—more than half of the time period—they had cooked the books in order to maintain their lucrative stock options and annual bonuses.

At first Baron rationalized that he'd only fudge the numbers once or twice, but that was irrational because the deception continued. He felt the fraud had continued for far too long, and as a result, his nerves were shot. As the CFO, he was solely responsible for the financial health as well as the reporting of the company. Despite his many self-explanations to the contrary, deep down he knew it was his fault. Furthermore, he knew one day the game would be up—that they could not continue to simply manufacture revenues. Sooner or later the charade would end and he would likely end up incarcerated, dead or possibly both, before it all panned out.

Baron popped two large *Prilosec* pills and washed them down with bottled *Evian* water. His drinking had increased considerably over the past two years as the fraud grew exponentially, and he felt it. At 57, he wasn't supposed to feel eighty. The only way he knew to effectively kill a hangover was to start drinking again, and for him, 5:00 p.m. couldn't come early enough most days, as he was always out the door and at the bar of one of his favorite local watering holes in order to help him forget about the fraud—and more importantly—his inability to stop it.

Baron had gone over more than a half dozen or more scenarios in his head of how he would finally confront Philip and convince him that it was time to report legitimate numbers—that there was a better way. But, he never could muster the courage to do it. To Baron, Philip was a really scary guy—a diabolical Southern cross between Hitler and Hannibal Lecter—and just the kind of guy that would do anything to protect his accumulated wealth, power and status. He feared for his life. Moreover, Baron, like the other founders of the company and upper level management, had become stinking rich as a result of the company's success and subsequent fraud. And so like the others, as his income and wealth grew, so did the pace of his lifestyle, taking on homes and cars and vacations he'd only previously dreamed of. Now, caught between greed and fear, he was precariously petrified into an alcohol-induced state of inaction, which was the easiest way for him to cope, given the circumstances.

Baron's spreadsheet reflections were interrupted by a quick, recognizable knock on his doorframe. He looked up and saw Mack Dawkins. Mack always knocked the same way. Therefore, it was easy to know who it was without looking because only he and Mack and Philip occupied the top floor, with Philip's office taking up more than half of the available square footage at the building's zenith. Baron's door was open, so he saw Mack standing in the doorway wearing a brand new gray business suit and colorful tie. His flowing brown hair was combed over to the right. He was clean-shaven, physically fit and looked extremely energetic—the veritable portrait of the successful CAO.

"What's up Baron?" Mack asked with an upbeat smile.

Baron shut his laptop.

"Nothing much. What's going on?"

"We've got some new hires that need to be added to the payroll."

"Oh yeah?"

"Yeah. We signed two new doctors today from the Birmingham Sports Clinic. Here are their names and social security numbers along with their compensation agreements."

"Alright," said Baron, quickly looking over each folder. He didn't recognize the names Leach and Palifax.

"And I have one more," Mack said.

"Yeah?" Baron asked.

"Yeah." Mack sat down before Baron's desk.

Baron could tell he had something to tell him. Mack looked behind him toward the door and looked back, as if he were concerned about someone eavesdropping.

"Me and Philip went honky tonking Tuesday afternoon. He and Amanda broke up—you heard?"

"Yeah. I was listening to Bierbaum's show when the news broke."

"Well, we hit this little haunt over in South Points and picked up this nympho."

"Really?" Baron asked, seemingly incredulous.

"Yeah! It was fucking unreal! Philip and I walked into the place and they had this young blonde sitting at the bar—and she looks pretty good. There was nobody else in there. We ordered drinks and the bartender gave us popcorn. Philip, who's now single, had to showoff. He picked up the popcorn and his beer and walked over to the girl. He asked her if she wanted some popcorn—and get this—she turned to him and asked him—'you wanna fuck?'"

"No way!" Baron said.

"Just like that!"

"Oh God," Baron said. "What happened next?"

"Well, we took her to some cheap hotel and double-teamed her for a couple of hours. Turns out she needs a job. Philip wants to keep her around, so I thought we could put her in the mail room. I've already talked to Bobby down there and he said he could find something for her to do. So, Philip said to go ahead and put her in for $15 an hour."

"Well, okay," Baron said. "I'll take care of it."

"Unbelievable!" Baron thought.

"And Baron, I was thinking…"
"About?"
"Next time you see Philip…"
"Yeah?"
Mack grinned from ear to ear.
"Go up to him and ask him if he wants some popcorn!"
"Oh man!" Baron laughed.

*** 

Ron Barton reported to work on Friday morning and Amelia was waiting near his office door. He could tell by her countenance and posture that she had bad news.

"Good morning." Ron said.

"Not so fast." She replied.

"Let me guess," he said. "All of them are gone."

"Furman just left here. He stopped by to tell me in person. Leach and Palifax both handed me typed letters by their secretaries. I guess it was too tough for them to explain in person that they are greedy bastards. At least Furman was honest. He said he was only going to work five more years at the higher salary and retire. He said it was 'just too good to pass up.'"

Ron was disheartened, but he saw it coming.

"Well, I hoped for better, but I certainly expected it, given what Lucci was offering."

There was a moment of silence. Amelia's face wore the same fearful look that normally preceded tears.

"It looks like we need to find a new place to practice medicine, right? There's no way we'll be able to make the lease payment without their help."

"Absolutely. We need to start looking now. All four guys said that they would honor their lease—Lucci is apparently picking up that tab for them—but, that only gives us three more months to operate here."

"Good enough," said Ron. "I say once we get payment from them we'll go ahead and pay off the lease and be done with it. We'll find a new place and move and start over. Let's both start looking. I guess if we're going to be solo we can operate just about anywhere. We could even renovate an old residence if we had to."

Ron could tell she was getting uneasy again. Her lip was nearly quivering. He'd have nothing of it.

"Remember what I told you Amelia—I am going to take care of you and your boys—okay?"

"Okay," she said, taking a deep breath.

"We're going to be fine."

"I'll talk to a real estate agent." She said with a smile.

"Good idea," he added.

"You've got some messages. I put them on your desk. Your first appointment is at 8:45."

"Thanks Amelia."

She walked away. Ron checked his watch. It was 8:30. He had fifteen minutes. He walked to his desk and sat down. He picked up the three messages awaiting him. One was Dr. Leah Thompson asking him to call her.

"Don't want to go there." He thought.

The next one was from Dr. Pete Goldman. "I need to get back with him," He said to himself.

The third was from a Dr. Stan Troutman, Director of the Alabama Medical Association, asking him to please return the call.

Ron wondered what Dr. Troutman wanted. He'd heard of him, but did not know him. He felt it might be important. He dialed his number.

His secretary answered.

"Dr. Troutman's office, Beth speaking, may I help you?"

"Yes, this is Dr. Ron Barton returning Dr. Troutman's call."

"Dr. Barton, please hold. Dr. Troutman is expecting your call. I'll put you right through."

Ron waited a moment or two.

"Dr. Barton?"

"Yes?"

"Good morning!"

"Good morning."

"How are you today?"

"Fine sir. How may I help you? I have an 8:45 appointment."

"Dr. Barton, I'm calling to inform you that you have been nominated for the award of Outstanding Orthopedic Surgeon for the State of Alabama granted by the Alabama Medical Association. The award will be presented at our annual convention in eight weeks, and we of course would like you to attend."

Ron was flattered.

"Well, this is certainly an honor Dr. Troutman. I definitely plan to attend."

"Excellent. I've heard a lot of great things about you Dr. Barton. I look forward to meeting you."

"I look forward to meeting you as well, Dr. Troutman. Could you do me a favor?"

"Certainly—what is it?"

"Could I have my secretary call yours and get the specifics related to the convention? I really need to get going."

"Absolutely."

"Terrific. Thanks for the call Dr. Troutman."

"You are welcome Dr. Barton. Have a great day."

"You do the same."

Ron hung up the phone.

"That's nice to know I was nominated," he thought.

Ron wasn't someone who craved recognition, but he felt that winning the award would really benefit him and his career during what could only be considered a trying time.

# 13

On Friday Amanda was able to finally, with the help of a moving crew, get the last of her things from what was now her former residence. Her attorney had been dealing with Philip's, and it looked like Philip was willing to give her a divorce settlement of $100,000, her vehicle, all of her clothes and only selected pieces of jewelry and furniture that valued under $3,000 per item. Because of her infidelity she wasn't in a position to collective bargain, but she was also simply glad to finally be done with Philip; so in all she felt the tentative agreement was acceptable. She just wanted to be with Ron.

Ron helped Amanda move her things into his house. In the end she decided to only keep a few pieces of furniture, so the bulk of it was items like clothes, electronics, pictures, personal effects and beauty aids. Amanda felt liberated to finally be away from Philip, and according to her attorney, her divorce would be final in about two weeks, as Philip was just as ready as she was to move on.

Ron loved the idea of Amanda moving in with him. After a few dream-like mornings, days and nights with her, the humiliation and pain associated with the extremely public revelation of the adultery and losing his medical clinic, were, in his mind, worth it. She was the most beautiful thing he'd ever seen, and he was also beginning to understand that she was also a good person—one who had been repeatedly traumatized by an overbearing, self-consumed husband.

In short order Ron received the rent payouts of the four doctors who left the clinic. He paid off the remaining balance on his lease and began to aggressively look for a suitable office space. He and Amanda even spent time in the evenings driving around looking for a working alternative. The entire experience was humbling to Ron. Prior to his collision with Lucci, everything had always gone like clockwork for him. It was the first real bump in the road he'd encountered.

In the meantime, Amelia retained a realtor. The search yielded two solid prospects. One was an old veterinarian's office near downtown, that was a little small and would need an addition to accommodate a larger waiting area and office space, and the other was an office building in the same area that would also require structural improvements. After visiting each locale with Amelia, Ron decided to allow her to make the decision, knowing well that either choice would require additions. Ron felt it was better that she decide, since she would handle everything.

Amelia decided that the veterinarian's office was the more suitable of the two, although it required significant improvements. Ron told her to go ahead and find an architect and a contractor and build it out to suit once the deal went through. He made an offer $10,000 below the asking price and the owner countered halfway in between at $5,000 below the asking price. Ron again countered with $6,500 less and the deal was done. He had a new office for his now-solo practice. Oddly, he was doing what his father did for years in Fairhope.

Ron thought long and hard about the decision to go solo. If it was not for Amelia, he would have seriously contemplated heading home to Fairhope, where his father's office was for sale. It would have been an easy transition. He and Amanda could have moved into his parent's home on Ono Island for a few weeks until they found a place. It would have been a breeze compared to life in Birmingham. Of course, he wouldn't have made as much money in Fairhope, but he figured he could be just as happy—or even happier, as the pace of life was slower there, and it had the polo fields of his youth, Mobile Bay, and the talc-like powder and good times of Orange Beach. But, to return home would have meant defeat, and deep down he knew it.

## PROFESSIONAL BONE

Dr. Ron Barton was a fighter. He was above average in every respect, and he had never been a quitter. In his young life he'd succeeded by facing fear--by getting up after being knocked down, by persevering with a devout belief in himself. As far as he could tell, he'd run into bad luck and in the end the law of averages would prevail and he'd again be back on top. Regarding Amanda, however, his feelings were still somewhat mixed. He felt bad for having sexual relations with a married woman. He knew that it was morally wrong. However, he was quickly falling for her, as she fulfilled a part of his life that was previously unsatisfied. In making a mistake he had found happiness, and he felt she was also happy as a result of the adultery, so he could deal with it. Moreover, his worldview wasn't so pious that he felt he could not be forgiven by his Creator. With seemingly the worst behind him, he looked forward to a bright future with Amanda, intent on enjoying himself without any pressure to marry, as he knew she wouldn't want to rush into anything given her plight.

Amanda's divorce went through as planned and she received her nominal settlement from Philip. She began interviewing and within two weeks landed another pharmaceutical sales job with a new drug company called *Pfizer*. The salary and hours were great and she and Ron settled in nicely together, enjoying each other's company in the evenings and on weekends.

Amelia did a great job of renovating the old vet's office to suit their needs. She and the architect collaborated on a façade build-out that added 750 square feet to the front of the building and her idea to knock out an interior wall created a great office space in which she could work. Furthermore, with Ron's consent she found an interior decorator to help with paint, wall artwork and furnishings, and when it was done, everything looked great. Ron couldn't believe the transformation when it was finally finished. A crowning accent Amelia added was an ornate, hand-painted wooden sign for the front yard that read, "Dr. Ron Barton" with "Orthopedic" underneath.

The relocation turned out to be a real success, because Ron was able to retain many of his former patients after he sent out a letter explaining that he was going to practice alone and had been recently nominated as Alabama's Top Orthopedic Surgeon. The new office was not only close to the hospital where he would regularly perform surgery, it had an adjacent side lot that provided adequate parking for visiting patients.

Ron's parents came up shortly after he moved into the new office. His mother brought flowers she got from the City of Fairhope Public Works Director. Fairhope spent millions on flowers each year for their flower beds on nearly every street corner and because Ron's mom had important friends, she got free chrysanthemums, lilies, pansies and tulips to plant in Ron's office's front yard. However, his parents really made the near four-hour drive to Birmingham not to plant flowers, but to meet Amanda, as they were thoroughly intrigued by her story and reported movie star looks.

Although he was 35, Ron was still a little squeamish about having his parents meet Amanda, as they had really liked Leah and had hoped he would have married her and given them grandkids before her biological clock stopped ticking. He knew his mom really liked Leah and that it would be difficult for her to immediately like Amanda, especially since she looked like the consummate gold digger for marrying Lucci.

Ron met his parents out at his office earlier in the day and helped his mom and dad plant the flowers they brought for his new office lawn. His mother made a nice arrangement around the wooden sign with his name, and he really liked the way it looked. He thanked her. His parents were staying at the *Wynfrey*, the place they usually stayed when they were visiting Ron, as it was Birmingham's only decent hotel. He told them that he had reservations at *Bodega*, an upscale eatery for Birmingham's "pretty people," and his mom and dad's favorite, for 8:00 p.m., and that he and Amanda would meet them there.

***

Ron and Amanda arrived at the restaurant early, at 7:45. Ron wanted to make sure they weren't late, and also, he wanted to be there before his mom and dad so he could scope the place out beforehand to see who was there. He was nervous. He and Amanda had not yet been to *Bodega's* as a couple, and the fact that his mom and dad were going to be there made him even more anxious. It was a Saturday night. The place teemed with life. When the beautiful couple entered, they turned many heads and created as many or more whispers.

Ron wore dark blue jeans, polished black loafers, and a black, long-sleeved button down with a tee shirt underneath. Amanda wore blue jeans, cowboy boots and a lovely multi-color cashmere sweater that made her look more busty than normal, even though it showed none of her cleavage. She wore no earrings and little makeup or jewelry other than a modest bracelet and a watch. Her shiny dark brown hair—which she had rolled and brushed, hung to her shoulders.

"You look terrific tonight." Ron said after they were seated.

"Thanks," Amanda answered. "I'm a little nervous about meeting your parents."

"Don't talk to me about being nervous," he said with a funny look. She smiled.

They ordered cocktails. Just as the waitress was bringing them to their table, Philip Lucci walked through the front door with Mack Dawkins. High on nearly two grams of cocaine, a sunburned Philip and Mack wore sunglasses, golf shirts, slacks, and Dixie Rehab visors. Ron faced the door. Amanda faced him. She had no idea Philip was at the restaurant. Philip did not immediately see Ron. He and Mack made their way to the bar and ordered drinks. Ron elected not to say anything to Amanda. He didn't want to make her uncomfortable as well.

Moments later Ron's parents entered the restaurant. His dad wore a baby blue seersucker suit with a white bow tie and his mom wore an expensive gold evening gown. They were dressed a little nice for the locale, but they looked good. Ron told Amanda they had arrived.

"Here they are," he said. He stood and waved to them. His dad saw where they were seated. He smiled, waved and led his mother in their direction.

When Ron stood Philip Lucci saw him. He also saw his ex-wife, Amanda seated next to him at the table. He surveyed the scene and realized that the two older folks were Ron's parents. The resemblance was there. Philip became enraged with jealousy. He nudged Mack.

"Look at this—It's Barton and Amanda—and his parents. They're meeting the new girlfriend. How sweet is that?"

"Oh really?" Mack answered. "Maybe we should buy them a round of drinks?"

"Good idea," said Philip. "Send them a bottle of *Don*."

Mack ordered the expensive champagne from the bartender and instructed him to have it sent to the Barton's table.

Ron continued to stand until his mom and dad made it to their table. Amanda stood once they were at the table, next to Ron.

"Hey Mom. Hey Dad." He hugged his mother and pecked her on the cheek.

"Hey sweetheart," she said.

He shook hands with his dad.

"Mom, Dad, this is Amanda."

Amanda gave them a million dollar smile and greeted them in her most congenial drawl.

"So nice to meet you Mrs. Barton, Dr. Barton."

Ron's mother shook her hand and graciously smiled. His dad shook her hand.

Everyone sat.

"How are y'all doing this evening?" Ron's dad asked.

"We're just fine. We've been enjoying our drinks, just waiting for y'all," said Ron.

Their waitress walked up to the table with a chilled bottle of *Don* and four glasses. Behind her was one of the busboys placing an ice bucket and stand.

"Good evening everyone. I'll be glad to take any additional drink orders in a second, but you have a good friend at the bar who sent over champagne."

Amanda looked toward the bar. She spotted Philip and made eye contact. Philip and Mack raised their glasses as if they were toasting them, and smiled. Amanda's heart sank into her stomach. She wanted to cry.

"That's awful nice of them," said Ron's mother.

"No it's not," Ron interjected. "It's Philip Lucci! That sonofabitch! Take it back! We don't want it!"

"Excuse me?" asked the waitress. She was incredulous. No one ever refused free *Don* before.

"Take it back!" Ron ordered, pointing toward the bar. "I don't want champagne—especially from him!"

She got the point.

"Yes sir. I'm sorry." She left with the bottle and glasses and her accomplice followed.

"I ought to go over there and let him have it," Ron said.

Ron's mom and dad were shocked. Everyone in the restaurant stared at their table. Everyone at Ron's table stared at Philip and Mack, who were laughing like high school kids along with two bleached blondes they'd met and treated to Patron Tequila shots.

"Please don't, Ron." Amanda asked in her sweetest voice. "Please, just ignore him. All he wants is attention. Ignoring him is the best thing you could possibly do."

Ron swallowed his pride and did his best to salvage the evening. Amanda recovered well from the pain Philip caused. She was pleasant and composed throughout the hour-long dinner. Philip left shortly after the incident, along with Mack and the two blondes they picked up at the bar; finally giving the Bartons time to get to know Amanda. Everyone relaxed when Philip left. It was like a weight was lifted from their shoulders.

When dinner was finished, Ron's dad picked up the tab. By this time, Ron's mother had warmed to Amanda, and the two couples had separated and paired with the other. The girls went to the restroom to freshen up before they left. Ron and his dad walked outside so his father could puff on a Cuban cigar. By this time night had fallen, but it didn't stop the many revelers that had gathered on the umbrella-strewn porch outside. Two dozen or more people enjoyed cocktails and laughter as well as the evening mountain breeze.

"You weren't kidding about Amanda," Ron's dad remarked as he lit his Cuban. "She's a real looker."

"Thanks Dad. Isn't she beautiful?"

"Stunning, as a matter of fact. I didn't anticipate how beautiful she really is."

"She's a good girl, too, Dad. She grew up dirt poor. Her dad was a boozer and her mom was crippled. She only married Lucci to escape all that. She made a mistake—and so have I—but it's brought me close to her, so that's a good thing. I'm happy."

Ron's dad puffed on the cigar.

"Just be careful, Ron. Remember what I said about Lucci. The guy's extremely dangerous."

"Dad, she's done with him. Her divorce is final. I'm going solo. It's a fresh start. I'm excited."

The two women burst through the front door laughing uncontrollably.

Ron and his father turned to them.

"What's so funny?" the older Dr. Barton asked.

"Oh my God!" Amanda said. "We were coming out of the stalls in the women's room and there was this short man standing there peeing in the sink!"

Ron's mom took over. She was nearly hysterical.

"He was almost like a midget—he could barely reach the front of the sink. He was peeing all over the place! He was terribly drunk. He said, 'Excuse me ladies, but I had to pee.' He almost fell backward. He stumbled. We died laughing and ran out behind him!"

"Was he shorter than Lucci?" Ron quipped.

"Much shorter," replied Amanda, frowning at him. She quickly smiled again. "It was ridiculous."

They all settled down after the hearty laugh.

"We had a great time tonight, Dad. Thanks for dinner." Ron said.

"Yes, it was wonderful," chimed Amanda.

"You're welcome," Dr. Barton answered. "We enjoyed it thoroughly. Amanda, it was a pleasure meeting you."

"It was lovely, Amanda," Ron's mother added.

"Well, y'all be careful going home," his dad said.

"Y'all are driving home, tomorrow?" Ron asked.

"Yeah," his dad said. Ron could tell he still wanted to talk to him.

"I'll call you this week Dad, okay?"

"Alright, son."

# 14

Philip Lucci, Mack Dawkins, Baron Scream and Will Bowens rode down the Intracoastal Waterway near Gulf Shores, Alabama on Philip's brand new 96-foot yacht named "Chez Partay." Earlier that morning Philip had flown the men down in his helicopter to take them on what he termed a much-deserved "Gulf Trip" to go snapper fishing. Philip told them that they had all worked hard lately, and that the trip was his way of rewarding them and celebrating their continued success with the company. But really, it was just a massive ego trip for Philip—who simply wanted to show off his new yacht.

The weatherman said the night before that the weather on the coast would be nice for the entire weekend. He was wrong. It was overcast and windy, with a chance of rain, transforming the normal emerald gulf waters the color of milk chocolate. However, the owners of the marina where Philip kept his yacht said that because of the size of Philip's boat, they'd have no problem getting to the deeper blue water where the snapper were biting some 15 miles offshore. They instructed the group to take the vessel to the east down the protective waters of the Intracoastal until they got to Orange Beach where they could then exit underneath Highway 98 into the Gulf of Mexico.

Baron Screem and Will Bowens, dressed in bathing suits and tee shirts, sat in sun chairs and drank cold, bottled *Budweiser* beer on the covered deck of the huge boat. They had picked up a styrofoam ice chest, a case and three bags of ice at the marina store. They were finally glad to be alone, away from Philip.

"Can you believe Philip made us listen to his country and western CD all the way here in the helicopter?" Will asked.

"Are you serious?" Baron answered. "Yes, I can believe it. Get real, Will—and get me another beer."

Will handed Baron another cold *Bud*. They had each already killed a couple.

"I have a more important question," Baron said.

"What's that?"

"Does Philip know where he's going?"

"I guess," Will said, popping another cold one. "Who gives a damn?"

Philip and Mack took turns driving the yacht while they finished off the last of several fat lines of high grade, uncut Columbian cocaine laid out on the flat part of the mahogany dash that encased the instrumentation panel and steering wheel. Philip snorted the last, eight-inch line in one long pull, holding the cut plastic straw to his nose as he tilted his head back to get every last grain of the chalky white substance into his sinuses where it would quickly melt into his bloodstream and enter his brain. Philip placed the straw in his front pants pocket. He felt invincible. Mack was at the wheel.

"Mack, I am really excited about where we're going with Dixie. Along with Muster and Appleton we've signed some pretty good doctors. We're going to really be able to work the sports injury marketing angle to the hilt, and I truly think it's going to do wonders for us."

Mack was as high as a kite. His entire head was numb.

"I'm thrilled about all of it!" He managed.

"Mack, I'm telling you, once we get this digital hospital built, we're gonna be rollin'—rollin' I tell you! We're gonna be on a monster roll!"

"How's the hospital coming along?" Mack asked.

Philip didn't want to shift his lofty line of thought to such a mundane topic.

"The hospital? I'm not sure. I saw the other day the foundation was done. It's moving along."

Philip looked across the bow to get a bead on where they were.

"We'll be at Orange Beach in about another five minutes or so, Mack. Keep her steady. I'm gonna go and screw with Baron and Will."

"Sure thing," Mack smiled.

Before Philip headed out of the cabin down to the deck, he flipped on the boat's professional-grade stereo system with fourteen different speakers and a ridiculously large amplifier. He pressed play on the CD player that held his band's album of country and western songs—the same CD he'd played repeatedly on the way down in the helicopter—just so the guys could enjoy the great lyrics as much as he did.

Baron and Will were both nearing the consumption of a six pack. The table between them held ten empty *Bud* bottles.

"How much longer do you think we can keep the fraud going, Will?" Baron unexpectedly asked.

Will was finishing his sixth beer of the day. As the suds trailed the beer's neck into his throat, he looked directly at Baron. When he was done he put the bottle next to the others and spoke.

"Don't go there, Baron. Not now. Not this weekend. We're supposed to be relaxing. This is a celebratory trip, remember?"

Will stood and trudged to the nearby ice chest and grabbed another bottle.

"Well, Will, it's just a matter of time until somebody figures it out. We can't keep doing what we're doing. That's all I'm trying to say."

Will guzzled the beer to avoid Baron's comments. As he was halfway through another healthy chug, the ten or more embedded outside *Bose* speakers came to life, blaring the now all-too-familiar hit, "Honk if you wanna Honky Tonk!"

Baron and Will looked at each other.

"Oh no!" Will moaned. "Not again!"

Baron grabbed his forehead with his free hand.

Philip burst through the stairwell door onto the deck.

"Don't drink too much, damnit!" Philip yelled. "You'll be too drunk to fish!"

"We're just having a couple of beers!" Baron answered.

"How y'all like the sound system?" Philip asked.

"Pretty sweet!" Will lied. "It sounds great."

"Guys, I'm really pumped about the company! We're really moving and shaking now! With all the new doctors we've signed and the digital hospital being built, I can see where we're really gonna make up for a lot of lost ground here in the coming months. I think we're moving into a whole new level."

Baron cringed at Philip's enthusiasm.

"Make up for lost ground must mean not having to cook the books?" Baron thought.

"Philip, I'm totally excited about everything that's going on. Everywhere I go in town everyone is stoked about where the company is going. I think the sky's the limit for us." Will said.

"Right on!" Philip replied. "Hey—look—I gotta get back up there and help Mack turn the boat. Get ready boys—we're goin' fishin'!"

Although inebriated, Baron quickly thought of something.

"Hey Philip!" He yelled.

Philip had turned and was almost to the stairwell door. He stopped and spun in place, facing Baron.

"Yeah?"

"You want some popcorn?"

Philip thought for a moment. He was surprised Baron knew. He smiled from ear to ear.

"You wanna fuck?" Philip replied with a sneering laugh. He forthwith turned and disappeared through the door and up the stairwell as quickly as he'd entered.

Will looked at Baron and asked, "What is that all about?"

"Nothing. It's an inside joke."

Philip got back into the cabin. Mack was still carefully steering the yacht.

"Alright Mack," Lucci said. "We're coming up on the turn. Let me take her over."

Philip steered the massive boat into the broad opening underneath the elevated highway that opened into the Gulf of Mexico. The wind violently whipped the Crimson Tide flag that flew on the deck. Philip hardly noticed, but Mack saw the whitecaps on the waves coming toward them after they made the wide right turn and headed into the turbulent gulf waters. Furthermore, it had started drizzling.

"It looks pretty rough out there, Philip," said Mack.

"Nah. Don't sweat it," Philip answered. "We'll be just fine. The guys at the marina said the boat is plenty big enough to handle these seas. Besides, it's gonna clear up later and we'll be on the fish!"

Philip gunned the boat's engines and cleared the channel leading to the gulf. The boat broke through the waves just fine initially, until an easterly wind gust caught its broad side and spun the ship off its course, swinging the entire vessel 90 degrees. Philip panicked. He had never driven the boat before. He had little experience with wind or turbulent seas.

"Damn!" Philip yelled. "I've lost control!"

Philip turned hard on the wheel, straining to get it back on course.

"Hang on to her!" yelled Mack.

On the deck, Baron and Will flew out of their chairs—beer bottles crashing on the deck--when the wind took control of the vessel.

"Holy shit!" yelled Will.

"Damn you Philip!" Baron yelled.

Philip again gunned the engines and turned hard against the direction they were spinning. The boat jerked forward and picked up speed, but it did not make a full recovery toward the way they needed to go.

"Philip, slow down! We need to take it easy!"

Philip didn't listen. He pushed the engines full throttle and the yacht churned through the rough waters in a southeasterly direction. Philip yelled, "Yahoo!" as he pushed the craft to its capacity. Baron and Will held on to the sides of the boat and sat directly on the deck. They were scared shitless.

"He's gonna kill us!" Will yelled. "Honk if you Want to Honky Tonk" still blared, as it was on repeat.

"He might," Baron thought, too scared to say anything, watching broken, golden brown beer bottle glass slide across the slick deck.

The boat picked up its speed and reached 35 miles per hour. Philip loved the power derived from driving the massive craft—of conquering the waves, of being the captain of his brand new ship. Suddenly, the boat came to a quick, firm stop. Philip lunged forward with a thud into the wooden, spoked steering wheel. Mack flew forward as well, hitting his head firmly on the window with a loud thump. Baron and

Will rolled across the deck unharmed, but still fearful of what was happening. They were helpless.

"What did we hit?" Baron asked, struggling to gain purchase on the deck.

Will sat in place.

"God only knows!" Will yelled. "What a buzz kill!"

Baron stood and walked to the bow of the boat. He looked down and saw a sand bar underneath two feet of choppy, murky water.

"We've hit sand! We're on a sand bar!" Baron yelled.

Baron and Will ended up drinking the rest of their beers before Philip and Mack were able to successfully radio for and get help. Philip called the owners of the marina and they sent a smaller boat out to get the four of them. Mack needed an ice pack for the bump on his head. Back at the marina Philip chewed out the owners for not telling him about the sand bar he hit. He later sued them unsuccessfully. Instead of fishing, the men wound up at a popular beach bar, *Live Bait*, where they got shit-faced drunk, Philip sang karaoke badly on stage, and later he and Mack picked up two sluts from Houma, Louisiana and brought them back to Philip's ridiculously large, posh house on Ono Island.

In a bizarre twist, Philip just two months later bought the same marina from the owners at what everyone thought was a ridiculously high price of $2.8 million, since its appraised Baldwin County Assessor's Office value the prior year was $1.9 million. Six months later he sold it to the City of Gulf Shores, Alabama for $13 million--over four times the investment price. A year later the Mayor of Gulf Shores who theoretically signed the check to Richard Scrushy was arrested in a separate land kickback scheme involving a multi-story condo developer that landed him a ten-year prison term for racketeering, taking a bribe, malfeasance in office and drug possession.

# 15

Several weeks passed. Dr. Ron Barton and Amanda grew closer during the time period. In January Ron was named Most Outstanding Orthopedic Surgeon for the State of Alabama at the Alabama Medical Association's annual convention. It was a huge boost to his psych and his practice, as it was as redemptive as it was honorable. The *Birmingham News* ran a half-page article replete with a photo showing him accepting the award.

During the rest of the winter Ron and Amanda enjoyed practicing and playing polo, snow skiing in Vail, the beaches of Cabo, the shopping and night life of Cancun and an impromptu trip to the Bellagio in Las Vegas that Amanda planned as a surprise. By the summer of 1996 Ron's practice had grown to where he was again busy and nearly making the same amount of money he made when he had the Birmingham Sports Clinic. Things had settled nicely for both he and Amanda, as she was one of *Pfizer's* top salespeople.

One morning in early June Ron was on his way to surgery at the downtown UAB Hospital when he unexpectedly ran into Dr. Leah Thompson. She was coming out of another section of the surgery wing when she saw him. Ron was talking to one of the other orthopedic surgeons, his former colleague, Dr. Palifax, who had just come out of surgery. Leah was furious. Of course she knew about him and Amanda.

It was old news. She was simply mad that he had never returned her call right after the news broke. He basically wrote her off—now that he had his upgrade—the beautiful Miss Amanda Lucci.

"Hey Ron," she said, standing right behind him. Ron never saw her approach. Her voice rang particularly high. Ron recognized it. The northeast accent was distinct. He panicked. He had never returned her calls. It had been months.

Palifax knew their past. He wasted no time bugging out.

"Talk to you later, Ron. Give me a call. We need to talk."

Ron turned to Leah, and back.

"Later Jim," he said. "I'll get with you." He squared his shoulders and faced her.

Strangely, he had butterflies. He felt intimidated.

"Hey Leah. How's it going?"

"Fine. Just fine," she answered sarcastically.

Ron focused on her eyes and face. He thought she looked good. She had a familiar glow.

"Good." He said.

"So you can't pick up the phone and call me? Am I not worthy of a phone call? After all we've been through? What's wrong with you, Ron?"

Ron was deeply embarrassed. The pain associated with the affair had humiliated him. He never called her back because he was ashamed. He simply couldn't face her. Now he had no choice. He looked around to see who was watching. He lowered his tone.

"Leah, I was ashamed. I couldn't face you. I was scared to. I'm sorry, okay?"

Leah was somewhat shocked. He was honest with her. He admitted he was wrong and seemed sorry. He didn't try and talk his way out of it. She immediately wanted to forgive him, to renew their friendship.

"Well, you could have called me. I mean, I was shocked like everyone else, but I wouldn't have judged you, Ron. I'll never judge you."

Ron appeared vulnerable. He said nothing, but to Leah he looked like a scolded child.

"She's absolutely gorgeous." She added.

Ron's countenance changed. He felt somewhat vindicated from the remark.

"We weren't dating, Ron—remember?" Leah said. She was making it easy for him.

"I know. It's just that I felt like I let everyone down."

"You didn't let anyone else down, Ron. In fact, if you're happy, you let no one down. It's your life."

Ron contemplated her words. He'd been through it all so many times in his head, but he'd never distilled it so well like she had.

He realized it really wasn't his fault. He fell for Amanda—like almost any other man would have.

"Leah, I appreciate your reaction to all of this. I'm really sorry about not calling you back. I wanted to, but I just couldn't. Please forgive me. I want your friendship."

Leah was still attracted to him. He was a good man—one of the best she'd known.

Her face came to life. She smiled.

"I forgive you, Ron." She said, nodding her head for emphasis.

"Thanks," he said with an equally broad smile. "How have *you* been? Are you seeing anyone?"

Leah was caught off guard. She'd been brooding since she heard the news about Ron and Amanda—so much so that she hadn't dated. Her life had been on hold because she was still in love with Ron.

"I've dated here and there," she said, lying. "But nothing serious. I'm still waiting for Mr. Right."

Ron laughed.

"You'll find him, Leah. Keep looking. You're worth the wait. Don't settle for just anybody, either."

"Don't worry," she said.

"I've got surgery in a few minutes. I have to run. Let's stay in touch, okay?"

"Let's," she said.

# 16

Ron's meeting with Leah served as an awakening. He'd become somewhat of a recluse as a result of all that had happened. Since being forced out of his clinic his days were spent working out, seeing patients, playing polo and spending time with his new love, Amanda. Stung with embarrassment, he had purposely tried to avoid his old colleagues.

Leah made him realize that he needed to come out of his shell. Furthermore, Leah made him understand that all that had happened to him really wasn't his fault—it was Philip Lucci's. He was the villain--not him. Ron's dad had repeatedly told him to stay clear of Philip, but he was now determined to exact revenge. Moreover, Ron felt that someone needed to stand up to Philip Lucci, since no one else seemed willing or able. That evening while relaxing at home he vowed to learn as much as he could about Dixie Rehab, how it operated, its key employees, and ultimately, its weaknesses. Dr. Ron Barton endeavored to do to Philip Lucci what he had tried to do to him—ruin him.

The day after running into Leah, Ron got into his office early and called Dr. Jim Palifax. Jim was an early riser and was already at work checking emails and doing paperwork before he had to start seeing patients. His phone rang and he answered. His secretary was on the line.

"Dr. Palifax, Dr. Barton is on hold."
"Put him through."
"Ron? Good morning."
"Jim?"
"Yeah. It's me. What's going on man?"
"Hey, I'm sorry about yesterday. I didn't see that coming."
"Look, no problem. I totally understand. Why do you think I'm still single? Don't sweat it!"
"Well, I wanted to talk to you about how you like your new work arrangement. How is it working for Dixie?"
"I'm glad you called, Ron. I want to talk to you about it, but not on the phone. Let's get together today after work, okay?"
"Sure, man. Where do you want to meet?"
"Let's meet at South Points Grill. We'll have a drink and chat."
"What time?"
"I'll be out of here around 4:00 or so. How about 5:00 sharp?"
"I'll see you there."

***

On a sunny afternoon Philip Lucci and Mack Dawkins hung out beside the banjo-shaped pool behind his Mountain Brook home. The men wore bathing suits, sunglasses and each held a frozen margarita with a flexible straw. Both men were in a supine position on a padded reclining layout chair.

"What are we doing tonight, Mack?" Philip asked.

"We could head down to Five Points South. There's always talent there."

"Nah. I'm tired of that scene. I need something strange."

Mack laughed.

"Well, we could always call up Chastity Jones. I'm sure she's up for a good time."

Philip looked at Mack like he was crazy.

"I'm not bringing that nut job over here!"

Mack grinned, but said nothing.

"I need to find another steady girl, Mack. Being single ain't all it's cracked up to be."

"No pun intended, right?"

Philip smirked.

"I'm serious. I'm too busy with Dixie to be running around looking for love all the time. I need to find somebody new and settle down."

Mack was silent. He liked running around with Philip. Philip spent money like it grew on trees. They always got laid when he did.

"Bierbaum called me yesterday and said that he's got a friend in the TV business, a news anchor from Montgomery, he wants me to meet. He said she'll be at his studio on Tuesday for some charity promotion. He said she asked him about me. She's really young—28, I think he said. Get this—she was an Auburn cheerleader and a former Miss Alabama."

"You're kidding?" Mack answered.

"Nope."

"She's a younger version of Amanda."

"Well, I understand she's a blonde."

"I doubt if she's a true blonde." Mack laughed.

"None of em' are," squealed Philip, sipping his drink.

***

Jim Palifax was from Missoula, Montana. As a youngster his parents moved him and his brothers and sisters to El Paso, Texas. The valedictorian of his high school class, he attended the University of Texas at Austin where he was a double major in business and biology and later the LSU Medical School in New Orleans. A consummate playboy, Jim was a regular on the Five Points South bar scene and he enjoyed the company of the opposite sex. He was fairly handsome, and of course, was viewed as a wealthy, successful physician by women. He drove a candy apple red *Corvette*, wore a 14-carat gold *Rolex* watch, tailored suits and always the latest designer menswear. At 44, he was the consummate player, and a pretty damn good doctor as well.

Ron arrived at South Points Grill at 4:45. Unbeknownst to him, Jim Boudreaux was there, buying dinner and several drinks for the popular Chastity Jones—who had predictably become the company doorknob. Ron had never met or seen Jim Boudreaux, so he was oblivious to his presence. Jim, however, knew who Ron was, as he'd seen his picture recently in the *Birmingham News* when he was written up for being named the Most Outstanding Orthopedic Surgeon for the State of Alabama. Moreover, he was the guy that stole his boss's beautiful wife.

Ron found a table outside in the courtyard adjacent to Jim and Chastity's table. Large, green umbrellas provided shade above each. Ron ordered a *Bud Lite* and waited. He couldn't help but notice Jim and Chastity. The two stood out from the regular young, upwardly professional crowd. Chastity's polka dot halter barely covered her undersized breasts and it was more than obvious that she was braless, as her nipples were on high beam. Furthermore, Ron couldn't help but eavesdrop during their conversation. Seemingly every other word was an expletive. Chastity's language was particularly nasty, as she used the "F" word more liberally than her cheap makeup, which appeared to have been applied with an ice cream scoop. Dinner for the couple consisted of loaded nachos and two-for-one margaritas with salt. Ron took particular notice of Jim Boudreaux's ponytail, and how creepy he thought the couple looked.

"Trailer park trash," he thought. Then he remembered that Amanda grew up in a trailer park, and he felt guilty.

Dr. Palifax arrived just before five o'clock. He spotted Ron in the courtyard as he entered the main entrance. He walked through the main dining room and exited onto the courtyard. Ron stood and greeted him.

"Jim—good to see you! Thanks for meeting me!"

"No problem, Ron. My pleasure."

"Want a beer?" Ron asked.

"Absolutely!"

"What do you want?"

"*Heineken.*"

The waitress was bringing Boudreaux and Chastity another round. Ron motioned to her. She noticed him.

"Could we get a *Heineken* when you come back around please?"

She nodded and smiled.

"Thanks," Ron said.

"So you want to talk about Dixie, huh?" Jim asked.

Ron was glad to see he was willing to talk.

Jim Boudreaux, three feet away, heard every word. He listened intently.

"What's it like over there? You've been there almost nine months now, right?"

"Going on nine, yeah. It's crazy, Ron. I mean, the money is great—don't get me wrong. Lucci gives me an "Orthopedic Director's Fee" and a "Departmental Fee" that basically doubles my income from when I worked with you, but I of course in my contract must refer all of my patients to Dixie for rehab. Regarding my office and work area, it's a step down from what we had at the Birmingham Sports Clinic. It's an older facility, and much smaller. Plus—and get this—because it's directly related to what I'm getting to—we are always short on necessary supplies for the facility. For instance, we are constantly low on toilet paper and paper napkins for the patient areas and we have even felt it from time-to-time in the doctors' and nurses' bathrooms. It's gotten so bad that we all keep a spare roll in our desk drawer. We have complained to the Dixie V.P. who oversees the administration of the facility but he just says that 'They're trying to cut costs.' It's pretty ridiculous. I don't know what's going on, but something's not right. Why are they trying to cut costs with toilet paper? It's fishy. I am wondering if the company is strapped for cash?"

"They're not providing toilet paper for the customers and doctors and nurses?"

"Well they are, but we're constantly running out and having to ration what we have. It's ridiculous. It's a real problem. The facility is super busy. Plus, I noticed that we don't have a janitorial service. Get this—the V.P. who handles administration and the other administrators have to stay late one night a week and vacuum, mop and clean all of the bathrooms."

Jim Boudreaux and Ron hung on every word.

"It sounds like they are trying to cut every cost imaginable. Things must be pretty bad financially for the company. Otherwise, they wouldn't be acting like that." Ron said. "I mean, toilet paper?"

Palifax sipped his beer.

"I've thought about it a good bit," Palifax replied. "The past four or five years the company has grown considerably, acquiring hospitals and physical therapy clinics left and right. Lucci is as ingenious as he is bold. He's been able to do it by not having to borrow money. The way he's done it is by issuing Dixie Rehab stock—which he has in abundance, to the company he is buying. This allows him to operate with his own de facto currency. He's not dealing with money—he's dealing with a devout belief in Dixie Rehab's success—and in the court of public opinion, perception is reality. Everyone perceives Dixie as wildly successful because of Lucci's media savvy. He's an icon."

"So you're saying that everything's not what it really seems?"

"I'm not sure, Ron. But I've thought about it a lot. For instance, I look at the company higher-ups—all the executives like the CFO, CAO, the controllers and the area V.P.'s-- among them I see not a single M.B.A. They're all undergraduates of directional universities in Alabama, Louisiana and Mississippi. It makes a reasonably intelligent, business-minded individual seriously wonder."

"They have no M.B.A.'s? But they're a publicly traded company..."

"It's all Lucci, Ron. He's a master manipulator and the ultimate face man. I think he's got everybody fooled. He operates like a benevolent mafia don. He pays everybody well—too well. He's not only bought their allegiance and effort, I think he's also bought their silence as to whatever's going on. Something's up is all I can think."

Dr. Palifax finished his beer. He switched his gaze from Ron to the inside area of the restaurant. He recognized someone, smiled and waved. Ron looked in the same direction and saw a petite blonde with blue eyes. She was adorable.

"She sure looks a lot better than us." Ron quipped.

"No kidding. She's one of the new drug reps in the area. She's smoking hot. I told her to meet me here. You don't mind, huh?"

Ron could tell he was ready to end the conversation.

"Are you kidding? Get after it!" Ron answered.

"Thanks pal. By the way, how are you and the former Miss Alabama coming along?"

"Quite well, thanks, Jim."

"Good to hear it. I'll catch up with you, bud. Oh, and I ran into Pete Goldman today. He told me he tried to call you a few months back and was never able to get in touch with you. He asked me to tell you to please give him a ring."

Ron remembered the unreturned phone call, and the one before it.

"Sure thing, Jim—I'll give him a ring."

Dr. Palifax stood. Ron stood and they shook hands. Ron dropped a twenty-dollar bill on the table and walked out behind Dr. Palifax. Jim Boudreaux fully contemplated the potential ramifications of the conversation and who within the company he should talk to about it.

# 17

Butch Bierbaum greeted Philip Lucci inside his radio studio. The two were used to working together, as Lucci had been appearing on the show on Tuesdays and Thursdays for the entire first hour for many months. The show aired daily from 2-6 p.m. Butch wore a white satin shirt without a collar and a houndstooth overcoat without a tie. Bald on top with hair only on the sides, he looked like a much thinner, and bolder Bob Newhart. Philip wore one of his three thousand dollar *Armani* suits. His shined, designer black leather shoes were fitted with lifts to give him an extra inch in height. His pencil-thin moustache was expertly tweaked by his barber earlier that morning. His hair was combed over deftly to make it appear fuller than it really was.

Bierbaum could tell he was dressed to impress.

"What's up?"

"Hey Butch."

"Looking sharp today, Phil."

"Thanks Butch."

"Looks like you're up for making a good first impression on Miss Clara."

"You never get a second chance, Butch. When is she getting here?"

"She'll be here any minute. I told her she'd be sitting in with us during the entire first hour. She's here to promote breast cancer awareness. She's the spokesperson for the State of Alabama's Breast Cancer Awareness Campaign."

"Oh, I see. You said she asked about me. Is she single?"

"Well, she didn't really ask about you. I told her you'd be on the air with me. She asked what you were like. She said that she had reported on you and Dixie many times, but had never met you. And yes—she's single."

"And you told her what about me?"

"That you are rich and powerful—and single—recently divorced."

Philip smiled, showing teeth.

"Strong work, Butch. I appreciate it."

"No problem."

Butch's producer, Patrick Tidmore, stepped into the studio. He wore a station I.D. and headset.

"Butch, Miss Clara Roberts is here."

Butch and Philip looked toward the door where Patrick stood. Behind him was a shapely, blue-eyed blonde in a royal blue dress. She wore matching high-heels and a large pink ribbon on her heaving left breast, the universal symbol for breast cancer awareness. Her presence completely lit the small radio broadcasting studio.

Clara Roberts was born in the state capital of Montgomery, Alabama in 1968. The daughter of a former state representative and state senator turned Chair of the Alabama Republican Party, she grew up in the shadow of state politics. During her junior year on the plains of Auburn she was elected student body president and homecoming queen. A year later she was named Miss Alabama. After graduating from Auburn in broadcast journalism she took a job with the NBC affiliate in Montgomery where she covered state politics. Over the six years with the same station she had moved up to news anchor and was increasingly being courted by the national news networks for her exceptional looks, intelligence, and delivery. However, Clara had a dark side that kept her close to home. She was weaned on the mother's milk of Alabama state politics—greed—and as a consequence, she was adept at getting what she wanted—like the finer things in life—by asking or manipulating others for it. This was easily done in her home state, where everyone in her father's rich and powerful circle made things happen to her liking. Nevertheless, her champagne taste had cost her daddy much in overdue credit card bills through her formative years, and her father's similar flair for the expensive and the excessive did little to curb her penchant for all that glittered. Clara was spoiled rotten, and as a result, she took much in life for granted.

Butch and Philip stood.

"Come on in Clara," said Butch Bierbaum, motioning with his right hand. "It's great to see you. How have you been?"

"I'm doing great Butch. Give me a hug!"

Butch opened his arms and took her in. She embraced him and gave him a peck on the cheek. They were old friends, having met four years earlier at a War Eagle Supper Club fundraiser.

"Clara Roberts, this is Philip Lucci. Philip, Clara Roberts."

They shook hands.

"It's a pleasure to meet you, Clara." Philip politely smiled.

"Likewise," she answered, returning the gesture.

"So, Clara," said Butch, "we're going to be talking about Alabama and Auburn's football schedules to start the program and we'll be sprinkling in a little Dixie Rehab news as always, but we wanted to bring you in during the second segment to talk about breast cancer awareness. What were you planning to talk about specifically? Is there anything you need me to do in terms of providing a segue for you?"

"Well, I was going to talk to the audience about the importance of encouraging their wives to either get a breast exam, or to at least self-exam for cancer."

"Oh really?" Butch replied. "That could get interesting."

Philip chuckled. Clara giggled.

"Butch! You are so bad!" Clara squealed. She motioned toward him as she spoke.

"It'll be fine, don't worry," Butch said. "We'll get the word out."

Philip interjected.

"I know your father, Clara. I'm a republican and I always support conservative candidates. I helped him with the Fob Smiley campaign four years ago. In fact, I plan on helping him again with the campaign this fall. I've gotten a few letters from the party, but I'd like to talk to your dad. Please have him call me."

Philip handed her his card, from a 14 carat gold case he'd earlier readied.

Clara was immediately intrigued by Philip. She'd heard so much about him—good and bad, but she knew that he'd bankrolled Fob Smiley's gubernatorial campaign four years earlier to the tune of $375,000 through the Republican Party. Her father had bragged to her about his ability to get that kind of money from one of Alabama's most successful businessmen. While Clara didn't see Philip as the most physically handsome man, she saw him nevertheless as the consummate rainmaker—which made his physical shortcomings seemingly nonexistent to her insatiable psyche.

"I'll definitely have him call you. I know for a fact he appreciated your help during the last campaign. It will be welcomed again. You'll hear from him soon."

"Thanks, I appreciate that. I look forward to talking to him."

Pat Tidmore stuck his head into the studio.

"Guys, we're on in one minute."

"Okay, let's get ready. Pat let's get a microphone test on Phil and Clara," Butch said.

Butch opened the program in the usual way. He and Philip chatted about the major sports items of the day and Dixie's progress on the digital hospital, as well as their continued efforts to revolutionize health care. After the first break Butch introduced Clara as the Breast Cancer Awareness spokesperson. After that, things quickly got interesting.

"So Clara, what should the average guy out there listening do if he loves his wife and cares about her trying to prevent breast cancer?"

"Well Butch, he should encourage her to consult with her physician, or if she's too busy or can't afford seeing a doctor she could conduct a self-examination of her breasts to check for recognizable, pre-cancerous lumps."

Bierbaum intervened, "Or, *he* could give her the exam, right?"

Philip laughed along with Bierbaum.

"Now Butch, as long as the exam is done, and the woman is consenting, I guess it's fine. You know this is all about prevention."

"Yes, of course," Butch said. "Could you please explain to our listening audience—which is predominantly male, how they would go about examining a breast for cancer?"

"I'd be glad to," she replied. "You want to slowly massage the breasts, feeling for any irregular masses, or lumps. Anything out of the ordinary in terms of texture should alarm you."

"Would you mind demonstrating for Philip and me?" Bierbaum asked.

"On you, Butch? Your breasts aren't quite big enough!"

Philip cackled loudly. Clara followed with her own high-pitched giggle. Bump music from the *Red Hot Chili Peppers* began.

"You're listening to the Butch Bierbaum Show. We'll be right back!" Butch sounded.

*\*\*\**

Jim Boudreaux called Philip's office but he was unavailable. He chose not to leave a message. He instead called Mack Dawkins on his office line.

"Mack Dawkins."

"Mack, this is Jim Boudreaux."

"Yeah Jim?"

"I've got some news."

"What's up?"

"I was at South Points Grill yesterday. I was sitting next to Dr. Ron Barton and Dr. Jim Palifax. Palifax is with us now."

"Yeah, I know who he is. Phil and I signed him."

"Well, they don't know me, and since I was right next to them I overheard their entire conversation. It seemed that Barton asked Palifax to meet him there to talk about Dixie, because he thanked him for meeting him there. Also, all they did was talk about the company."

"Really? What did they say?"

"Palifax talked about how he suspected the company was having financial problems because they never had toilet paper and napkins in the bathroom, even though he and the other doctors have complained. He said that the Dixie management staff has only said that they've been trying to cut costs."

Mack was concerned. He'd heard Philip and Baron go round and round about the finances before, but never really paid it any mind, since it wasn't his area of expertise. He was there to get things done, not to count beans or worry about finances.

"What else was said?"

"Nothing much else—something about us not having any MBA's running the company and how everything's not really like it seems. Is the company in trouble?"

Boudreaux knew nothing of the company's cash flow problem.

"We're fine, Jim." Mack reassured. "Don't worry about it. I'll pass this info along to Philip. Excellent work. He'll certainly want to know."

Mack Dawkins was from Dothan, Alabama. He met Philip when he was selling physical therapy equipment to UAB's Physical Therapy School where Philip taught before he became a health care business guru. A business graduate of Birmingham Southern, Dawkins maintained contact with Philip when he left to work for Southern Rehab and the two became fast friends as well as business associates. When Philip formed Dixie Rehab, Mack was one of the first people he called on to build a business development team. Mack was hardly a scholar, but he was street smart, charismatic and he knew well the art of human relations. Most importantly, however, he knew his boss—and he knew he needed to tell him what he'd just heard, as Philip Lucci, like he was with people, was a master at the art of war.

# 18

Dr. Pete Goldman read the pink message slip on his desk. "Call Dr. Ron Barton." He'd been wanting to talk to Ron for some time. It was 4:35 p.m. He wondered if Dr. Barton was still at his office. He picked up the phone and dialed Barton's number. His secretary answered.

"Dr. Barton's office, Amelia speaking."

"Amelia, this is Pete Goldman. I'm returning Ron's call."

"Hey Pete! How are you?"

"Fine, Amelia. Thanks, and you?"

"Doing great! Hold on. I'll get Ron. He's just finishing up for the day."

Amelia put Pete on hold. She stood and walked to the other side of the office. Ron was saying goodbye to his last patient of the day.

"Mr. Pemberton, remember it's important for you to exercise every day as hard as you can until the morning of the surgery. I need you strong heading in so you'll be stronger coming out, okay?"

"Yes sir, Dr. Barton. I will."

"Great. See you next week."

Amelia approached him.

"Ron, Pete Goldman's on the phone."

"Pete!" Ron thought. He rushed to his office, sat in his leather chair and took the call.

"Pete! Thanks for returning my call!"

"Ron! Good to hear from you, man! How have you been?"

"I'm well, Pete. Look—I'm really sorry about not calling you back from several months ago. I met with Palifax yesterday and he told me that you wanted me to call. I remembered that I hadn't returned your call. I'm sorry. It's been a tough few months for me, but I am finally getting back on my feet."

"Ron, I understand. Look, I realize what you've gone through. There's no need to apologize, really."

"Well, I feel bad about it."

"Don't man. Hey—you up for drinks at the *Highlands*? My treat."

Ron was supposed to barbecue at home, but he felt Amanda would understand. He'd simply call her and tell her something came up.

"Sure man. What time?"

"Let's go early so we can get in and out before it gets crowded. Can you meet me in thirty minutes?"

Ron checked his watch.

"Sure. I'll see you then."

Ron Barton parked his *Porsche* and strode into the front door of the *Highlands*. The air inside the popular bar and eatery was cool and a most welcome contrast to the humid, sticky summer Birmingham air. The maitre d greeted him.

"Good early evening Dr. Barton. How are you, sir?"

"I'm fine, thanks. I'm meeting Dr. Goldman. Has he arrived?"

"He has, sir. He's at the bar waiting for you."

Ron passed the maitre d and veered to the right where the circular bar was located. The bartenders and bar backs were readying for the evening rush. There were only two other patrons in the bar, two elderly women enjoying mint juleps. Ron purposely sat with his back to the wall at a corner high top table. He wanted to be able to see anyone coming in to the establishment. Pete sat across from him. The alert bartender immediately took their order from a distance behind the bar. They both ordered beers.

"I'm glad you called, Ron. I was the first to leave the clinic and I never really felt that good about how things went after I did. I mean, I didn't feel good about *how* I left—it wasn't easy, and then it seemed like everything went south for you after that."

"Pete, look—I don't hold any grudges. What happened, happened. It wasn't your fault."

"Well, I know it wasn't completely my fault, but I sorta got the ball rolling being the first to leave, and I want you to know that I regret it."

Ron was surprised by his statement.

"Why do you regret it?"

Pete looked over his shoulder at the bartenders. They were occupied. No one was eavesdropping.

"The whole place is a scam, as far as I can see, Ron. Lucci is a liar and a con artist—he's got to be one of the biggest ever."

"What do you mean?"

"Well, first of all, I don't think the company is as profitable as they claim. They are cutting every conceivable non-care related cost. From toilet paper to janitorial to even travel expenses for the upper-level managers—it's absurd. I think the company is bleeding. There's no other explanation. It's grown so fast and been so aggressive toward expansion, the hiring of new doctors at exorbitant pay hikes and the building of the new digital hospital, that I think it's terribly cash poor. I believe Lucci is playing a shell game with the numbers. It's pretty easy to see. Plus, all the while he's building monuments to himself and buying expensive toys like jet airplanes and helicopters, yachts and cars like the money grows on trees. Everything is out of whack, Ron. I can see the stress among the managers. It's obvious."

All of it struck an all-too-familiar chord with Ron.

"So you think the company's fudging its numbers—that it's not as profitable as it says it is?"

"I definitely think that. But that's not all."

From the way his countenance shifted, Ron sensed Pete had something big to tell him.

"Not only are the finances a likely lie, I have reason to believe that some of their doctors are lying about the care they provide. They're willfully violating the Hippocratic Oath."

Ron didn't understand.

"What are you saying?"

"You know Flo Thompson, right?"

"Well yeah—I played baseball with him at Auburn. What about him?"

Vincent Ed "Flo" Thompson was a native of Bessemer, Alabama. A two-sport phenomenon at Auburn University, he batted .401 in 1982 and he was the 1985 Heisman Trophy winner. His .864 slugging percentage playing college baseball is still a school record. As a dual professional athlete in 1989 he became the only person to ever start a Pro Bowl and an All-Star Game. Moreover, in 1990 "Flo Knows" became a popular NIKE marketing campaign to promote a shoe that that bore his name. Flo was also the most high-profile athlete Dixie Rehab ever treated—allegedly.

The bartender brought their beers. Ron was dying to know about Flo.

"Ron, what I'm about to say is confidential. It's the kind of thing that could cause major trouble for both of us just by knowing. Lucci is a real sonofabitch and no telling what he would do if this leaked."

Ron grew anxious. It was all so compelling to him. His understanding of everything about Dixie was growing.

"Do you know Dr. Tyrone Biggs?" Pete asked.

"Yeah, sure. He's got a great reputation--came from Tuskegee Institute. I went to medical school with him. He's smart. He was a great student. I hear he's a hell of an orthopedic."

"Well, I know him well. We go to the same church and we've worked together to raise money and help some of the more underprivileged members. You're right about him on all counts. He's a hell of a guy—a hell of a doctor."

Pete paused.

"What about him? What does this have to do with Flo?" Ron asked.

"He's good friends with Flo Thompson."

Ron wondered where he was going with the conversation.

"Ever wonder why Tyrone was never offered by Dixie?"

"Because he's black?" Ron answered, taking an educated guess.

Pete turned and checked the direction of the bar. All was cool. No one conspicuous or new had arrived.

"Flo told Tyrone that Appleton didn't perform his hip surgery."

Ron's eyes widened. His brow furrowed. Dr. Appleton was known as one of the country's top sports medicine experts. He and his partner, Dr. Muster, had both signed with Dixie Rehab within the last year. Shortly thereafter Dr. Appleton reportedly operated on Flo's hip. Lucci had subsequently used Thompson's star notoriety to develop an entire expensive ad campaign targeting male couch potatoes and sports fans. It was a brilliant marketing tactic that had generated thousands of new Dixie Rehab customers.

"You mean Appleton didn't operate on Flo?"

Pete looked him in the eyes and said nothing. He only nodded his head. He again scanned the bar room. He took a double-take as two gentlemen dressed in coats and ties entered. He did not recognize them, but he was leery of them regardless. He continued nonetheless, in a much hushed tone. Ron strained to listen.

"Word is that Lucci flew in some specialist from Chicago because Appleton was scared he couldn't perform the surgery, and the Chicago White Sox wanted another doctor—a hip specialist—to handle it. Apparently Flo's hip was really bad. But Lucci pushed the lie about the surgery and rehab because it benefited Dixie. Now, Flo has actually rehabbed here at Dixie, but Appleton didn't do the surgery. Some guy named Weinstein did. Yet, everyone thinks Appleton performed the high-profile surgery—all for the benefit of Dixie's glitzy marketing strategy."

"This is nuts." Ron said, shaking his head.

"You're telling me. And now Flo's hip needs more surgery. The first one went bad--and Appleton is supposedly going to do it. At least that's the word."

"Flo knows all of this?"

"He was tipped off. One of the nurses present for the surgery told him. She was too stressed out about it. She told him 'he had a right to know.' Apparently Appleton was there when the anesthesia was administered. He told Flo he'd be 'just fine.' He then went and played golf at Greystone and was back in the recovery room four hours later to tell him everything went 'as planned.'"

"This is sick." Ron said.

"And Tyrone told me that Dixie Rehab employs not a single black person—not even a janitor—and they have over 50,000 employees."

Ron's head spun like a top.

"God almighty. This thing is a time bomb, don't you think? Sooner or later the Feds will move in. It's inevitable."

"Don't be too sure, Ron. Lucci's walked the tightrope without a balancing pole for a long time. That's how he rolls."

"What are you going to do?" Ron asked.

"What can I do? I'm under contract. Believe me, I'm not happy about it. I wake up everyday and have to live with the decision I've made. We had it great, Ron. I'm sorry I fucked it all up. I completely sold out—and that's why I regret it."

"I think somebody needs to do something about all of this. This can't continue." Ron answered. Pete shrugged his shoulders and finished his beer.

"Ron, don't mess with Lucci. He's a serious character. You should know that by now."

Ron gritted his teeth. He refused to succumb.

"Ron, I've got to run. Remember—everything we've talked about is confidential, right?"

Ron was lost in thought.

"Ron?" Pete asked again.

"Oh sure, Pete. It stays between us."

Pete went for his wallet.

"I got this, Pete."

"You sure? I said it was my dime."

"Yeah man, I'm sure. I got it."

"Well, look—let's stay in touch. Don't be a stranger."

"I'll definitely be in touch, Pete."

"Thanks for meeting me."

\*\*\*

Philip Lucci and Clara Roberts rode at 30,000 feet aboard Air Birmingham One—Dixie Rehab's newest, $25 million jet airplane en route to New Orleans. At the end of her time on Butch Bierbaum's show Philip asked Clara if she had ever had Banana's Foster at *Commander's*

*Palace* in New Orleans. She replied that she had not. He immediately insisted on taking her. She was somewhat intimidated by the boldness of his offer, but her curiosity was equally piqued.

"I'd love to go with you to New Orleans," was her eventual reply.

Two days later they were in the air heading to the Big Easy—all on Dixie Rehab's dime, of course.

"I spoke to your father last night, Clara," said Philip, sipping on recently-poured French champagne. His on-board chef was busy preparing hors d'oeuvres for their enjoyment. Clara was enamored with the entire extravagant experience. She had never been lavished upon so freely. Money seemingly did not matter to Lucci—and she loved it.

"Really? He called you then. I had asked him to like you wanted."

"He did, thanks, and we feel strongly that we can get Smiley elected this go round."

"But only with your help, right?"

"He did say something to that effect," Philip said. He grinned.

"That's daddy," she replied, "the consummate pitchman."

"Well, it's time for a change, Clara. We need a good conservative—someone who cares about family values—the values that have made this country so great—back in the governor's mansion in Montgomery."

Like everyone, Clara loved the sound of her name. But to hear Lucci—a multi-millionaire, say it with such endearment and meaning—made her feel even more important, and especially lucky. She was already dying to tell her girlfriends back in Montgomery of her amazing time with "King Philip." She was already envisioning herself as his queen, even though she had not even kissed him.

"Oh I agree wholeheartedly. We can do so much better than that Demo-Rat we've suffered at the hands of for four years," she said.

"I've pledged a half million dollars to the party this time," said Philip. "I've upped the ante considerably. There's just too much at stake for the good people of Alabama. They deserve so much better."

\*\*\*

Two days later Mack caught up with Philip in his penthouse office. Philip was whistling a happy tune, as he had just returned from a two-day jaunt from the Big Easy with Clara. Philip was a gentleman the entire time, ensuring that they sleep in separate beds inside adjoining rooms at the W Hotel on Poydras. Philip and Clara enjoyed the colorful, harmonic trappings of Bourbon Street, Café Du Monde and the shops at the River Walk before returning on his jet.

"What's up Mack?" Philip asked, smiling from ear-to-ear. To Mack, he seemed to be happier than a lark, with hardly a care in the world. He was extremely upbeat, a welcome change from recent relations.

"A lot. Where have you been the last couple of days? I was looking for you."

"I was in N'awlins with Miss Clara Roberts." Philip answered.

"Oh really? How did that go?"

"Quite well, thanks. I got to second base," he bragged.

"First date, huh?"

"Yeah, but we're going to Vegas this weekend—to Caesar's Palace—I should get a four-bagger for sure."

"Nice, Phil."

Philip reclined in his massive leather desk chair. He placed his hands behind his head and crossed his ankles upon the desk.

"So what's going on?" Phil asked, obviously switching the conversation to business by the tone and intonation of his voice.

"We've got a developing problem."

Philip focused on Mack.

"I spoke to Boudreaux the other day. He was at South Points Grill and Ron Barton and Jim Palifax sat at the table next to him. He overheard their entire conversation. Palifax told Barton that he thinks Dixie is in financial trouble because we are cutting costs left and right. He told Barton that he thinks something funny is going on with the company."

Philip sat up straight and dropped his feet to the floor.

"Palifax met with Barton and told him that we are having trouble, huh?"

"That's what Boudreaux said."

Philip fumed. He balled his fists. His forehead wrinkled. His eyes darkened. His face reddened. He breathed deeply.

"Are we having trouble Phil?" Mack asked.

"No!" He yelled. "Of course not!" He qualified with an intimidating scowl. The right side of his face twitched uncontrollably. He appeared almost rabid.

"I thought not," Mack answered, fearing what he might do to him for bearing the news.

"That little prick, Palifax! Tell Boudreaux I want to talk to him!"

\*\*\*

Ron thought long and hard about what Drs. Palifax and Goldman had told him. Both had painted an unfavorable picture of Dixie—one that pointed to larger problems within the organization. The information fueled his confidence and zeal toward uncovering the truth about the company. He surmised that if Dixie was so desperately cutting costs then there was a good chance that it was indeed cash poor and an even better chance that it wasn't as profitable as it was reporting to the public through its quarterly earnings statements. He decided to contact Furman and Leach—his two other former colleagues, to see if they had similar stories to tell.

Ron called Dr. Furman under the pretense of just wanting to say hello, and to see how he was doing. However, Furman was older, and was by nature extremely reticent. He simply said that he was busy but really he had little to offer about Dixie when Ron asked how things were going with his practice. This was no major surprise to Ron, as he and Furman had never been buddies because of the age difference.

To his surprise, Ron learned that Dr. Leach was no longer with Dixie. All he could discover from his former Dixie office secretary was that he had hired an attorney and successfully negated his contract and was now working in Florida. However, the young woman who gave him the information about Leach also told him that shortly after Leach began working there he started dating one of the Dixie hospital managers. She said that the manager left with Leach when he fled to Florida. He asked her which city. She said that she thought it was Gulf Breeze. Ron immediately hired a private investigator to find Leach and the number of his new office. By the end of the business day he had his contact information. Dr. Leach had a solo practice in Gulfport, Florida, near Tampa Bay. Ron gave him a call. His girlfriend, Laura, now his office manager, answered the phone.

Paul Leach was born in Los Angeles, California in 1958. He grew up surfing at Santa Monica Pier, skipping junior high and high school to watch Dodger Double-headers, and playing little league and American Legion baseball. A National Merit Scholar, Paul attended UCLA on academic scholarship, and later UCLA Medical. Paul moved to Birmingham because it was his first wife's hometown. When that didn't work out he decided to stay. He and Ron met when he heard that Ron was getting together a group of orthopedics to create the Birmingham Sports Clinic. Ron and Paul weren't close friends, but they were respectful of one another.

"Dr. Paul Leach's office," Laura answered.

"This is Dr. Ron Barton. I'm calling for Dr. Leach, please."

Laura knew exactly who he was.

"Hold please."

Moments later Leach came to life on the line.

"Hello Ron Barton." Leach said in monotone.

"Paul! What are you doing down in Florida?"

"I needed a change of scenery, Ron. It was time. Let's just say I kinda started over."

"Sounds wonderful—no more B-Ham—no more trouble. How did you manage to shake Lucci so easily?"

"Easy--I threatened to sue with a talented attorney."

"How didn't he comply?"

Leach laughed.

"Why do you want to know, Ron? Haven't you had enough of tangling with Lucci?"

Ron was reminded of how intelligent Leach was.

"I don't think Lucci is as good as he and everyone else thinks he is."

"He isn't. He's a con man."

"That's what I hear."

"They're cooking the books, Ron."

Ron liked what he was hearing.

"Laura can corroborate that, can't she?"

There was a pause.

"Don't bring her into it. All that is behind us now. That's why we moved. We don't want any more trouble with Dixie Rehab."

"So it's all a lie, huh? They're manufacturing revenues to maintain the stock price?"

"Put it this way—and I would rather you not repeat any of this—but if you want to go after Lucci—get to the bottom of the revenue picture. There's two separate sets of books—what the company really does—and what they tell Wall Street. It's so bad that the managers at the individual clinics have to keep their own set of books because they're not allowed to report bad numbers. The thing is that the numbers aren't that bad—the company is profitable—it's just they're not as profitable as they're reporting."

There was a pause.

"It's just that Lucci's a greedy bastard." Leach added, sounding perturbed.

"Well, it's just a matter of time until it unravels, don't you think?"

"It won't just unravel, Ron. Somebody will have to blow the whistle. Remember—Lucci is the darling of Wall Street."

Ron contemplated his remark. He was right. The Feds needed a reason to investigate.

"I appreciate the call Ron, but I'd also appreciate you not mention to anyone that we talked. I've put Dixie firmly in the rearview mirror, understand?"

"Roger that, Paul. You've got my word."

"And Ron…"

"Yeah?"

"Be careful."

\*\*\*

Jim Boudreaux reported immediately to Philip Lucci's office as requested by Mack Dawkins. Philip was at his desk, reading over a press release prepared by the marketing department. Philip's door was open. Jim stood at the threshold. Through his peripheral vision, Philip saw him.

"Come in Jim. Please close the door and have a seat."

Jim entered the office and sat before Phil.

"What do you think of this ad copy, Jim? Let me read it to you."

Phil held the page a few inches from his face and spoke.

"Dixie Rehab—work with us and we'll get you going again—back to work, back at play—back in shape. Dixie Rehab—give us a chance to get you back where you belong—healthy, happy and strong."

"I like it Phil. I like it a lot."

"Thanks. I wrote it."

"It's good."

Phil dropped the page back onto his desk and looked directly at Jim.

"Alright, Mack told me about Palifax and what he told Barton."

Jim intently listened.

"First, Palifax is full of shit. The company is fine. He's just saying that because he feels bad about leaving Barton's clinic. So forget about anything he said. Got it?"

"Sure."

"Alright, now about Palifax—I want him taken care of. I want it to look like an accident, or a suicide, but I want him out of the picture."

Boudreaux winced. He was at a loss for words. He stammered.

"You, you want him killed?" He asked.

"Yeah," Philip panned. "I want him dead—finished."

Philip's brow furrowed and his right temple twitched uncontrollably.

"I'd like to do Barton as well, but I'd be a prime suspect. It's too obvious. He's with Amanda. But if I take out Palifax, he'll realize I mean business—and that I could easily do him as well. I'm afraid that Dr. Barton may be a problem for us if we don't act. I need to send him a message."

Philip gauged Boudreaux's physical reaction. He appeared shocked.

"You don't have to do it yourself, Jim—but you need to find someone to do it. Just get it done, alright? Let me know how much it will cost."

Jim realized he was deadly serious.

"I'll find somebody, Phil."

"Good. Let me know when you do and when and how it will go down."

"Alright boss."

Jim Boudreaux left Phil's office with the realization that his life was about to drastically change. His boss had ordered him to become an accessory to premeditated murder—and because of the ridiculous money he was making as head of security he knew was going to carry it out. He was pissed.

"This isn't going to be cheap," he thought. "And I'm going to skim some off the top. This is a whole new ball game now. He's fucking crazy if he thinks this fits my job description."

# 19

Ron met Amanda for dinner at their favorite restaurant in nearby Homewood. The couple had settled. They were beginning to become familiar with each other's idiosyncrasies and habits. Furthermore, the two became even closer than they were from the onset. In the beginning of their relationship both of them experienced trauma resulting from the tumultuous circumstances surrounding the adultery, its extremely public revelation and the subsequent divorce. Nevertheless, over time the pain and humiliation of the affair's onset subsided and the two were able to enjoy the bliss of their newfound relationship.

Ron kept little from Amanda; although he had little to hide—except for his plans to bring down Philip Lucci. He simply couldn't share his increased understanding of Dixie. Moreover, Ron could not avow her of his intentions, for he knew well that she would fear for him and would certainly be worried sick about what Philip would do if he discovered his malicious intentions. For all practical purposes, Ron was on his own on his mission to bring down Philip Lucci.

"How was your day today?" Amanda asked, sipping on her white wine. She smiled at him.

"It was productive," answered Ron. "I felt like I covered a lot of ground today."

"Great," she said. "I always love it when I feel like I get a lot done in a day. It makes it all worthwhile sometimes. It keeps you going."

"Indeed," he countered. "I think it's important to celebrate the small wins."

Ron lifted his *Amstel Light* bottle in a toast. Amanda followed his lead. She raised her glass to his.

"A toast," Ron offered. "To us—to ten months of bliss."

His bottle touched her glass, producing a "clink."

They both drank and smiled. Their hands joined between them.

Amanda's eyes watered slightly. Tears hung on the lower tips of her droopy lids. She looked down shamefully, and then looked to him.

"What's wrong?" He probed.

"Ron, when I was a little girl," she hesitated, "and when everything was going so wrong in my life—when my mama was at her sickest point before dying, and my dad was too drunk to care anymore; I'd hope and pray that some day I'd have a man who made me feel safe and content; and more importantly--who loved me."

She paused and began crying. A single tear quickly ran from her right lid down the side of her face. Another under the left lid welled and threatened to fall.

"You've made that dream come true for me, Ron. Thank you."

The other tear fell, preceding more.

"Amanda, don't cry," he said, not wanting to see tears when she wasn't really sad.

"I know," she said, it's just that I'm so emotional right now. I'm so glad the way things have turned out. I finally feel content. I have my life back."

"I'm happy too, Amanda."

She wiped her face with the back of her hand.

"I love you, Ron."

"I love you too."

***

Philip Lucci, Mack Dawkins, Baron Scream, Will Bowens, three controlling accountants and Laura Becnell, the new Director of Risk Management—a title created by the company's Board of Directors, were present in the company meeting room one early Monday morning.

The purpose of the meeting was to introduce Laura to the executive management team and to allow her to discuss her planned efforts to reduce risk across Dixie's many departmental responsibilities.

Philip, as Chairman of the Board had gone against the board membership's interest in creating Laura's position, but the majority of them voting decided it was a prudent move because of the company's recent growth spurt. Given this, Philip was not excited about the meeting, which he was used to leading and dominating. Moreover, he had not hired Laura—she was hired directly by the board, as Philip said he was dead set against it and would prefer them to fill the position, as it was theirs.

Philip began the meeting with a brief introduction and a welcoming of everyone. He explained that Laura had been on the job for four weeks and that the purpose of the meeting was to introduce her and to allow her time to outline a risk management plan, as well as related objectives, strategies and timelines for implementation. After going around the table in a clockwise fashion, introducing each member of the upper level management team, Philip introduced Laura and she stood to address everyone.

Laura Becnell was the only upper level manager at Dixie with an advanced degree. She had an undergraduate degree in business from UT-Austin and a master's degree in economics from Vanderbilt University. A former human resources manager for IBM, and later an HR guru for an internationally-acclaimed business consulting group stationed in Washington, D.C., she was arguably the most qualified of any of Dixie's management team. Nevertheless, she was hardly a part of the company's long-standing inner circle. In fact, she was considered an outsider by Philip and his faithful minions. Philip had already expressed his disliking of her hiring to both Mack and Baron before the meeting started. They were both altogether receptive to his angst as the last thing they wanted was a woman with a master's degree telling them what they needed to do with the company.

"Good morning everyone," Laura began. "It's good to finally match faces with names I've heard repeatedly over the last few weeks. Also, it's good to finally be able to address each of you and hear first-hand your concerns about the important, encompassing topic of risk management. I have targeted three specific areas of concern for the company: Growing receivables with respect to recurring revenues, a severe lack of handicapped-compliant clinics in keeping with the Americans with Disabilities Act recently passed by Congress, and most importantly—and utter lack of minorities within the ranks of the Dixie Rehab workforce. As far as I can tell—there simply aren't any, which is a direct violation of Federal Affirmative Action legislation requiring minority set asides for a company as large as Dixie Rehab. This violation could potentially cost millions of dollars in lawsuits. I recommend that Dixie Rehab upgrade its insurance liability accordingly, as it currently stands in non-compliance and at severe risk if a lawsuit was brought forward. Does anyone have any comments regarding these areas I've designated? Before I get into larger strategies to correct them, I would like to hear from you."

Philip fumed. He shook his head and made himself heard.

"Laura, I appreciate your expertise. Your track record is impressive. However, you must understand that Dixie has operated for over ten years without instance. We have avoided lawsuits successfully because we take care of our business. We are good at providing world-class health care and rehabilitative services—so much so that we are viewed universally as a sort of business Samaritan of sorts. Furthermore, we are seen by many of our peers as corporate stewards. We're trendsetters in our field. And because of that, I want all of you here to understand—but especially you, Laura—that as long as I am CEO and Chairman of the Board of Dixie Rehab, we'll *never* have a single nigger working for us! And that's that! Does everyone understand?"

Philip said what he did with righteous indignation. He wanted to twist the barb once he stuck it. He was adamant. When he was done speaking, Laura Becnell, who was still standing, gasped. Her mouth fell agape.

Philip repeated himself, raising the intonation of his voice. "Does everyone understand?"

A smattering of low audible "Yes Philips" was heard; among them were Mack Dawkins, Will Bowens and the controllers. Baron Scream's face was red. He was deeply embarrassed; yet, he said nothing. Laura Becnell mustered courage theretofore unbeknownst to her.

She spoke confidently, "I resign my position effective immediately. I have nothing else to say. Thank you."

Laura removed her lanyard with its Dixie Rehab photo identification card attached and placed it on the table in front of where she stood and walked out of the room. In doing so she had given up a six-figure salary, stock options, a bonus package and benefits.

Philip continued.

"That's just the way it's gonna be, folks. If anybody else doesn't like it—they can leave also—and don't let the God-damned motherfucking door hit you in the ass on the way out!"

No one said anything.

\*\*\*

Philip Lucci and Clara Roberts frolicked on the Strip in Las Vegas, Nevada in front of the fountains at the *Bellagio* Casino and Hotel. Philip hugged Clara from behind while they looked upward and enjoyed the rhythmical, spraying undulations of the rooster-like columns of pressurized water that painted such a beautiful, albeit brief image for tourists, bystanders and passersby of the multi-million dollar resort built by billionaire developer Steve Wynn. They had just finished eating sushi and steak at one of Caesar's Palace's many posh restaurants. Afterward Philip took Clara shopping at the famous *Shops at the Venetian* and bought her an $18,000 diamond choker necklace, which she wore after the purchase. She couldn't believe how beautiful it was. She repeatedly checked her look in every storefront window and mirror they passed. Clara was quickly swept off her feet by Philip. Never had a man spent so much money and paid so much adoring attention to her. Although she knew it was premature, she increasingly visualized herself as his adoring, catered-to wife.

When they returned to Caesar's Philip and Clara went to the bar where they had drinks and talked. Philip confided to her that he had dreams of becoming a billionaire and that one day after that he might run for governor of the State of Alabama. Emboldened by the drinks and the fact that Clara was coming on strong to him, they left the bar and walked arm-in-arm to the High Roller Salon.

They sat across an aging Asian male blackjack dealer and Philip called to the pit boss. He asked for a $100,000 marker. The marker was brought immediately and Philip signed for it. He asked for 20

$5,000 chips. The dealer placed a stack of 20 five grand denomination chips in front of the groping couple.

Philip quickly doubled the allotted chips by playing two hands against the dealer. Unlike most gamblers, he promptly cashed out. They walked straight back to the jewelry store where Philip bought Clara the scintillating pair of diamond earrings and the accompanying bracelet that matched the necklace. The checkout slip totaled $19,000. Clara realized that she had scored nearly $40,000 in jewelry on one date in a single day with Philip Lucci. She could only wonder what a Christmas, birthday or anniversary could bring. That night they slept together for the first time. In the morning she awoke naked, but still wearing the jewelry. She slept with Philip three nights in a row in all, totally giving herself to him like she had no other man before.

# 20

Ron Barton pumped away at the pedals of the stationary bike while he watched the *Fox* morning news. He was 45 minutes into a 55-minute workout when the news anchor switched to a topic of interest.

"Dixie Rehab CEO Philip Lucci said in a news release today that the company's future is brighter than ever—that the construction of its digital hospital is going well ahead of schedule and that its revenue projections continue to increase, despite grumblings of an ultra-competitive rehabilitative health care market. Lucci cited his company's increased investment in human capital and facilities as well as their operational efficiency as reasons why they repeatedly meet Street expectations. Lucci added in the release that while his company's stock is currently trading at $18 per share, he feels it's undervalued and should be around $24 or $25."

Ron was incredulous.

"What a liar! He's a sociopath!" Ron thought as he continued pedaling. He couldn't believe the audacity of Lucci. As he saw it, the man had no scruples. He now knew that the company wasn't on the move like Lucci insisted. If anything, the company was on the retreat, according to what he'd recently learned. He thought of the stockholders—the many thousands of Alabamians who'd invested their life savings with the company. He knew their money was at serious risk.

"I've got to try and stop him," he thought. But he also knew he needed more information. He decided it was time to call Flo Thompson, his old teammate, to see what he had to say.

*** 

Philip Lucci and Jim Boudreaux met in Philip's office at the Dixie Rehab headquarters.

"You've got some news for me, Jim?"

"I do."

"What's the word?"

"I found a guy to do the job."

"Really?"

"Yeah. He's my second cousin. He's an ex-con from Bogalusa, Louisiana. He did six years for an aggravated murder charge. He's been living in Mobile for the past two years, laying low and working different jobs since he was released from Angola Penitentiary. I told him about our job and he said he could do it for twenty grand."

Boudreaux wondered if it was too high.

"That's a fair price," Philip said. "How will he do it? What do you have planned? Have you looked into it, or given it much thought?"

Jim crossed his legs and relaxed. He wasn't sure if Philip would go for that amount, but Philip didn't even blink.

"I did an extensive background search on Dr. Palifax. He's single, as you know. He has two residences—one here and another—a cottage in Gulf Shores. He's pretty clean—nothing comes up in terms of past offenses except for a few speeding tickets. He likes fast cars and women, but he's also a gambler. It appears that he's really into sports gambling and casinos so much so that it's caused him financial trouble."

"How?"

"Well, he spends more than he makes. He's got several credit cards that are maxed out—seven to be exact. He gets cash off of them to play, because he can't borrow from the banks. He has two mortgages on the home here and two on the one in Gulf Shores."

"He sounds desperate."

"He likely is. I think we should make it look like a suicide. I've surveyed his neighborhood. There's a cul-de-sac in the back. I talked to my cousin about the layout and the plan. Through my friends with special abilities I can acquire copies of Palifax's financial statements. We can make it look like he dressed to go to work, drove to the back of the neighborhood, parked in the cul-de-sac, and blew his brains out with a pistol or revolver. I have one with the serial numbers filed off already. His house has no security and no gate. He doesn't have a garage. He parks out front. My cousin said he'll wait for him to come out of his house. He'll approach him and put the gun in his back, get in the car with him, and force him to drive out back where he'll finish him with a single shot to the temple. My cousin will be wearing rubber surgical gloves. He'll then turn off the car, place the pistol in the doc's hand, place a manila folder with his financial documents on the passenger seat, and leave the scene. I'm confident he can handle this. It's an easy job."

Philip opened his desk drawer and retrieved a checkbook. He placed the book before him, opened it and wrote a check to "Cash" for $20,000. He tore the check from the book and handed it to Jim.

"Here you go, Jim. You have my full approval. Make it happen just like you said."

Jim immediately thought, "That's the easiest $10,000 I've ever made."

# 21

Ron Barton played baseball at Auburn with Flo Thompson. While to many Alabamians Flo Thompson was looked upon as a God, to Ron Barton, he was simply his old teammate. Ron was a couple of years older than Flo, and therefore Flo always looked up to him as a team leader when they played together. While they weren't good friends, they still shared the inseparable bond of Auburn Baseball.

Ron got Flo Thompson's number from a friend in the Auburn Athletic Department who handled fundraising. Ron was an annual contributor to the athletic department and he made a special donation each year to the baseball team, helping to make sure that the coach had an adequate discretionary spending fund to purchase necessary equipment and supplies. The number he got for Flo was his cell number—which was really the only number they had for him, as he was seemingly always on the go—living the fast-paced life of a high-profile sports celebrity.

From his office phone Ron dialed Flo's number. It rang twice and clicked.

"Hello," the low-pitched voice said from what sounded like a deep well.

"Flo? Is that you? This is Ron Barton."

"Barto! What's going on, man?" He sounded enthusiastically.

Ron's nickname on the baseball team was Barto.

"Nothing much, Flo. I wanted to talk to you. It's been quite a while. How you been?"

"I'm good, Barto, and you? You got a family now?"

"I'm still working on that one, Flo. Still working on it."

Flo was so busy he didn't even know about Ron and Amanda. He was oblivious to all of it.

"I hear you, man."

"Well, Flo, I called because I wanted to talk to you about your hip injury. I'd heard that you've had trouble with it. I might be able to help you."

"Man, I forgot you're a bone doctor, Barto. Come to think of it, I have heard from several people that you're really good, though."

Flo paused.

"My hip is bothering me a lot. I just don't think the surgery went well. I'm looking for a second opinion right now. I've been seeing Dr. Tyrone Biggs. Do you know him?"

"Yes. I do. I don't know him personally, but I understand he's a good doctor."

"He's great, but I don't know if he's the one to open me up again. He says it's a tough fix."

"Flo, I'd be glad to look at your x-rays and examine you, if you like. We could even do it at Dr. Biggs' office. I don't mind at all."

"That's cool with me, Barto. I just know I don't want Appleton touching me again."

Ron was perplexed with his statement. He thought about what Goldman had told him.

"Maybe only Biggs knows," he thought.

"I tell you what, Flo—I'll call Tyrone and set up an appointment where I can come by and check you out, okay?"

"That sounds good, Barto. I appreciate it, man. I look forward to seeing you. I'll be back in B-Ham next week. Give Ty a call and set it up."

"Will do, Flo. Will do. I'll call him today. Later man."

"Later Barto."

Once he hung up Ron immediately called Dr. Biggs' office and left a message for him to call him back.

\*\*\*

In early September, Philip and Clara stood at the precipice of Niagra Falls in Canada. They had flown there on Philip's jet via the Buffalo, New York airport the night before. Days earlier Philip had asked Clara if she had ever been to Niagra Falls and she said no. Since he had never been either, he booked a trip. However, Philip had another motive—he wanted to propose to Clara. The week preceding their trip Philip had Amanda's old 32-carat diamond reset in platinum. To make the ring uniquely Clara's he added a ring of six one-carat diamonds around the base of the new setting, creating a dazzling presentation that he knew would make her melt.

At dinner overlooking the falls on their first night in Canada, Philip proposed to Clara. Without her noticing, he retrieved the ring case from his right coat pocket and placed it on his right thigh. They had been enjoying a $250 bottle of red wine recommended by the chef.

"How do you like the wine?" Philip asked.

"It's divine," Clara answered. "I love it!"

She wore a low-cut, red sequined dress.

"I'm glad you like it."

"Clara, we've grown close these past few weeks—wouldn't you agree?"

He had her full attention.

"Yes, Phillip. We have. I'm crazy about you."

"As I am about you, Clara—I want us to be together all the time. It's difficult having to work around your work schedule, and for you to have to constantly drive up from Montgomery."

She hung on his every word.

"I want to marry you, Clara. Will you marry me?"

Philip deftly slid from his chair and pulled the ring box in front of him and opened it as he hit one knee.

"I want to be with you forever, Clara—just you and me, always."

Clara couldn't believe her eyes. The size of the ring was amazing, but it was equally, if not more beautiful due to clarity and cut. It was unreal.

"Oh, Philip, it's gorgeous!"

"Will you? Will you marry me?"

"Yes! Yes! Yes! I will marry you!"

She held the ring box with one hand and hugged him tightly with the other.

Philip was all smiles. He had another, even younger, trophy wife. Life was good.

***

Ron finally caught up with Dr. Tyrone Biggs. They played phone tag in between their busy schedules until Tyrone finally asked Ron to call him at home after business hours. Ron called him at 7:00 p.m. on a Monday, from his home.

"Hello, this is Dr. Biggs."

"Dr. Biggs, Ron Barton—how are you this evening?"

"I'm well, sir. How are you?"

"Fine, just fine, thanks. I spoke with Flo the other day…"

"Yes—I know. He told me. I went ahead and set an appointment for early Wednesday morning. Flo has to fly out before lunch so I figured you would be able to come by before work hours started. I tentatively set it for 6:45 a.m. Is this a problem for you?"

"No, Doc. Not at all—I normally don't start seeing patients until 8:30, so that gives me plenty of time to get back to the office. You're near the main hospital downtown, right?"

"Correct. I can get my secretary to fax you directions if you like."

"That would be great."

"Alright then. I look forward to meeting you Doc."

"Same here."

"Oh, and Doc, I've got a question."

"Yes?"

"What's this I hear about Appleton not conducting the initial surgery?"

"I'd rather talk about that on Wednesday if you don't mind."

"Sure, Doc. See you then."

***

Bump music from Steely Dan preceded the auspicious Tuesday afternoon opening of the Butch Bierbaum Show. Philip Lucci, dressed in jeans, a denim cowboy shirt and cowboy boots, sat with an irrefutable smile glued to his clean-shaven face. In the waning seconds preceding the show's opening by its esteemed host, Bierbaum quipped, running his forefinger under his nose, "You shaved the stash, Phil—I like it!"

Philip only smiled and nodded his head. He placed the headphones that hung around his neck onto his ears while Bierbaum opened the program.

"Good afternoon everyone, we've got a great show for you today. Philip Lucci is in studio with us as usual. We'll be talking about Alabama and Auburn's victories this past weekend in football as well as looking forward to this Saturday's opening SEC contests. Alabama will face Vandy and Auburn will be squaring off against LSU. You're listening to the Butch Bierbaum Radio Network, the Deep South's sports authority."

There was a pause for effect.

Dr. Ron Barton, who on a rare occurrence, was out of the office at 2:10 p.m. on his way to see his dentist, tuned his radio in his Porsche to the Butch Bierbaum Show. He wasn't exactly a fan of Bierbaum, since he felt he was Lucci's mouthpiece, and was largely responsible for the loss of his clinic and the subsequent tumult his personal life experienced.

"Philip, what's new on a Tuesday? What's new at Dixie Rehab?"

"Well Butch, we must be butter, because we're sure on a roll!"

Butch chuckled but he didn't think it was funny. He was just trying to placate Philip, who paid him tens of thousands of dollars a year to sit in with him two days a week.

"How so?" Butch asked.

"Butch our stock price continues to climb and our cutting-edge digital hospital continues to escalate on the campus near our headquarters. Better days and higher stock prices are sure to come. Things are really looking up."

Ron listened and shook his head.

"So, if I were a potential investor out there should I consider purchasing Dixie Rehab stock as an investment?" Bierbaum quizzed.

"I highly recommend it. The sky's the limit for our company. We are really making things happen right now."

"You heard it straight from *The Man* at Dixie Rehab, one of the most influential businessmen and highest-paid American chief executives, Philip Lucci. Anything else you would like to add, Philip?"

"Yes, Butch, as a matter of fact, I do want to say something."

Lucci paused, following the lead of his accomplished host.

"I'm engaged."

"Whoa!" Butch commented. He knew Philip and his friend and colleague, Clara Rogers, had been dating pretty seriously. He and Dr. Barton, who was still listening, were equally shocked.

"Let me guess—Clara Rogers?"

"How'd you guess, Butch?" Philip answered with a grin.

"Well, being that I introduced you two here on this show a few weeks ago, let's just say I had a slight hunch."

They both laughed.

"You're listening to the Butch Bierbaum Show. In case you're just joining us, Philip Lucci, CEO of Dixie Rehab, just announced that he's engaged to Montgomery TV Personality Clara Roberts. When's the wedding, Philip?"

"We've set a date for early November, in Jamaica, right after the gubernatorial election."

"Really? That soon?"

"Well, Butch, we're in love. We want to be together forever, and we just think eternity should start sooner rather than later."

"What a line! You can only get that kind of copy here on the Butch Bierbaum show, folks! My oh my! Philip Lucci and Clara Rogers—a match made right here—live—on this program! I guess that makes me a matchmaker, huh, Philip?"

"You did well, Butch. You did well. I guess we can start calling you Cupid!" He chuckled. Bump music in the form of Billy Idol's "White Wedding" began.

"I want you to know I expect an invite, Philip! You're listening to the Butch Bierbaum Radio Network. We'll be right back."

Dr. Ron Barton was surprised at the news, but the more he thought about it, the less he was really surprised at anything Philip Lucci did. Ron was beginning to see Philip for what he was—a truly complex, quirky individual who was a classic narcissist and an egotist of the highest order. To him, it made perfect sense that Philip would want to trade an older trophy wife for a younger model. Nevertheless, as a result of the revelation of Philip's impending marriage to Clara, Ron thought more seriously of the prospect of marrying Amanda. They had been together nearly a year, and while he had pondered hard about making things official between them, he still had reservations.

Before he fell in love with Amanda, marriage seemed like such a final formality—almost like death to a bachelor of his stature. But in recent months, and particularly over the last few weeks, he'd definitely experienced a change of heart. He'd contemplated fully marrying Amanda and having a child before she became too old. Amanda was a year older than Ron. At 37 a pregnancy would already be risky at best. His paternal grandmother before she died had encouraged him to marry and have children, so it was something that had always lingered on his conscience.

Ron realized that he had lived with Amanda longer than he had with any other woman. He and Leah had only lasted six months before he called it quits. He and Amanda, on the other hand, had made nearly eleven. Above all, he didn't want Amanda to hear that Philip was engaged and subsequently wonder about them and their future together.

"Marriage wouldn't be much different than this," he wishfully reasoned.

After his dentist appointment Ron visited a respected jewelry store. He looked specifically at wedding rings. He remembered something someone once said about engagement rings. It was along the lines of having to spend two months of your annual salary on a ring. He quickly did the math. "25,000-30,000--gee whiz," he thought. Ron looked at several rings. He told himself he was only going to shop. However, like most men, when he saw what he wanted, he decided to simply go ahead and buy it. He paid for it--$26,000 for a 2.4 carat ring in an antique platinum setting--with his *VISA Gold Card*.

He asked the salesperson's opinion.

"Do you think it's a pretty ring?"

She looked at him with wanton eyes.

"Honey, that ring is to die for. Any woman would love it! Let me tell you somethin'—you done good!" She smiled and winked.

Ron blushed. He remembered Amanda's previous ring was more than 12 times larger. He reminded himself that it was also ridiculously gaudy.

"You don't want it wrapped, do you?" The salesperson asked. She held the ring box at eye level.

Ron thought of what he was doing. He would need ready access to the ring in order to propose.

"How will I do it?" he thought.

"No thanks. I'll just take it in the box."

"Thanks Dr. Barton. Good luck!" The salesperson smiled.

Ron was somewhat embarrassed as he walked out of the store.

"What am I doing?" he thought.

\*\*\*

Ron went to the *Whole Foods* grocery when he left the jewelry store. He bought two dozen red roses, two filets for the grill, fresh green beans and a bottle of merlot. He got home before Amanda, marinated the steaks and placed them on a low flame on the patio grill. He and Amanda both liked their steaks rare. He cut the roses and placed them in a ceramic vase on the center of the dinner table, set the table, sautéed the snap beans in vegetable oil and opened the wine to let it breathe. He poured two crystal glasses full. He checked on the steaks outside. They were doing fine. He walked back inside to find Amanda admiring the flowers. They made eye contact. Amanda beamed. Ron blushed.

"I love the flowers! They're beautiful! Thank you so much!" Amanda said. She rushed to hug him. They embraced.

"You're welcome," Ron said.

She smelled the steaks through the gap in the sliding glass doorway.

"And you're cooking?"

"Yes, I am," Ron answered with gusto. She noticed the wine on the center island.

"And wine? How nice."

She walked to the glasses and grabbed one. She handed the other to Ron.

"I know you like merlot," he said.

"I love it, like I love you," she answered.

"A toast," she stated, raising her glass. He raised his.

"To us," she said.

"To us," he repeated. They touched glasses and drank.

They finished it with a passionate kiss. Ron placed his glass on the island and embraced her. Amanda maintained her grip on the wine glass and stroked the back of his neck with her other hand. The ring was in Ron's pocket. With one hand on the side of her face, he reached for it. Once he had it within his grasp he disengaged their kiss.

"Amanda," he said.

She was startled he pulled away in the middle of their embrace.

"Yeah, baby, what?"

Ron dropped to one knee. He placed the ring box in full view before her.

"Amanda, I love you. Will you marry me?"

He opened the box.

Amanda started crying. She nodded up and down twice, holding the sides of her face with her hands.

"Yes, Ron. I will marry you." She shook with excitement.

She pried the ring from its padded mooring and slipped it on her finger. It was a little large, but it didn't matter.

"It looks a little big," Ron said.

"It's fine. Don't worry. We can get it sized," she said.

"Oh Ron, it's absolutely stunning! I just love it!"

She tightly hugged him.

## 22

Ron made it to Dr. Biggs' office early, around 6:30 a.m. Biggs had just arrived. Ron saw him through the double glass doors of the façade. He lightly rapped the door with his fist. Biggs quickly came and unlocked it and let him in. The office was empty except for the two of them. Biggs was a slender man with glasses and a small fro. He looked brainish, and was the former student body president at Tuskegee University.

"Good morning Dr. Barton."

"Morning Dr. Biggs."

"Please, call me Ty."

"Fine, call me Ron."

"We had classes together in med school, I think," Ty said.

"We did. I'm sure of it. I remember you."

Ron looked around the austere office.

"Nice place you have here."

"It works for now. I'm planning on moving, actually. I'm going to build a new place."

"Really? Where?"

"I've bought a lot in South Side."

"That sounds great."

Ron wanted to talk business.

"Where's Flo?"

"I told him 6:45." Biggs checked his *Rolex* watch. "He should be here any minute now."

"How's his hip?"

"It's tough to tell. I'm anxious to see what you think."

Ty was well aware of Ron's growing professional reputation.

"I believe he's going to need additional surgery to remove scar tissue. He's got some problems with his range of motion. I'm also afraid he might need a replacement. He's such a powerful athlete, that it's both a blessing and a detriment. He's really torn it up."

Ron thought of Dr. Appleton and his round of golf, and then of Flo.

On January 13, 1995, during a Raiders playoff game against the Bengals, Flo suffered a hip injury while being tackled. The injury ended his football career and seriously threatened his baseball career. After Flo was tackled, he writhed in pain on the ground. Nevertheless, he mustered unforeseen strength and courage and amazingly popped his hip back into place. Flo later told a TV reporter that he felt his hip come out of the socket, so he just "popped it back in." Athletic trainers and physicians everywhere were amazed. Such a feat required almost superhuman strength.

"Let's talk about who performed the original surgery."

Ty's face grew serious.

"I've got coffee brewing in my office. Let's get some."

"Sure."

The two walked to his office.

"You married, Ron?" Ty asked as he prepared coffee for both of them. "Cream and sugar?"

"I'm engaged—as of last night—and yes, to one cream and one sugar."

"Well, congratulations! Or, should I say 'my condolences?'" He quipped.

Ron chuckled.

"That's what I'm wondering."

Ron noticed Ty's ring.

"How long have you been married?"

"Eight long years," he said, with the finality of death.

"Just kidding," Ty added, perking up. "It's been great. My wife is the best thing that ever happened to me. She keeps me straight."

"Super." Ron said.

They both sipped their coffee.

"Who performed the initial surgery on Flo?"

Ty's countenance shifted. He was serious.

"Some Jewish guy. I don't even know. I just know what Flo told me. One of the nurses from Dixie told him the truth about it. The whole thing pisses me off. I can't stand Philip Lucci."

"You're preaching to the choir," Ron said. "You think I like the sonofabitch?"

Ty had pieced Ron's story together from what he'd heard.

"I guess you have your reasons to hate him too." He said and smiled.

"What's up guys?" The deep, bellowing voice of Flo Thompson sounded. He walked right into Ty's office.

"Good morning!" Flo added.

"Good morning Flo," Ty said.

"What's happening old buddy?" Ron asked.

The two old teammates shook hands soul style and hugged.

"Man, it's been a while, Barto! You lookin' good, man. You must still be working out, huh?"

Ron blushed.

"I'm just trying to keep up with beasts like you, Flo! Look at you! My God, you're huge!"

"Pro ball is the real deal, man. I gotta keep that edge, you know?"

"I can only imagine. Hey—let's have a look at you. I've got patients starting in an hour or so and I want to give you a thorough exam. Doc—you've got his recent x-rays, right?"

"Yeah, Ron, they're over here…"

Ron spent nearly an hour with Flo. He began by taking him through a host of range of motion exercises, concentrating on his hip's flexibility and strength. Flo explained that while he still had good strength in his hip, the explosive speed he once had was no longer part of his legendary repertoire. As a result, he was no longer an NFL football player. The Raiders had released him earlier in the year. As he examined Flo, Ron admired his unique muscle tone and size. He recalled a baseball play Flo once made that personified his legend.

Early in his professional career, when he performed free from the restraints of his injury, against the Baltimore Orioles, Flo accomplished his famous "wall run," when he caught a baseball on the run approximately two or three strides from the outfield wall. As he caught the ball in full stride, Flo looked up and noticed the wall quickly closing. He simply ran up the wall—with one leg after the other reaching higher as he ascended. He actually ran along the wall--nearly parallel to the ground--and came down with the catch, to avoid impact and the risk of injury from the fence. Ron knew normal humans weren't supposed to be able to do such things. Flo was truly gifted.

Ron studied Flo's x-rays. He quickly came to the conclusion that Flo had avasular necrosis, a condition resulting from a decreased blood supply to the head of his femur. This debilitation caused deterioration of the femoral head. Ron felt the only alternative to salvage his professional sports career was hip replacement. This was a difficult decision for Flo because it would require him to sit out a year to fully heal and rehabilitate. However, Ron felt that if he worked hard—which he knew he would—he could come back and compete in baseball at nearly the same level as he had before the replacement. This of course wasn't going to make Flo "brand new" again like he was when he was a two-sport, pro superstar, but it would keep him in the game. Ron explained all of this to Flo, and Flo agreed to allow Ron to do the surgery after Ron insisted that Dr. Biggs assist him during the operation. Ron liked Biggs and he wanted to help him.

Flo explained that he had complained directly to Philip Lucci regarding the botched surgery—and to the fact that a strange doctor had actually performed it, instead of Dixie's preferred orthopedic, the over-hyped Dr. Appleton.

"You talked directly to Lucci about this?" Ron asked.

"Yeah. I told him just because I'm under contract doesn't mean I'm a piece of meat. I told him I could sue him if I wanted to."

"You certainly could," Ron commented.

"Yeah, but Lucci has given me crazy money, Ron. I mean—lots of money."

"So?"

"So? I have a contract with them and they've paid me big money to be a part of their marketing team. Besides, when I mentioned suing him he right away gave me two million."

"He gave you two million dollars to keep it a secret?"

"Yeah."

Flo shamefully grinned.

"Ron, look, I know I don't have much longer in the bigs. I've made a ton of money—more than I'll ever be able to spend. I figure after you fix me up I've got one, maybe two or three years left and then I'm done. I want to get into business. I've always wanted to. I was thinking I could start my own company."

Ron couldn't believe what he'd heard.

"So what is Lucci going to do when he hears I'm performing surgery on you?"

"I could care less. I just need to get it cleared through the White Sox. If they say it's cool, it's cool; but look—it's gonna be cool, because Ty told me you're the best there is, and besides, me and you go way back. I trust you."

They set a date for the surgery. It would be performed six days later. Ron encouraged Flo to continue his workout regimen until the eve of the surgery.

# 23

Felton Boudreaux had done hard time in the unforgiving Louisiana State Correctional System; and he looked it. At 34, he was 6-1, 190 pounds of thin, corded muscle. He had a blurred, dark blue ink tattoo of a teardrop falling from his left eyelid, coupled with a high and tight, pomade-greased haircut. Acne scars riddled the surface of his face and forehead. The tattoo signified his allegiance to an Angola prison gang—the same gang that raped him repeatedly as part of his initiation into their despicable ranks. Strangely, he always wore a sterling silver crucifix on a leather lanyard around his neck—a constant reminder of the friend he'd found in Jesus while in prison.

Felton served 72 months of a 120-month sentence and was pardoned due to prison overcrowding and the fact that he had never been written up for violence. It wasn't that he was an angel while he was on "The Farm," it was just that he was never caught. Once during his incarceration, upon directive by his gang leader, inside the shower he took a planted black diamond file turned into a shank and mutilated an inmate's genitals. The New Orleans native bled to death before any of the on-duty guards found him. Prison life had hardened Felton in many ways, as had his backwoods Bogalusa, Louisiana upbringing.

When Felton was 26 he and his girlfriend of two years got into a fight over the fact that she looked at a black man's butt. The fight ended with Felton bludgeoning her with an aluminum softball bat so badly that her wake required a closed casket. Felton's court-appointed attorney argued that he acted in self-defense—evidenced by the many deep scratches in his face and neck, but in the end the jury found him guilty of second degree murder and returned a sentence of 12 years. Felton never apologized to his girlfriend's parents for taking her life and ruining theirs.

In the days preceding the hit, Felton thoroughly cased Dr. Palifax's residence in an upscale neighborhood. He learned his morning routine. Palifax ran religiously at 5:30 a.m. for thirty minutes. He returned for a shower, breakfast and the newspaper and was always out the front door around 7:15 a.m. He drove a candy apple red 1993 Corvette that was always parked in front in the semi-circular driveway.

On Wednesday morning at 7:05 Felton parked a white van he'd rented in Mobile a week earlier across the street from Dr. Palifax's house. Before driving to the neighborhood he removed the plate and replaced it with a phony he'd purchased at the Greater Mobile Flea Market. He wore a gray painter's suit, an aged Alabama baseball cap, old *Sperry Topsiders*, dark *Ray-Ban* style sunglasses and latex gloves. He waited behind the wheel for Palifax to exit and lock his front door. Moments later the front door opened. Out came Palifax carrying a briefcase and his coat. He wore business attire—navy slacks, white shirt and a red tie. Felton turned off the van's engine and exited the vehicle. He made a bee's line to where Palifax stood locking the door. By the time Palifax turned to walk to his vehicle Felton was upon him—with a nine millimeter pistol in his right pants pocket.

"Excuse me, sir," Felton asked. Palifax was startled. He never heard him approach. Palifax was three feet from Felton and only paces from the *Corvette*.

"Yes?"

"I am looking for 585 Buckingham Lane. I'm painting their house. Where is that?"

Palifax lived at 581 Buckingham Lane, two houses down. He turned and pointed to the address. In doing so he left himself vulnerable from the side. He felt something jab him hard in his right rib. He smelled the stranger's bad coffee breath.

"Get in your fucking car and don't try anything or I'll kill you—quicker than shit," Felton said in a low, Louisiana drawl. He sounded deadly serious.

A petrified Palifax complied. Although nauseous, he walked straight to his vehicle. Felton closely followed, the weapon still pressed to the doctor's side. A mockingbird in a nearby maple chirped a morning salute. The day was just beginning, a large orange dot slowly rising in the East.

"Open the passenger door automatically—now!" Felton ordered, knowing Palifax could open it with the clicker on his key. Palifax again complied. The doors unlocked.

"Don't try anything! I only want your car." Felton assured.

Palifax was somewhat relieved, for he thought for sure it was his day to die. The car was insured, and besides, it was time for something new. Felton adeptly opened the door for Palifax, concealed the gun and walked briskly around the front of the car and entered through the passenger door. Once inside he retrieved the weapon and held it once again to Palifax's ribs. Palifax looked down and saw the surgical gloves the robber wore, which he thought was strange.

"What do you want me to do?" Palifax questioned.

"Drive to the cul-de-sac in the back of the neighborhood. We're gonna meet a friend of mine."

Palifax started the Corvette and slowly drove out of his driveway. As he left his house he looked to see if any of his neighbors were out in their yards. He saw no one. He was never more scared.

"So you want my car?" Palifax asked.

"Yeah. Just keep driving," Felton answered, sounding bored.

They approached the cul-de-sac. It was a newer part of the neighborhood, without homes. For Sale signs dotted the front of each contiguous, vacant lot.

"Park here," said Felton, his breath exhaling as he spoke.

"Is this where your friend is going to meet us?" Palifax asked.

"Yeah. He'll be here in a minute."

The gun was pressed firmly against the doctor's ribs.

"Who is he?"

There was a pause.

"*Your maker.*" Felton answered in his most sinister tone.

Palifax panicked.

"Please don't kill me," he pleaded, his voice cracking. "Why are you doing this?"

"For money."

"For money?"

"Yeah—Philip Lucci's money."

Palifax's mind raced finally, "I asked for this."

Felton removed the gun from Palifax's ribs and placed it on his right temple and fired. The blast was muffled by a silencer. Brain and skin tissue exploded in a red blob on the roof of the car. Blood and spittle trailed down the driver's side window. Palifax slumped forward and to the left. He perished instantly.

Felton acted fast. He unzipped the front of his painter's jump suit and removed from the front of his gripper underwear along his washboard stomach a manila folder with copies of Palifax's financial records and placed them on the floorboard. He took the pistol and placed it into Palifax's limp right hand, ensuring that he had his prints on the grip, barrel and trigger. He opened the passenger door, placed the records on the passenger seat, and shut the door. He walked normally back to the van, unnoticed, and drove away straight to Mobile to return the vehicle with its original plate.

***

Jim Boudreaux strode into Philip Lucci's office at 9:35 on Wednesday morning.

"What's the good word, Jim?"

"It's done."

"You sure?"

"Positive. I just spoke to my cousin. He's gone—just like you wanted."

"Good work. Let's just hope he's in the clear."

"He's on his way back to Mobile now. He stopped and called me from a pay phone a while ago. He said he saw none of the neighbors before or after he did it. It sounded like everything went off without a hitch."

"Solid," Lucci replied. "This is going to scare the shit out of that little prick, Barton. He'll know better than to even think about jerking around now."

Boudreaux said nothing. He was beginning to see a different side of Philip—one he didn't like.

Philip sensed it.

"You paid your cousin the twenty grand, right?" Philip asked, looking deep into Jim's dark brown eyes.

Boudreaux twitched a little.

"Yeah—yeah, I paid him."

Philip nodded.

"Good."

\*\*\*

Word of Dr. Jim Paifax's death made breaking news on the local *Fox* affiliate's noon report. A city street sweeper happened along the cul-de-sac where Palifax's car and body were left. Palifax's blood and brain matter on the driver's side window were clearly visible from the high perch of the street sweeping machine. The city employee used his C.B. radio to report the crime. Birmingham's finest reported shortly thereafter, finding the body, the weapon with his fingerprints, his briefcase and the financial documents detailing his many debts. The police completely took the bait. No investigation was necessary as they saw it. It was reported to the media as a suicide.

Dr. Barton's secretary, Amelia, was eating lunch in the office when she saw the breaking news report regarding Palifax's death.

"*Fox News* has just received word via the Birmingham Police Department that Dr. Jim Palifax, a local orthopedic surgeon, was found dead in his vehicle in a cul-de-sac in the back of his Vestavia Hills neighborhood. Initial detective reports indicate that the doctor took his own life with a single gunshot to the head. We'll have more information on this story during our five o'clock report, but again— tragic news today--Dr. Jim Palifax, a local orthopedic surgeon, was found dead this morning. He apparently took his own life."

Amelia stopped eating. She pushed her lunch aside and rushed to the room where Ron was with a patient. She knocked on the door. Ron opened it and stuck his head through the small crack.

"Yeah Amelia? What's up?"

He could tell something was wrong by the look on her face.

"Jim Palifax was found dead in his car in a cul-de-sac behind his neighborhood. The cops are saying it was a suicide. He had a single gunshot wound to his head."

Ron's face registered shock.

"Hold on," he said to Amelia.

He closed the door and told the patient he needed to tend to an emergency. After he explained that a nurse would be with her momentarily, he quickly instructed the elderly woman to exercise diligently in the days leading to her surgery. He re-emerged from the room. Amelia was still standing there.

"Walk with me to my office," he said. "Judy—please visit with Mrs. Smith and go over the pre-surgery routine with her."

"Sure Doc."

Judy was one of their nurses.

"Where did you hear this?" Ron asked Amelia.

"*Fox* noon report. It was just on."

Ron shook his head.

"Jim wouldn't commit suicide. He loved life too much."

"That's what they said the Birmingham Police Department reported."

They entered his office. He closed the door behind them and sat in his desk chair. Amelia remained standing. Ron put his hands on his face and propped his elbows onto the desk. He slowly ran his fingers through his brown wavy hair.

"They said they'd have more info on their five o'clock report, but that it looked like a suicide."

"This is bullshit!" Ron yelled, gesticulating wildly with his right arm. He was obviously exasperated.

Amelia had never seen him show such emotion.

"You think he was murdered?"

"Absolutely! And that it was Lucci!"

Amelia gave him a puzzled look.

"Trust me." Ron said. "I know."

# 24

The news of Palifax's death spread like kudzu throughout the medical community. Ron was so shaken he cancelled the rest of his afternoon appointments and drove to the Police Department. He wanted more information about what happened. When he got there he had zero success of getting facts related to Jim's death. He explained to the front desk attendant that he was a colleague of Jim's and that he wanted to speak to the lead detective on the case. The woman told Ron that he wouldn't be available until later in the day and that he'd call him if he had time. Ron pressed her unsuccessfully to give him the detective's name and number, but she didn't budge. He left disgusted. His anger with Lucci had reached a fever pitch. He knew somehow Palifax was murdered for passing along information to him. Strangely, he experienced the same feeling he had when Lucci discovered Amanda was seeing him. It was eerily identical.

When he got home Ron made himself a highball and called Pete Goldman. Pete didn't answer, but he called him right back after he left a message.

"Ron?" Pete asked.

"Yeah man—I just called you."

"I know, I was on the other line."

"I guess you heard about Jim, huh?"

"Yeah."

"Do you really think he killed himself?" Ron asked.

There was silence on the line for a full two seconds.

"Ron, of course I do. What are you saying—that the cops are lying?"

He sounded unnatural.

"I'm saying that they think he committed suicide but he didn't."

"You're cynical, Ron. Look, I've got to run. Let it go, Ron. He's dead."

He hung up the phone.

Dumbfounded, Ron rewound the brief conversation in his mind.

"Goldman is scared shitless. He knew I met with Palifax. He's fearful for his life. He's afraid of Lucci."

There was noise at the front door. The lock clicked.

In came Amanda.

"I'm home!" she said, making a grand entrance.

She was dressed in a gray business suit with a white blouse and black heels. Her hair was in a pony tail. She looked dynamite as usual.

"Hey honey," Ron said, still sipping his drink.

"I met with a wedding planner today."

"Really?" he asked.

"I did."

"And?"

"I think I would prefer something smaller and really nice compared to a bigger wedding."

That sounded good to Ron.

"Okay."

"Are you alright?" She asked, sensing something was wrong. She knew Ron only drank when he was a little edgy or if something was the matter.

Ron didn't want to talk about Jim. He thought of home.

"I'm alright. You know I haven't told my parents?"

"You haven't?"

"No. You wanna go down to the beach house this weekend? We could drive to Fairhope on Sunday and tell them."

"Sounds like fun. You know I love the beach—especially with a hunk like you!"

She playfully punched him in the stomach. Although it was late September, the weather in Lower Alabama was semi-tropical.

Ron knew he'd have to pay for the wedding, as both of Amanda's parents were deceased. He thought it was sweet of her to say she wanted a small wedding. At their age they really were past the age of having a big wedding. Ron cringed at the thought of having to create a list of invites and to make all the arrangements.

"Maybe Vegas?" He thought.

\*\*\*

Philip Lucci got word about Flo Thompson's planned surgery with Dr. Barton on Friday morning. He received a call from his contact with the Chicago White Sox organization saying that Barton was approved to perform the surgery. Philip was predictably livid. Barton was stealing some of his big thunder, and he was pissed. He objected but the White Sox said that Barton checked out well and aside from that—Flo really wanted him to do the surgery. He assured Philip that Flo would still rehab with Dixie, but Lucci was still madder than hell, and the news ruined an otherwise great morning for him.

Before he received the call from Chicago, Philip learned that his newest music venture—an all-girl teenage glam band called "Phase One" had scored a record deal from *Sony* Records after Philip gave the company Vice President a gift of 500,000 shares of Dixie Rehab stock. The stock also ensured that Phase One would open for Britney Spears on her next nationwide concert tour.

Philip had failed miserably as a country and western star, but he felt that his newest music venture would be an eventual hit since it had such an auspicious start. After all, Phase One already had a record deal, a star-studded concert tour and first-rate boob jobs--all paid for by Dixie Rehab, of course. Philip felt they were destined for success—success that he would undoubtedly take full credit for if it somehow materialized.

\*\*\*

Detective Frank Swansen called Ron on Friday afternoon, two days after he'd requested a call back from him. Amelia took a message and Ron called him back.

"Frank Swansen, Birmingham Police, may I help you?"

"Detective, this is Dr. Ron Barton. I'm returning your call."

"Yes, Doc, thanks. You called me requesting information, right?"

"Yes sir, Jim and I were former colleagues."

"Well, there's not much information to give."

"How is that?"

"He killed himself."

"You know that for a fact? Is there evidence supporting that theory?" Ron sounded presumptively.

Swansen was a bit perturbed. He disliked people who tried to tell him how to do his job.

"His prints were on the 9mm pistol, Dr. Barton."

"Okay. What else was there?"

"There was a folder on the seat next to him with his financial records. It appears he had a gambling problem and was in serious debt because of it. It all checked out."

Ron had no idea Jim was a gambler. He felt bad for prodding the detective like he had.

"Really? I did not know that about him. I'm sorry if I sound pushy. I'm truly shocked that he would take his own life, Detective. Jim loved life to the fullest."

"Dr. Barton, you don't have to apologize. Your reaction is normal. Tell me something—did Dr. Palifax have any enemies? Would anyone have a motive to kill him?"

Ron couldn't go there.

"Not yet," he thought.

"No Detective, I don't. If I can think of anything I'll give you a call. I appreciate you getting back with me."

"Alright Doc. Have a good day. You've got my number, right?"

"Yes. Thanks."

After he hung up the phone Ron thought about Jim being a gambler and how it caused him financial trouble. Although it was surprising, he still didn't think Jim Palifax was the suicidal type. It just didn't fit. The more he thought about it, the more he kept coming back to the odd fact that a folder with his financial records would be beside his corpse.

"Was it Jim's way of explaining why he did it?" he thought, or "Was the folder placed there by the killer to make it look like a suicide?"

"They're professionals," he recalled. "They're capable of anything. Lucci and his thugs are capable of anything."

\*\*\*

Ron and Amanda went to his family's house on Ono Island near Orange Beach, Alabama for the weekend. After a day of leisure at the beach as well as shopping at the outlet mall on Saturday they watched the sun set. The next day they had lunch with his mother and father at *Julwin's*, a popular family restaurant in downtown Fairhope. They shared the good news about their engagement and Ron's parents gushed over the beauty of the engagement ring. As always, they were proud of their son. Of course, his parents pressed him about a wedding date, and he simply said they were still discussing dates and times. Ron explained that he and Amanda were both busy and really weren't in a hurry. He added that they wanted the wedding sooner rather than later, and that they'd be the first to know once they had a date.

On the drive back to Birmingham on Sunday afternoon Ron revealed to Amanda that his former colleague Jim Palifax committed suicide and that the services were scheduled for early Monday, the next day. He explained to her that he discovered Jim had a gambling problem. Amanda did not know Jim and she had no reason to be overly concerned since she didn't know that Jim had told Ron so much about the problems Dixie Rehab was having, and that Ron surmised that Lucci could have had him murdered. Ron felt there was no reason to make her unduly worry; as he had determined before toward settling the score with Lucci—he was on his own.

\*\*\*

Amanda had a sales meeting early Monday. She offered to attend the funeral with Ron, but he insisted that she make the meeting, that there was no need for her to miss work. Jim was his former friend and colleague, not hers. He told her thanks for wanting to support him, but that it was more important that she make the meeting.

Jim was a Catholic. There was a mass where his younger brother beautifully eulogized him. Nevertheless, it only further confounded Ron, because his brother echoed the dominant theme repeatedly that Jim loved life like few others. At the mass Ron noticed Pete Goldman was in attendance. Later, at the funeral he caught up with him. Walking with his wife, Pete did not notice Ron approach him.

"Pete, hey man," Ron said.
Pete was startled.
"Ron, hey. Do you know my wife, Laura?"
"No, I don't believe we've met. Hello Laura."
"This is Dr. Ron Barton," Pete added.
"Hi Ron."
"Pete, do you have just a minute to talk? I really need to talk to you." Ron said. Laura could tell Ron wanted privacy.
"Go ahead Pete. I'll be at the car."
It was a cool, cloudy day. A light mist began to fall, foreshadowing certain harder rain.
"Okay honey." Pete answered. I'll be there in just a minute. I don't want to get wet."
As she walked away Pete turned to Ron.
"Make it quick, Barton."
Ron was unsettled by his tone.
"What's the problem, Pete?"
"What's the problem? You talk to Jim and me about Dixie, and Jim dies. You really think I believe Jim committed suicide?"

Pete looked around as if he was being watched. He was frantic. He lowered his tone, but he was still super serious.

"There's no way Jim Palifax committed suicide! That hardleg sonofabitch would have never done that! No way, no how! I don't care how much debt he was in from gambling! I don't like it, Ron."

Ron said nothing. He only stared at Pete as the drops grew larger and steadier, bouncing off their hair and shoulders.

Pete continued, "All I'm going to say is you better watch yourself. Lucci has you in his crosshairs. You may have taken his wife, but you're not going to take his business without a fight! You're in over your head, Ron Barton. You're an army of one. You can't fight him—he's got goons that carry guns and aren't afraid to use them! They're everywhere. How do you think he found out about you and Amanda?"

Ron knew everything he said was correct. He was at a loss for words. Pete recognized his shock.

"Look, Ron—just leave me out of your little crusade. I don't want to wind up pushin' up daisies, okay? I've got kids, man."

The rain fell heavier, exploding in small droplets on their clothes.

Ron didn't have kids. He couldn't relate.

"Later man," Pete said. He trotted off in the direction his wife had earlier walked, leaving Ron standing in the cool deep clutches of the pouring rain.

# 25

It was late September. The weather had grown chillier over the last few days, with the temperatures falling into the low fifties at night, which was perfect high school football weather. In all of the South's big cities, high school football is king. Birmingham is no exception. Gridiron battles are the Friday night main event at high school stadiums across the metropolitan region.

Philip Lucci's motorcade of him and Clara and his entourage of bodyguards and overpaid sycophants lumbered its way into the Briarwood Christian stadium grounds. Two volunteer parking attendants with flashlights approached the large black *Escalade* carrying Philip and Clara. The driver lowered his automatic window.

"How many vehicles in your motorcade?" the forty-something soccer mom asked. She wore heavy makeup and dark red lipstick.

"Three M'am," he replied.

"That'll be 15 dollars, please."

Philip yelled from the backseat.

"Give her 50. Tell her it's a donation from Dixie Rehab."

The driver pulled an envelope from his coat pocket that he kept for such charitable occasions. He handed the woman a $50 bill.

"Thank you!"

The driver's window rose electrically. The tricked-out black *Escalade* with shiny dark limousine tint pulled forward. Two identical vehicles followed holding Lucci's security team. They parked amidst the throng of hundreds of vehicles arranged in crude rows in the grass field behind the school. Philip and Clara exited their vehicle and were surrounded by six armed men wearing black sunglasses and black suits with white shirts and black ties. Their weapons were concealed. Philip was in a suit. He also wore an overcoat with a ridiculous fur-lined collar that stood up on the back of his neck. Clara wore a dark mink coat and literally millions in gold and diamond jewelry. Excitement stirred the nearby stadium. Kickoff was approaching.

Pony-tail wearing Jim Boudreaux stepped into the circle.

"Weapons check." He yelled, his cigarette-hot breath slightly misting the air.

Each man retrieved his weapon and checked it for ammo. A cacophonous exchange of sliding metal on metal screeched in the cool autumn air.

"Watch out for the weirdos," Boudreaux instructed. Three in front and three behind the principal at all times."

Just after kickoff the group walked to the gate where it was met by two uniformed police officers. Lucci's security team showed their concealed weapons permits and the group moved into the field compound along a gray chain link metal fence in front of the entire home team crowd. An eerie hush came over the throng as Philip's conspicuous entourage, like a freak show, made its way up the middle stairs leading to his reserved seats all the way at the top, just below the press box and just below his Dixie Rehab logo emblazoned underneath the press box windows.

Philip's power and range of local influence was vast. The veteran head referee's wife worked for Dixie Rehab. When he saw and heard the hushing commotion bubble through crowd when Lucci arrived, he stopped play in the game, adding to the ridiculousness of the moment. The Hillbilly Prince had made a full arrival to Briarwood Christian.

Once he was situated in his seat, Philip Lucci stood and waved to the adoring crowd. They obliged him with raucous applause, his armed gunmen waiting anxiously for weirdos in the wings, while the head referee allowed play to once again begin.

Philip was at Briarwood Christian to see his son, Nathan, a senior defensive end, play football. Nathan was the starting defensive end that night. However, Nathan was only starting because his father had built the team a new 5,000 square-foot training facility replete with free weights, machines, cardio devices and physical therapy rooms. The building was named after his father and noted as such on a plaque above the front door of the weight room. It was Nathan's last game of his senior year, the swan song of a non-existent high school athletic career, as his father had barely shown theretofore interest in his ever-sporadic play. The new training room and Lucci were recognized at halftime, with Lucci at midfield to accept a plaque designating a prestigious local annual philanthropic award.

***

Ron and Amanda caught the last flight out of the Birmingham Airport on Tuesday evening--a 9:35 p.m. flight to Las Vegas, Nevada. Earlier in the day Ron performed a complete hip replacement on Flo. It went exceptionally well. He was extremely happy with how the surgery went and was confident Flo would make a great recovery with Dr. Biggs' help and oversight. With his spirits tremendously buoyed by the accomplishment, on his way home he decided he could wait no longer to marry Amanda. When she got home shortly after him that evening he told her to pack her bags, that they were in a few minutes catching a flight to Las Vegas to get married—and that they were staying at the Venetian.

Amanda was slightly apprehensive at first, but after contemplating the fact that if she chose to go, in a matter of hours she'd really be Ron's wife—she couldn't get packed fast enough. She was more excited than a kid at Christmas.

In the early evening the next day Ron and Amanda were married just off the legendary Strip in Las Vegas before a signed and sworn Justice of the Peace according to all pertaining laws and regulations required of the married within the State of Nevada. Both felt that they had outgrown a larger, traditional wedding, and during their many weekly conversations about one they both mentioned eloping to Vegas as an option. Amanda thought it was romantic and so less painful, so when Ron said he was ready to do it, she gladly went along. It fit.

After three nights and three days Ron and Amanda returned home as Dr. Ron and Mrs. Amanda Barton. Ron called his mom the first day back and gave her the news. She was not happy at first, but relieved completely and moreover excited to hear that they were already trying to have a child. She was actually ecstatic, since she had in the last few years given up on any real prospect of grandchildren. Ron and Amanda both agreed to have one child as soon as possible.

Another upside to having eloped was the fact that the *Birmingham News* didn't even cover it. Had they had a large wedding in a church it would have made the Society Page and the resulting gossip would have run for weeks. Eloping made the only news of their wedding an uneventful surprise, which was exactly how Ron wanted it.

A small blurb on the *Birmingham News* Sports page did appear regarding Flo Thompson's hip replacement. Ron deferred all media correspondence to his assisting physician, Dr. Tyrone Biggs. Biggs told the media that the surgery was an early success, and that Flo responded well to therapy in the days following the operation. It was reported once in the article that the surgery was performed by Dr. Ron Barton and assisting physician Dr. Tyrone Biggs. Thereafter it only mentioned Biggs.

***

Even with Philip Lucci's help to the tune of $375,000 to Republican candidate Fob Smiley's campaign coffers, he lost his attempt to unseat Democratic incumbent Dan Siegel. Philip was terribly upset that his candidate did not win, as he held an important membership on the Certificate of Need Board for the State of Alabama, the six-member body that controls the scope and direction of health care in the state. With Siegel's election, Philip feared Siegel might in retaliation for backing his opponent try and ouster him from the board. Nevertheless, Lucci had other concerning matters.

As planned, Philip and Clara were married in Jamaica in early November, 1996, just after the gubernatorial race. Philip flew 250 people to the event and provided resort accommodations for each of them for four days. Among the dignitaries attending the grand soiree were Governor Dan Siegel and his girlfriend, Jimmy Buffet, Randy Owen, Michael Jordan, Troy Aikman, Michael Jackson, Rod Stewart, the members of Phase One and their families and Martha Stewart, among other Dixie-Rehab wanna-be notables, including Baron Screem and Mack Dawkins. In a strange twist, Butch Bierbaum was knocked off of the invite list at the last minute to accommodate dining diva Martha Stewart. The entire bill for the wedding was reportedly a little under $2.2 million.

The Birmingham media covered the wedding extensively. They got photos of the entire event as Philip also flew in many of the media members to enjoy the fun. Multiple articles replete with dozens of color Jamaica wedding photos of the bride and groom and lavish reception made the Birmingham paper and television news rotation many times. King Philip had been married. He ensured the moment would live in film and print far beyond him.

In the days after the wedding Butch Bierbaum published in his statewide sports column carried by more than 30 Deep South newspapers, and read by thousands, that even despite being snubbed for attending the wedding, Philip Lucci was still unequivocally, "The Most Influential Man in the State of Alabama" for his "far-reaching stroke and power from business, to sports to health care and back to business," and that, "everything he touches seemingly turns to gold." The next day, Dixie Rehab's stock was up five percent to an annual high of $22.30 per share.

# 26

After Jim Palifax's death and funeral, Ron tried to take a reprieve from investigative work. His enthusiasm had been tempered by the senselessness of it all. Jim Palifax's death hung high on his heavy conscience. He didn't want anyone else to be hurt; although, he still wanted Lucci, and he did not want to give up the noble fight against him.

The endless local coverage of Philip and Clara's wedding from Jamaica nauseated Ron. Moreover, it made him again focus mentally on Philip and how he might affect his demise. Ron knew that Philip had to be under some sort of scrutiny from the Federal Government, as he was just too defiant of the laws that governed business. He felt that with a little more information—like something related to the company's finances emanating from someone with rank inside the company—the revelation could be explosive—and the very thing he needed to help the Feds put the bastard away.

When Ron checked his messages at lunch on Monday he found a pink slip asking for a return call to Dr. Frank Quitman, the chiropractor from Phoenix City who knew Philip. He had not talked to Frank for over a year. He dialed his number.

"Dr. Frank Quitman," was the answer.

"Frank, this is Ron—returning your call."

"Ron—thanks for getting back with me so soon. Listen—can we meet for lunch today? I really want to talk to you."

"Sure, Frank. How about our usual place—the Mediterranean Café?"

"I'll be there at 12:30."

"See you then."

Ron entered the Mediterranean Café and Quitman was already seated with their food. He'd ordered the same thing they had the last time they were there, more than a year earlier. Ron was surprised he'd remembered exactly what he had.

"Hey Ron, I hope you don't mind, but I went ahead and ordered for us. I figured it was the only way you were going to let me buy you lunch."

Ron chuckled and sat down. Frank had only begun working on his potato chips.

"What's been going on Frank?"

"A whole lot. My life is pretty complicated these days, Ron." He crunched the potato chips.

"Really? Tell me about it." Ron said, opening his chips.

"Ron, remember the last time we were here you asked me about Lucci and whether or not I thought he would be able to build a digital hospital and impose his forced monopoly on Birmingham health care?"

"I do."

"And remember I answered, "Only if we let him.""

"Yes."

"Well—we can't let him!" Frank vehemently said.

Ron wondered what he was leading to. He was so matter-of-fact.

"What do you know?" Ron asked. "Tell me."

Frank's countenance changed. He seemed confessional.

"My wife had an affair with one of the higher-ups at Dixie Rehab. She and I have gotten through it through counseling and prayer—we've made it, but she shared some things with me that she learned during the affair that would bring down the company if they were to get out."

Ron hadn't touched his food.

"Who was it?"

"The CFO—Baron Screem."

"The CFO?"

"Yeah."

"What did she find out?"

"They had an affair that lasted almost two years. It ended about four months ago. She started just going out with coworkers to bars after work for drinks, then it was music clubs and more bars. I let it get out of hand. I wasn't paying attention to her. Baron was."

Ron listened.

"My wife's name is Rachel—Rachel Quitman. She works in accounting at Dixie. Baron got her several promotions and she makes great money now, but she swears the whole place is a lie—that they're cooking the books to meet Wall Street expectations—and get this—that it's been going on for years. Baron told Rachel that he's sick about it all. He said it's terrible to live a lie like he has. He told her he regrets not standing up to Philip. He and his wife are still together too, but by the hardest. Baron's apparently a real mess health-wise because of his nervous stomach."

"Frank, I'm sorry about the affair, I'm sure that's tough. But it sounds like you guys are working through it."

Frank appreciated the gesture.

Ron continued, "Now, let me get this straight--you mean that they're just *making up* their numbers?"

"Yeah—they're just lying about their revenues. It's all false entries. They are fabricating revenue entries. They're not nearly as profitable as they claim."

Ron knew this was the final piece of information required. Now he simply needed to talk to the F.B.I. and then get them to listen. Securities fraud on the scale Lucci was committing was a massive crime—Ron surmised that it was easily one of the largest accounting frauds in American history. It had gone on for years. The imminent negative repercussions to both the stockholders and the larger Birmingham and Alabama economies were staggering.

"That's why they have been cutting every conceivable cost," Ron said.

"Exactly. They're hurting for cash. The company's earning statement is a bold-faced lie just so Philip and the rest of them can keep their stock options, bonuses and ridiculous salaries."

"Frank, I've been suspecting something like this. I now know even more about Dixie Rehab that I don't like. Lucci is really bad for Birmingham."

Quitman grimaced.

"He's bad for America! What do you mean? The guy is a real jerk to boot!"

Ron couldn't argue.

"I'm going to figure out how to bring him down, Frank. I can do it. I just need to find the right person within the Federal system. Someone in the U.S. Attorney's Office would surely love to bring Lucci down."

"You think?" Frank answered, chewing on his gyro. "God, I would hope to hell so!"

"Would Rachel testify in court? Better yet—would she talk to the FBI and corroborate what you've said?"

"I think she will. I think she's ready. From what she's said, I think Baron is close to his breaking point. He's got a chronic stomach condition because of his nerves. Maybe he's ready to roll over?"

***

Christmas time quickly descended on Birmingham. In mid-December Baron Screem sat at his desk and pondered his life. He was so literally sick to his stomach from the stress related to the fraud that he couldn't even get into the Christmas spirit. He seemed incapable, even unworthy of holiday bliss. He'd hit a disgusting, new low.

He shut down his laptop with the legitimate Dixie Rehab numbers and left his office to go shopping. He went to the *Galleria* Mall and purchased five silk *Hermes* ties for the five accountants reporting to him. Each tie cost $135.

When Baron and Philip were raising venture capital for Dixie they learned of a particular silk tie that all the big investment bankers wore. The brand was French—*Hermes*. Baron eventually bought over 300 of the neckties and Philip, not to be outdone, purchased over 800, totaling nearly $100,000 in retail value. It was one of the true hallmarks of their staggering excess.

On December 22, 1996 Dixie Rehab had its annual office Christmas party. This party, which took place during normal working hours after lunch, unofficially lasted until quitting time. As the last workday before the holiday, it was always fun.

Baron presented the five accountants under him their wrapped French ties. Each of the guys opened their gifts in front of all the other invited upper-level administrative workers to many "oohs and ahs." They were a huge hit. The accountants were all appreciative, and told Baron as much. With all that was going on in his life, Baron found great solace in being able to give to others that had helped him, and whom he truly cared about. Although it was a small and simple gesture, giving the ties made him feel good. He was a little closer to feeling the wonder the holiday season can bring.

After the party was over Philip walked over to Baron, who was enjoying a scotch and water with Will Bowens and Mack Dawkins. Most of the others had left for home to be with their families.

"Baron, what were you thinking earlier today?"

Baron was caught off guard.

"What do you mean?"

"The neckties."

"What about them?"

Philip's brow furrowed and the color seemed to drain from his face, making his already dark eyes seem devoid of light. Philip also did the strange twitching thing that made him appear so ominous.

"Those are *our* ties, Baron! Those low-level guys aren't supposed to have them! I can't wear mine anymore, and what am I going to do with nearly 800 designer French silk ties?"

Baron was more hurt than he was stunned. After all it was Christmas.

"Merry Christmas, Philip." Baron said. He placed his half-full drink on the table next to the punch bowl and left without saying another word.

# 27

On a Monday in late January 1997 Philip Lucci saw two breaking news stories that immediately caused him great consternation. In the morning a $14.8 million judgment was announced by a Federal Appeals Court relative to a lawsuit filed by the U.S. Government against Dixie Rehab for using Medicare and Medicaid money to "kick back" money to doctors and other specialists who referred patients to their rehab clinics. It affirmed an earlier court rendering. Moreover, the court's findings declared that all doctors within the Dixie Rehab network would all have to forfeit certain monies and/or pay taxes on unreported monies paid to them by Dixie Rehab for referrals. This created great financial problems for all of the Dixie Rehab network doctors like Ron's former colleagues. It meant that each of them would have to forfeit some of the cash they'd recently made from Lucci as well as pay taxes on much more. It would be a huge check to cut for some, and it was a major blow to their ego and job security, as the announcement was made public.

If that nugget of doom wasn't enough, Philip Lucci's luck turned from bad to worse when it was announced that same afternoon that Medicare and Medicaid would no longer be reimbursing physical and rehabilitative therapy on the cost basis that it once did. The end result was negative--Dixie relied heavily on the steady stream of Federal cash related to government health care assistance. The major reimbursement change spelled doom to Dixie Rehab profits, which in turn meant that the stock price would suffer. Amazingly, it turned out to be the beginning of the end of Dixie Rehab under Philip Lucci's reign.

Following the two unfortunate developments, an emergency meeting of the Dixie Rehab executive management team was called on Monday afternoon at 2:45 p.m. Philip met with Baron Screem and Mack Dawkins in his office, overlooking the construction of the new trend-setting digital hospital. The 20-floor edifice was slowly climbing its way above the rock-hewn city. The monolith was really taking shape, its strong metal lines and glass ornamentation its most striking early features. Philip stood before his large office window staring directly down at the rising progress.

"The hospital's really coming along, huh Philip?" Mack asked, pouring himself a drink.

Baron walked to a daydreaming Philip. The CEO gazed. He was unbeknownst of Baron's presence nearby.

Philip, still staring at the hospital, murmured, "Hopefully I'll get to see its opening."

Baron couldn't believe it—Philip seemed remorseful, at least for a moment. Moreover, he seemed to realize that the game was up. This made Baron somewhat hopeful of what was to come, although, Philip had disappointed him before. He was used to it.

Philip really turned on the charisma and charm to talk to Mack and Baron.

"Okay guys, let's talk." He yelped, moving behind his desk for authority.

Mack and Baron found comfortable chairs.

"Each of you know what this Medicare/Medicaid reimbursement shift means, right?"

Baron truly wondered.

Philip continued, "It means we have to get really aggressive in our reporting strategy."

Baron was disgusted beyond belief. This obviously meant to keep lying about their revenues—at an even larger rate of deceit. It was the breaking point.

"I quit Philip! I retire immediately!"

Philip was incredulous.

"What?" he asked. "You can't just leave!" His face registered shock.

"Watch me! I'm done! The game is up. It's time I retire. I have plenty money. I don't need this shit anymore! I've made up my mind. I am at this moment officially retired!"

Mack was more shocked than Philip. He knew better than to say anything.

Baron got up and walked straight to the door.

Philip ran and caught him. He jerked Baron to him, grabbing his arm above his elbow.

Baron jerked back his arm.

"Get your hands off me, Philip. I'm done. I'll clear my desk out by the end of the week. I'll also be sending you—as a fellow founder of the company—a retirement proposal. I'll expect your cooperation. Thanks Philip, but it's all yours now."

Baron walked away, shutting the door to Philip's office behind him.

When the door closed Philip stared out of his window and transfixed once more on the escalating monolith that swelled beneath him. He thought of Baron walking away and leaving it all to him to sort out. He seethed.

"Mack, get Jim to get somebody on him immediately and that we want hourly reports on his whereabouts."

"Sure thing, Philip."

The next day at the opening bell of the New York Stock Exchange, moving on news that the Medicare reimbursement shift would negatively impact its earnings, and amidst abounding rumors that Philip Lucci was mentally unstable, and in financial trouble, Dixie Rehab stock halved its price, tumbling from an all-time high of 22.86 per share to just 10.96 by day's end.

In what was literally a New York-minute, Birmingham and the rest of the State of Alabama was devastated by a wealth-draining Tsunami. Tens of Millions were lost in a day's trading, with many more to follow. Philip Lucci--in an instant--went from hometown hero to hillbilly huckster and con-artist. It was a drastic turnaround when the bottom finally fell; and when it did it took no prisoners in its vacuous wake.

\*\*\*

Ron Barton stepped into his guest bedroom where most of Amanda's stuff that never found a home in the rest of the house was stored. He focused on a box of loose photographs. Shuffling through the photos he saw one that caught his eye. The image captured a familiar face. It was the cheesy, pony-tail-wearing guy he'd seen at South Points Grill with the trashy-mouth, flat-chested, bleached-blonde. Next to him in the photo were Philip Lucci and Amanda.

Amanda arrived home minutes later. Ron asked her about the singular photo.

"Who is this guy?" he asked, pointing to the pony-tail-wearing suspect.

"Jim Boudreaux, why?"

"Who is he?"

"Philip's bodyguard and head of Dixie Rehab security."

Ron was cratered. He couldn't believe how unfortunate he was.

"He likely heard everything," he thought. "He was right next to me and Palifax."

"Really? So this guy is the head of Dixie Rehab Security?" Ron asked.

"Yeah. He's not one of my favorite people, either."

\*\*\*

Ron Barton dialed Frank Quitman's house line. A female voice answered.

"Hello."

"Is this Rachel?" Ron asked.

"Why yes, it is. Who's speaking?"

"Ron Barton—Dr. Ron Barton."

"Oh, hello Dr. Barton."

"Rachel, Frank told me about Dixie. Can you get Baron to call the Feds? It's the right thing for him to do. Can you talk him into becoming a whistleblower? If he comes clean and cooperates he may get immunity."

Rachel was reluctant to talk about it.

"Rachel?" Ron asked.

"I'll talk to him. I don't know what he'll do. Baron is stressed out more than anything. I just think he wants to call it quits. The last time I talked to him he told me he wanted to resign from Dixie. He said he wanted to retire and just walk away."

"Good. Please get back to me if you talk to him."

\*\*\*

From his bulky black cell phone inside his car Baron Screem dialed Rachel Quitman's cell. The two were still good friends and co-workers; they were just no longer intimate. Nevertheless, they shared the despicable bond of Dixie Rehab, and all of its sordid trappings. In this case, misery loved close company.

In his rearview mirror Baron saw a navy cruiser with dark window tint tailing him. Fred Foster was driving.

Their relationship was over, but Baron just wanted to tell Rachel, as he knew she was going through much of the same that he was, emotionally, with the company. Besides, she was one of the only people within the company he felt he could tell.

She answered.

"This is Rachel."

"Rachel, this is Baron."

"Baron? Hey, I was just gonna call you."

That fact fell on deaf ears. Baron had something to say.

"I'm done, Rachel. I wanted to tell you. I just walked away. I just told Philip I retired."

"You're kidding?"

"No. I told him I was done. It's just a matter of time until the fraud is discovered. The Medicare news was huge. It's going to put pressure on us to reveal the true nature of our accounting practices. I just figure if I retire now maybe I can distance myself from whatever happens."

"Baron, it's not going to be that easy. You should contact the Feds. Give them what they want. If you cooperate you'll get a light sentence, if any and avoid real jail time. Seriously, Baron, you need to protect yourself by doing the right thing. Come clean and go easy. Don't make it hard."

Baron thought about what she said. He knew she was right. It was time to really end it. It was time to reveal the massive accounting fraud to the United States Government.

# 28

As it turned out, the U.S. Government was already focused on Philip Lucci—for insider trading. In the past six months Philip had sold over $210 million in Dixie Rehab stock, exercising time-bound options not yet affected by the Medicare reimbursement fallout. That Philip was able to sell at such a premium price enraged duped shareholders and wildly piqued the interests of Federal investigators.

The day after Baron quit Dixie Rehab was contacted by a representative from the U.S. Attorney's Office. The Feds called to inform the company that additional agents from their office would be arriving with search warrants and affidavits to claim records relative to all of the recent sales of Dixie Rehab stock by Philip Lucci, the Board of Directors or any of the other company managers. Moreover, another Federal lawsuit was filed against Dixie.

Philip had created a computer company for his mother and father—J.J. Enterprises—to purchase and re-sell computers to all of Dixie Rehab's offices across the country and the world. They had made millions with the separate case of insider dealing. However, since Dixie had used Federal money to pay for some of these contracts, the government wanted their money back, with a penalty attached. Philip knew the noose was slowly tightening around his neck, yet he was obstinate to its related danger, stoically confident he would overcome everything thrown his way.

\*\*\*

Two days after he left the company, Baron Screem parked his car in the covered parking area underneath the *Wynfrey* Hotel. As instructed, he took a serpentine route through the shopping mall before getting on the elevator in the connecting hotel lobby.

Fred Foster followed Baron. He was only yards away when Baron pressed the button for the third floor. Fred stepped into the elevator just as the doors were closing. The men stood only feet apart in the elevator. Baron had no idea the man next him was one of Philip Lucci's goons. They were quickly taken upward two floors. The doors opened and Baron exited into the hallway. Fred followed him from a distance. Baron saw arrows pointing toward the right to room 209. He followed them. He knocked on the designated door. Fred slowed and pretended to fumble with keys and try to open a door much farther down the hall so as not to tip off Baron. Baron was oblivious. He stared only at the unopened door before him.

"Yes?" an unfamiliar voice answered. "Who is it?"

"Dale Murphy," Baron answered, as earlier instructed.

The door swung open to a room of suits. Baron entered and the door closed quickly behind him. An open chair next to the table awaited him. He left his coat on and sat down. Baron scanned the room. Now facing the door with his back to the window, he could survey everything. Four FBI agents—three males and one female-- stood before him in a strange hotel room.

"You guys ready to learn about one of the biggest frauds in the history of American business?" Baron asked with a peculiar smile. He was ready to come clean.

The lead male agent sat down across from him.

"Sure, tell your story," he said, without cracking a smile.

Fred listened through the door. He could tell Baron was talking to someone about Philip Lucci, as his name came up repeatedly in the conversation. A bellman made his way along the hallway and made direct eye contact with Fred while he had his ear to the door. Fred quickly stood and walked toward the elevator and left the hotel.

Baron told the F.B.I. agents everything—about the company's unrealistic growth, about its inability to maintain Wall Street expectations, and the diabolical, sociopathic nature of Philip to keep the accounting team motivated toward committing fraud. Moreover, he explained how simple the fraud was—that the Dixie Rehab fraud team labeled "the family" simply created "dirt" or false revenue to fill the "hole," or shortfall from the expected number of Wall Street. It was all news to the F.B.I., who only surmised that Philip was involved in insider trading. No one imagined Dixie was outright lying in the reporting of its revenues. This was securities fraud.

The next day Philip Lucci arrived at work via a three-mile helicopter ride when he was met by a swarm of government vehicles and armed agents. The F.B.I., with court orders in hand, acting legally on the motive of suspicion of securities fraud initiated by Mr. Screem, seized the Dixie Rehab Headquarters building as potential evidence. Philip of course protested, but there was nothing he or his army of attorneys could do. The powers of the United States Government were being unleashed unmercifully against them.

The *Birmingham News* headline read the next day: "Lucci, Dixie Rehab Accused of $2.8 Billion Accounting Fraud after former CFO blows whistle." As Ron opened the paper as he sought purchase on the treadmill he couldn't believe it. There was a photo of Philip being greeted by Federal agents at the side of his helicopter.

"Rachel got through to Baron," he thought. "He did the right thing. Yes!"

Ron experienced great relief over the news. He felt vindicated in many ways. All the inner-turmoil he dealt with trying to fight Lucci; thinking he was nuts for wanting to do so; wondering why no one else saw Lucci as a self-serving, manipulative crook, etc. He was just so glad that it was now just a matter of time until Lucci went to jail for his crimes. He thought of how sinful it was that he would probably take pleasure in watching Lucci go down in flames.

***

Just hours after his incident tailing Baron to the *Wynfrey*, Fred Foster caught up with Jim Boudreaux. He told Boudreaux that he felt Baron went to meet someone in privacy at the hotel. He did not know who it was, but he felt that Screem was talking to someone—and that it could be the authorities. Jim reported this to Philip, and the next day, of course, all hell broke loose with the FBI raiding the Dixie Rehab headquarters. Nevertheless, this incident reinforced Philip's need for Jim Boudreaux, as his intelligence relative to the FBI raid was one hundred percent correct. It gave Philip a much-needed advance warning so that he could contact and alert his legion of attorneys as to possible problems. This successful tip-off by Boudreaux also proved to Philip that he could trust Boudreaux.

Lucci wasn't treated like a regular criminal, however. Four days after the FBI seized his posh penthouse and headquarters, he was indicted on 32 counts of Federal securities fraud and conspiracy charges. Despite these many counts against him, Lucci was allowed to be free. He did not have to serve jail time awaiting his trial. He was, nevertheless, removed as Chairman of the Board of Directors for Dixie Rehab, as well as removed from his position as CEO. He was officially finished with the company, on his own to defend himself against the many mounting, pending lawsuits against him.

Meanwhile, Dixie Rehab stockholders were hemorrhaging—the stock hit 23 cents per share, damaging the company's survival chances, as bankruptcy was now a serious option for the mediators charged with taking over the company in Lucci's absence. If not for careful action at this difficult time, Dixie was in danger of dying.

# 29

After the fraud was revealed Ron thought again of Jim Palifax. He thought of what the detective had asked—if Jim had any enemies—anyone that would want to hurt him. Given what had happened, and the fact that Lucci was no longer seen as the benevolent, caring philanthropist, made the call much easier. Ron dialed Detective Frank Swansen's cell number.

"Frank Swansen, can I help you?"

"Detective, this is Dr. Ron Barton."

"Dr. Barton, yes, how are you? What can I do for you?"

"The last time we spoke you asked if there was somebody who wanted Dr. Palifax hurt or dead."

"Yeah. I did."

"Well, that person is Philip Lucci. He wanted Dr. Palifax dead because he knew Palifax had been talking to me about Dixie Rehab's business practices and that he thought they were fudging their numbers to continually meet Wall Street expectations. We now know this to be a matter of fact. I think Philip had him killed because he felt he was a threat—and to send a message to me that he isn't messing around—that he's willing to kill to protect his domain."

There was noted silence.

"Dr. Barton, you think it was *a hit*?"

"Detective, why would he have copies of his financial records with him? Also, why was he dressed for work?"

Swansen allowed it to settle.

"Who did it, then? Where do we look?"

"Jim Boudreaux is Lucci's security head—or former security head, who knows. I'd start there. Ever wonder why the CEO of a *Fortune* 500 rehabilitative health care company needs a gun-toting security team?"

\*\*\*

Frank Swansen used his desk computer's far-reaching database to find James "Jim" Boudreaux. He wrote his address and pinpointed the GPS setting, recording it alongside. He got into his vehicle and drove to Boudreaux's residence, a renovated hillside dwelling on the city's neglected South Side. It was 6:02 a.m. when he pulled into Boudreaux's driveway behind his large, shiny black suburban with brilliant chrome wheels.

In full uniform Frank exited his vehicle and knocked on Boudreaux's door. Moments later Swansen saw the doorbell behind a thick vine weaving its way across building material encasing the button. He pushed it. Moments later Boudreaux was at the door in his underwear, white socks and a muscle tee shirt, his unusually hairy chest, shoulders, arms and legs on full display.

"Can I help you?" Boudreaux asked, still bleary-eyed. He realized the guy was a cop. His heart pumped, as he once was one.

"James Boudreaux?" Swansen asked.

"Yeah—I go by Jim though."

"Jim, we need to talk."

"Want some coffee?"

"Sure."

Frank Swansen entered Jim Boudreaux's kitchen and sat at the breakfast table while Jim turned on the coffee machine twenty-five minutes earlier than usual. He had been interrupted in the deep, tail end of his sleep. Now he was alert. There was a cop in his kitchen. He flipped the switch and with his arms folded, faced the detective.

"What do you know about the death of Dr. Jim Palifax?" Swansen asked, focusing on Boudreaux's beady, shifty brown eyes.

Boudreaux was super-still except for a slight nervous twitch in his left eye.

"I know he worked for Dixie Rehab."

"And was he in good favor with the company?"

"As far as I know, yes."

"No one in the company wanted him harmed for any reason?" Swansen probed.

Boudreaux was slow to answer. He wondered if he had already said too much. The company was falling apart quickly. He had not reported to work the last two days and he doubted if he'd be paid for work done in the last pay period leading to the revelation of the fraud. He had not spoken to Philip since the raid and everyone told him that Philip was going to jail and he'd be lucky to escape jail time. He knew only he and Philip knew about his cousin Felton and the money they unknowingly split for Philip's ordering of Palifax's murder.

"Detective, as far as I know, he was liked by everyone." Boudreaux confidently stated, his nervous twitch returning. Swansen thought he was a tough sell. He just couldn't tell if he was truthful.

"Mr. Boudreaux, what type of work did you do for Mr. Lucci?"

"Security work."

"Explain fully what you were paid to do. Provide a job description."

"We existed to protect the physical integrity of the headquarters and Philip, of course; to run background checks on employees, to monitor *Yahoo* Finance and other Birmingham cybercommunity message boards, run interference for employees between their wives and their girlfriends— in general, stuff like that."

"Really?" Swansen asked.

"Yeah."

"Fascinating—tell me something Mr. Boudreaux—has your boss ever asked you to harm someone?"

Boudreaux twitched. He wondered if he should come clean.

"Never," he answered.

Swansen picked up on his nervousness.

"You know, Mr. Boudreaux, if you were to make statements that would be helpful in the successful prosecution of a contract murder, you'd likely be given clemency and I would doubt even any jail time. You would get off easy. Save yourself."

Boudreaux's mind ran wild. He needed a smoke—bad.

"I hate to tell you, detective, but you're barking up the wrong tree. You and I both know that Dr. Palifax committed suicide."

\*\*\*

Leading to the Dixie Rehab trial, the United States Government successfully tried and convicted two other high-profile executives—Kenneth Blutowsky of Tyco and Bernie Feathers of Worldcom were both sent to prison for 25 and 30-year sentences, respectively. However, their trials were held in New York City, where juries are more sophisticated and understanding of financial and business topics. Dixie Rehab's Philip Lucci was spared that expense. Because of the ego of his named prosecutor, Sarah Harkin, who loved to flaunt her success and clout among her peers, Lucci's trial took place in the South—in Birmingham.

Sarah Harkin was a Republican appointment who had never tried anything as significant as Dixie's case. Heading into the trial, she was as brash as she was self-centered. Harkin felt there was no way she could lose. She confided as much to all close to her. While it was a mistake not to try the case in New York, it was even more of a mistake by Harkin to underestimate Philip Lucci.

After the United States Government mistakenly chose to try their case in Dixie Rehab's backyard, Philip Lucci wasted no time in reinventing himself. The court of public opinion was quickly turning against him. He had to act fast, and he did.

Using his abounding wealth he purchased a small local television station and began hosting an hour-long religious program every morning titled "Perspectives" that entertained one prominent black Birmingham preacher after another, as well as their faithful watching congregations. Philip ended each program by giving a check to the preacher's church to build classrooms or additional church space, and to provide technology and computers for their people.

What at first puzzled many was a shameless, unscrupulous, planned, well-orchestrated, months-long move by Lucci to taint the majority black jury pool.

# 30

In the early morning twilight Butch Bierbaum drove his black deluxe *Eddie Bauer* Edition *Ford Explorer* into the predominantly African-American neighborhood. He parked in the empty, adjacent church parking lot. The only visible light was a fading Mercury-vapor corner lamp some twenty yards away. Butch walked with his coat and tie on a hanger as he approached the religious building. He knocked on the left side door, as instructed, and noticed that it was partially open. He pushed it and entered. He made his way into the church. When he discovered the guiding light of the large open space he found a beehive of activity. Philip Lucci and his wife Clara were getting ready for the shoot, along with several other production hands. There were bright stage lights aimed everywhere.

"Where's the restroom, Ronald?" Butch asked the older black man, Philip's attorney, Ronald Dawkins, a well-connected former City Attorney of Birmingham.

"Back there," Dawkins answered, pointing. "Good to see you Butch!"

Bierbaum went straight into the dingy, antiquated, poorly-lit men's restroom. Staring at his reflection in the mirror, he started tying his tie. The restroom door opened and closed. Philip Lucci walked into the space directly behind Bierbaum. Butch noticed him standing there. He looked into his reflection in the mirror.

"Philip." Butch said, slowly nodding his balding head.

Lucci just stared, brow furrowed, dark eyes glistening.

"Philip—I'm glad I could be here this morning, to do this for you."

Philip unblinkingly stared him down.

Butch finally adjusted his tie and turned and faced Philip.

"I said--I am glad I could help you, Philip." Butch iterated, just inches from Philip's face.

"You *owe* me, Butch!" Philip growled.

Butch said nothing. He rolled his eyes and casually walked right past Philip and back into the House of God gone mad. As requested, Butch sat in with Philip and Clara for their show, Perspectives, and true-to-form made several rash comments about his "awareness of Clara's breasts" and the "types of revealing clothing she was wearing in God's house," and that "her mere presence was turning the place into a bordello" and finally that it "reeked cheap wine and sex near the altar."

Philip announced on the Perspectives program following the Bierbaum appearance that he and his wife were, on behalf of their good viewership and sponsorship, and in defense of good taste, suing Mr. Butch Bierbaum for slander with specific malicious intent. Moreover, Philip ended his sponsorship of the Butch Bierbaum Show, making him thereafter perilously fair game for Butch.

Butch went after Phil not for being a charlatan—but a hypocrite—for courting blacks into his favor while he never found the fortitude to hire one while he was CEO of Dixie Rehab. Bierbaum was quoted in a related *New York Times* article saying "Philip Lucci must be desperate (for courting black preachers) because I never saw a single black person at Dixie for as long as I knew him as the CEO of the company."

Philip didn't stop at his religious television program. He employed a group of young black activists/journalists to write favorable articles about his ongoing philanthropic work with the leaders of the black churches. These articles appeared in a prominent, long-standing periodical of the black community. Fortunately for Lucci, many of the people behind the publication were also associated with the community's more prominent preachers and reverends. They all ran together. This cohesive group formed the crux of what was dubbed Lucci's "Amen Corner" in the courtroom that sat faithfully behind him every day as the trial dragged monotonously forward.

For the government, the task was not simple. However, heading into the trial many onlookers felt that the government's case was nonetheless solid, although there were many reasons why the prosecution had a difficult time trying Philip Lucci. One of the main ones was that unlike other high-profile securities fraud cases that were tried in New York City, Lucci's case was tried in the Deep South. It was on his home turf, where there was already a deep disdain for all things Yankee. Moreover, there was the money factor.

Most cases involving the Federal Government and a citizen are tremendously lopsided in terms of the resources expended for both sides. In Philip's case, his enormous wealth balanced the playing field considerably, as he was able to create a Southern dream team of high-priced, and better-connected attorneys. Furthermore, Philip would not spare money when it came to his defense, as he was banking on it. As a director of Dixie Rehab, Philip had many years prior taken out a Director's Insurance Policy that stated that if he ever had to defend himself in court and won he would be reimbursed for the cost of his successful defense.

The trial began in May and lasted 14 weeks. The first day of the trial began with testimony from former CFO Baron Screem amidst national news reports that Flo Thompson had amazed the sporting world by cutting short his rehab period and starting for the Oakland Athletics. In his first at-bat he homered over the center field wall. He was quoted on *ESPN* thanking his doctors, Ron Barton and Tyrone Biggs, both of Birmingham, Alabama.

***

The U.S. Attorney's case against Philip Lucci was apparently simple. Eight different CFO's ranging from Baron Screem to Will Bowens to Weston White—the last of the minions to hold the position—all testified that Lucci insisted that they cook the books. Granted, it was them against Lucci, but Weston White's testimony was particularly damning. Weston quoted Lucci as saying, "Are you guys fucking nuts?

We can't report the real numbers! We'll no longer be rock stars! Our dicks will be in the fucking dirt!" All of them talked about how Lucci certainly knew, as he was the consummate micromanager. All testified that Lucci was aware and expected the charade to continue. Lucci's defense, of course, said the exact opposite—that they did it without him knowing—that he was the unsuspecting, aloof CEO. Expert legal pundits gave Lucci's defense little credit and even less of a chance of working.

While Baron's testimony, as well as that of other Dixie Rehab employees cast Philip as the unforgiving, overbearing, hard-driving boss that forced them to cook the books to maintain a lavish lifestyle, Philip brought all of his wealth and influence to bear, pulling every string and favor he could muster among remaining supporters. Through his television program and newspapers Philip made huge public relations strides among the population he most needed to gain favor—the jury pool—the people who would decide his fate.

Lucci's defense was led primarily by two attorneys—Ronald Dawkins, the established, black mover and shaker of the Birmingham community who had formed a rock-solid reputation as the consummate "arranger and dealmaker," and James Darkman, a character as ominous as his namesake would foretell.

While Dawkins was undoubtedly the racial lynchpin of the duo, Darkman was perhaps the brains. Darkman's strategy was simple: Defend Lucci by saying that the CFO's were the ones who cooked the books and characterize all of them as dirty "rats" who drank excessively and did drugs, cheated on their wives, didn't pay millions of dollars in Federal income taxes and orchestrated one of the biggest frauds in American history. To bang home his point to the jury Darkman commissioned a cartoonist to produce a large placard with a rat on it. He played the rat card hard with the jury—holding it up to them repeatedly, reminding them of the kind of dirty rats they were dealing with. It was brilliant. Stereotyping the prosecution's main witnesses as filthy rodents was good strategy, as most of them had acted accordingly during their Dixie Rehab tenure.

In the end, the strategy worked. The working class jury of seven blacks and five whites found Philip Lucci not guilty on all counts, while most if not all of the CFO's had already agreed to relatively light jail sentences. Philip was triumphant on the steps of the Federal Courthouse. He and Clara hugged on the top step of the white stone column edifice and waved to the sea of media surrounding them. Reporters yelled questions from all sides. They all wanted a statement from Philip. With Clara clinging to his arm, Philip reached his neck out toward the throng of multiple microphones pointing toward his smiling face. He was visibly exhilarated.

"We placed our great faith in the Lord before the court and we were found not guilty. We must believe that we are pure, as we've been given new life. I am a man of faith, certainly a man of God. I am so thankful," Philip Lucci wept, placing his head in Clara's bosom. He was no longer able to continue. His crying young wife clung to him and cradled him, relieved from the outcome.

# 31

The shock from the outcome of the trial was viral, particularly among the Birmingham health care and vast Dixie Rehab hospital networks. Wall Street was rocked, as it appeared that one of the biggest capitalist crooks that ever lived—a Southern charlatan with a flair for the ultra-excessive—had fleeced them and gotten away with it. Stockholders were further devastated as Lucci's acquittal only served to pour salt on already festering wounds. Moreover, hate for Lucci grew exponentially. Most who saw him shamelessly manipulate a black community with television and the almighty dollar viewed him as scum. He had set Birmingham race relations back thirty years or more. He was no longer the favorite son. To the contrary, he was its unequivocal, prodigal son.

Strangely, the national networks did not cover the trial much. The verdict was released but little information about the specifics of the trial appeared in the national press. Perhaps it was because the trial was held in Birmingham, where there is hardly a decent hotel for a legitimate reporter to stay. Nevertheless, Philip was free, still extravagantly wealthy, and like always, capable of anything.

Ron was devastated by the outcome. He made his way into the courtroom on the day of the verdict. A friend from Auburn who worked at the courthouse got him a pass to attend. He wanted to see

Philip's face when the guilty verdict was read. He was certain it would be guilty. Like so many others, it was difficult for Ron to take the surprise. The verdict was not only wrong from the sense of injustice, but it was equally despicable that the CFO's were all going to jail and Philip got nothing. He wouldn't spend a day in jail. But more injustices were to come.

When it was reported in the *Birmingham News* a week after the verdict that Lucci would receive $19.75 million from his Director's Insurance Policy to reimburse him for his personal $25 million appropriation in his own defense, no one could believe it. The boy from Phoenix City had played everyone. Now, his persona was much bigger. Lucci was seemingly invincible, the ultimate Southern Teflon Don personified; and with the added ego boost he was even more dangerous.

Lucci reveled obnoxiously in his victory and the publicity it created. Moreover, he loved the opportunity for more publicity it allowed. He made the talk show circuit, appearing on *Hannity & Colmes*, *Rush Limbaugh* and the *Savage Nation* programs talking about how he somehow beat 32 Federal charges and how he had changed from CEO to evangelical preacher with his own daily television talk show and was reaching out to his growing ministry.

Lucci was great for TV ratings as he was as odd as he was amazing. The program directors received numerous calls from viewers commenting on him, and that they thought he was fascinating. Lucci even had the balls to attend the trial of Enron's Ken Fay and report afterward to reporters on why Fay's defense failed. Philip, now the fraud sidestepping expert, was again on a roll, in the limelight—the highly sought after one. He loved it. He was living hard and playing fast like he never had before and he was winning—winning big. He felt omnipotent, as he knew his detractors despised him all the more for pulling off what no one said he could. Lucci defeated the Federal Government in their court. In reality, less than five in a hundred are so lucky.

With his freedom, Lucci's incredible wealth remained a factor, although he had several ongoing lawsuits to navigate with surely more on the horizon. He told everyone and anyone who would listen that he was committed to his newfound ministry and bent on helping others, that he wanted more children with Clara and that he wanted to support Christian politicians at every level of government and help them get elected. He bought a small radio station and contemplated starting a newspaper to counter the increasingly negative *Birmingham News*, which no longer wrote of him favorably, despite his long record of spending ad money with the publication.

Baron and the rest of the CFO's all got short prison sentences. Will Bowens received the longest sentence of the group, because he failed to pay his income taxes for over ten years and was the apparent architect of the fraud.

Several hundred million U.S. dollars were spent on forensic auditors and accountants to reconcile the complete nature and scope of the fraud. Hundreds of millions in fines and returned taxes were administered. Dixie had overstated earnings so much in the last three years that the Feds actually owed them money in overpaid income taxes.

By the hardest, Dixie Rehab's mediators were able to save the company. However, stockholders weren't happy, as the stock hovered around $1.00 per share thereafter for some time. Many lost their retirements or life savings. Dixie Rehab investors across the State of Alabama were ruined when they gave in at the height of fear and sold way short.

The City of Birmingham was devastated by the trial and outcome. After the verdict public outcry was such that mobs of Philip Lucci haters defaced his name on public buildings and infrastructure across the city. His statue in front of the Dixie Rehab headquarters was pulled down from its perch and never seen again. Furthermore, the stainless steel statue of several stick figure men pulling a wagon that once stood in front of the Dixie Rehab Headquarters in the foreground of the luxurious, multi-stream fountain, was now a weed-surrounded, forgotten ornament at the Barber Motor Sports parade grounds outside of Leeds, Alabama, an eastern Birmingham suburb.

***

When the narcotic effects of Lucci's most unlikely victory over the Federal Government's securities fraud charges finally wore off, Philip realized that he still had problems. A class action lawsuit by Dixie Rehab shareholders was filed in Federal court. He still had lingering lawsuits related to his unlawful bonuses and stock options paid based on false earnings statements. While he enjoyed being on television daily and fulfilling the steep demands of his acute, malignant narcissism, Philip realized he was still not completely out of hot water. He knew there were still many questions that remained to be answered as far as the government would be concerned. He became increasingly paranoid of the belief that everyone was out to get him. He relayed his thoughts and fears daily to Jim Boudreaux, who remained his body guard and only paid employee outside of his house staff. But more importantly, Jim remained his confidant and personal advisor. Just like he had with Amanda, Philip confided little if any to Clara.

Philip Lucci, Jim Boudreaux and Mack Dawkins finished off the first two grams of a brand new eight ball that Philip scored. The three were inside his pool house at his Lake Martin home. Clara was on an Atlanta shopping trip, having taken one of their small planes. Three Mexican prostitutes mingled in the nearby anteroom, sipping Silver *Patron* over large square ice cubes. One of the girls had been to the lake house and entertained before.

Mack was no longer working for Philip, but they remained close friends despite their dissolution from Dixie. Furthermore, Mack owed all of his personal wealth to Philip, as he had become a millionaire entirely as Dixie CAO. Because of this, he wanted to support Philip to the end to try and help him through all of his legal problems. He supported Philip steadfastly through the trial and walked along with Philip--since he said what Philip said—that the accountants had pulled off the fraud without Philip's knowledge. It was wholly convenient. Besides, Mack was Philip's remora—he was also going to hang around for scraps until the end, as he had no intent of going back to the real working world.

"Guys," Philip said, catching a huge drip of the river of cocaine and mucous flowing through his burned out sinuses, "I have a feeling they're going to try and get me on something else," he said.

Boudreaux was unaccustomed to doing cocaine, but took it up under the pretense of pleasing Philip, his gourmet meal ticket and leader. He had his own thoughts on the subject.

"Philip, I don't trust Detective Swansen. I think Ron Barton is feeding him information. I've thought about it a lot and he's the only person I can think would have tipped him off. Amanda likely told him all about me."

Mack listened, grinding his teeth, sipping his *Pinch* and water.

"Barton? You really think he could be behind the detective calling you and going over to your house?" Philip asked.

"Philip, think about it—Barton gets the info from Palifax. Palifax dies. Barton freaks out—calls the cops to get their side of the story, as he doubts Palifax committed suicide, which he should. Somewhere along the way Barton gets my name as your bodyguard and turns it over to Swansen. Who else is there?"

Philip loathed Barton for all he had done to disrupt his life. It seemed he was always there at every turn to foil him.

"I hate that sonofabitch! Flo Thompson is singing his praises on national television—that little bastard thinks he's so God-damned smart!"

Philip's brow furrowed and his face reddened; his forehead flush with blood. Mack and Jim hung on his every word and expression.

"Do him—just like Palifax—get rid of him! I want Barton done—completely out of the picture."

Philip stood. Mack and Jim were in disbelief. Both thought it was crazy.

"But—this time, Jim…" Philip said, staring at Boudreaux and pointing to him.

"Yeah?" Jim asked.

"You're going to do it yourself. Don't bother calling your cousin. I want to cut out the middle man."

Jim could only stare, his face red with embarrassment, his heart full of fear. He knew Lucci had him pegged. Jim wondered if he could do the job.

Mack could only wonder what Philip meant.

\*\*\*

A child was something they wanted and Ron was disappointed that Amanda had not become pregnant. Three weeks earlier she'd had her period when they were anxiously awaiting other news. Ron felt that the stress from Lucci's acquittal had done little for him and Amanda's health. While disappointed, the two talked little of the pregnancy results, although Ron knew well that time was not on their side, so to speak, as Amanda was getting older and further into the age range of likely complications. Nevertheless, the two remained close. In addition to polo they began occasionally jogging together, visiting the park near the Vulcan statue as a favorite place to stretch their legs.

After receiving the order from Philip to eliminate Barton, Jim Boudreaux began following him. Boudreaux was not a contract killer. He was a former Louisiana State Policeman and Baton Rouge cop. Nonetheless, his role and worldview had changed as a result of his business alliance with Philip Lucci. He had changed—and he knew it. He knew it because he was ready to commit murder for hire. Philip promised him $15,000 for the job.

After careful surveillance, Boudreaux realized that Barton was most vulnerable when he went to the Vulcan Park to run. To reduce stress and improve fitness Ron began taking an intermittent afternoon run in nearby Vulcan Park. It was a time in which he was alone. Where he parked his vehicle to start his run was often desolate. The area was remote—a good fifty yards or more from the main road on an offshoot, winding, loose gravel trail. Ron liked the shade and privacy the area provided as he enjoyed stretching and cooling down protected from the sun.

Boudreaux figured the easiest way to do the job was to ambush Barton while he was still in his vehicle and make it appear like it was an armed robbery gone awry. He'd simply remove all of Barton's jewelry and clean out his vehicle, making sure to steal the stereo to make it look like it was a job done by young African-Americans looking for something to pawn to buy crack rocks and get their fix.

Boudreaux knew Barton's routine and surmised that he could wait for him farther down the winding gravel road from the main road, and approach toward him just as he drove up and parked. He planned to pull next to him and park so that he could roll down his window and face him. When Barton rolled down his window to talk he'd hit him with a couple of downward shots to the face with a .38, ransack his *Porsche* and drive away, leaving the body and scene untouched, as he would use latex surgical gloves to prevent fingerprinting.

At 56 feet, the Vulcan statue is the largest cast-iron statue in the world, and a universally recognized symbol of the City of Birmingham. Commissioned at the turn of the twentieth century by the Commercial Club of Birmingham for the city's entry into the Louisiana Purchase Exposition, the sculptor was the Italian-born Giuseppe Moretti. The unlikely statue depicts the Roman god Vulcan, the god of fire and forge, reflecting the city's roots in the iron and steel industries. Much of the steel components for the form were forged in the Birmingham area, although other parts were pre-fabricated and sent by railroad from the North.

The statue, which is the likeness of a standing, muscular, bearded male—presumably Vulcan--with a hammer in one hand at his left side and a spear point high in the other, also contains an anvil and block. In 1936 the statue found a home on a 126-foot sandstone pedestal on Red Mountain. The Vulcan was the intended crowning jewel of a new park funded and constructed by the Works Progress Administration of President Franklin Delano Roosevelt.

Ron liked to park his car about a quarter mile past the statue, away from the onlookers that often came from all parts of the world to get a glimpse of the area's most unique landmark. Ron's parking place while he jogged was secluded, making it the perfect place for an ambush. Ron liked to jog from about 5:15 p.m. to 6:05 p.m. every Monday, Wednesday and Friday, stretching before and afterward. Jim figured Friday would be the best time as there would be the fewest people on the mountain running trails.

# 32

On Friday morning Amanda was sick. She told Ron that she had a stomach virus or something, and that she wasn't going to work. On Friday afternoon around 4:45 p.m. Ron returned home to find a lethargic Amanda watching television on the living room couch. She wore only an Alabama tee shirt, panties and a wrap-around wool blanket.

"Hey! What's up?" Ron asked. "You feeling better?"

"I'm so tired. My stomach is feeling better but I'm just tired. I don't understand it."

"You're too lethargic," Ron replied. "You need to get up, get dressed and come running with me at Vulcan Park."

Amanda didn't want to go, but she wanted to be with Ron.

"Do I have to?"

"Yes! You must! Get up and get dressed. It'll be good for you! Come on!"

He ran up to her and pretended to tickle her toes. She got up and ran to their room and got dressed into her sweat suit.

It was a gorgeous early autumn evening. The azure sky showed only traces of wispy white clouds and the wind was a flutter. The air was crisp and neat. Birds were chirping. Ron was invigorated and anxious to run, as he loved to run with Amanda. She helped him relax and enjoy the exercise. Furthermore, she made for great motivation.

On the ride over in Ron's Porsche Amanda started getting nauseous. She rolled down the window but didn't get sick. She pushed the top of her chair all the way backward so she could assume a near horizontal, supine position. She placed her right forearm over her forehead and closed her eyes as Ron sped to the park with the car windows down.

\*\*\*

Jim Boudreaux waited and listened intently inside his black *Chevy Suburban* with super black window tint. The vehicle even had tint on the top half of the windshield, allowing extremely limited outside visibility of the Suburban's inside. Boudreaux sat on the gravel road facing the direction Barton normally used to get to his parking spot. He wore a generic black baseball cap, a black bandana around his neck, dark, pilot-style sunglasses, black eyewear retention, a heavy, four-day beard, black denim shirt, black jeans, black leather cowboy boots and latex gloves on both hands. The windows were cracked and the radio was off. A loaded .38 revolver rested on the curve of the passenger seat.

Ron pulled off the main road on to the gravel side path that led to where he parked. Amanda was still horizontal. She was miserable.

"Ron, I don't know if I'm going to be able to run," she said. "I'm feeling pretty queasy."

Ron was sympathetic. He was genuinely concerned.

"We don't have to run, babe. We can take a walk if you like. We'll just wait. If you feel up to it, fine. If not, don't sweat it. We'll just hang out and enjoy the air."

Amanda appreciated his understanding. She reached behind her and grabbed his hand and squeezed it. He squeezed back.

Ron pulled to where he always parked, near a small pine tree. Moments later he saw a large black *Suburban* pulling slowly toward him. He had never seen a vehicle there before. The black truck stopped next to him and the driver's window slowly rolled down halfway. Cigarette smoke filtered through the opening. Ron could only see dark sunglasses, a black hat, a lit cigarette and smoke. He rolled down his window. As he did he noticed above the vehicle, in the distance, like a looming specter, the large statue of Vulcan, his sharpened spear point lifted high into the air.

Because the *Suburban* sat much higher on the road than the *Porsche*, Jim Boudreaux never saw Amanda lying in the passenger seat. When Ron's window was halfway down, with his left hand Jim flipped the automatic window switch, lowering his window completely. With his dominant, right hand he pointed the revolver through the full opening directly at Ron. Ron saw the gun and reacted. With his left hand he flipped a switch and went directly backward into a supine position in concert with two quick, loud, blasts and the smell of cordite. Forthwith, he put the vehicle in first gear and gave it gas, pulling quickly forward down the loose gravel road. Ron shifted into second and was quickly on to third. Everything happened so fast.

Ron heard gurgling noises. He looked to his right and saw Amanda gasping to breathe. She had a gaping bullet wound in her neck and was bleeding profusely. Blood dripped straight down the front of her shirt and warm-up top. He quickly realized she needed help fast or she would die. She needed the emergency room.

Ron's heart pounded. He had to save her. He took a fork in the gravel road that led back to the main road. He gunned the engine, determined to get Amanda treatment. With his right hand he put pressure on her wound, trying to stem the massive blood flow. He saw she was unconscious. Her blood was running down his wrist and onto his forearm toward his bicep.

She gasped and made another gurgling noise.

"Amanda! Amanda! Can you hear me? Amanda! Amanda! Amanda! Can you hear me, Amanda?"

She was unresponsive.

Ron zoomed down the Red Mountain Parkway and blew through every red light on his way to the UAB Hospital emergency room, applying pressure to Amanda's wound as he could with his right hand as he steered with his left. He parked underneath the overhang and ran around to the passenger side, cradling and carrying her blood-soaked torso in his arms through the automatic glass doors.

"Help me!" Ron yelled as he breached the threshold of the room. "She has a gunshot wound to her neck. I think it got her carotid artery. I think she's bleeding out!"

Two nurses and a young doctor immediately came to his aid and pulled Amanda out of his arms. They placed her on a stretcher and wheeled her away. Ron collapsed into a kneeling position on the floor and wept, examining his right arm and shirt smeared with Amanda's blood, knowing well it was unlikely that she'd make it.

# 33

Ron was given Valium and was kept under observation before being released. However, the news of Amanda's death came fast. Within minutes of his arrival the young emergency room doctor came to him in the glassed-in, partitioned area where he was being monitored.

"Dr. Barton?" the young man asked.

"Yeah?" Ron replied, looking up from his chair. His feet were propped up on another.

"Your wife didn't make it. We tried to save her but she just lost too much blood."

Ron sat up and placed his hands on his head and cried uncontrollably. He had so many feelings rushing through his conscience—selfishness, guilt, arrogance, heartbreak—he was again alone.

"And Doc," the young doctor said through tired eyes.

Ron looked up. Tears trailed his face.

"I know this doesn't make it any easier for you—but she was pregnant."

Ron fell sideways into the chair next to him, weeping loudly.

\*\*\*

When Ron woke Detective Frank Swansen was sitting next to his hospital bed. After he passed out from the shock of the news of

Amanda and his unborn child's death three hours earlier, he was issued his own room for the night for continued monitoring. Moreover, he was put on an I.V. drip with a slightly higher Valium dosage.

"Hey Doc." Swansen said as Barton's eyes strained to focus. He felt sluggish.

Ron recognized Swansen's voice and the police uniform. His eyes finally worked like they were supposed to and he read the nametag and confirmed it.

"Hello Detective."

"Dr. Barton, I'm sorry about your wife. I know this has to be difficult. I heard the victim was your wife and I made sure I got the case. I want you to know that I am going to find out who did this. But, I am going to need your full help and cooperation."

Ron nodded. He was really looped up on the Valium, but it didn't come close to numbing the pain of losing Amanda. He was grieving.

"I know you're tired. You can rest now if you like. I can come back tomorrow."

"No Detective," he said. "Stay. Please."

"Do you want to tell me what happened?"

Ron nodded his head. He mustered the courage to speak with conviction. From a grimace he spoke.

"Jim Boudreaux tried to kill me and got Amanda instead."

\*\*\*

At 11:03 p.m. Frank Swansen drove straight to Jim Boudreaux's house and arrested him. Boudreaux was halfway through a bottle of green label *Jack Daniels* and several sleeping pills. According to the police report he appeared suicidal when he was apprehended and brought into custody for questioning.

Boudreaux sobered up and the next day took credit for murdering Mrs. Ron Barton. Shortly after Swansen lit into him and told him that Barton saw him pull the trigger on Amanda, he said he wanted to come clean. Surprisingly, he also took credit for murdering Dr. Jim Palifax, telling Swansen he committed both crimes out of malice. In the confessions he referred to Palifax as a "little prick" and Amanda as a "complete bitch."

Swansen was surprised at the double confession. He wasn't expecting Boudreaux to confess to Palifax's death.

"So you killed Palifax because he was a "prick" and Amanda because she was a "bitch?" He asked.

"You got it detective. That's exactly right." Boudreaux said.

Swansen didn't buy it. He figured he was covering for someone.

"Don't I get a phone call, detective?" Boudreaux asked.

"Yeah, you do," said Swansen. "Who do you wanna call?"

"Philip Lucci."

\*\*\*

News of Amanda's death reached Philip Lucci via television before he refused to accept Boudreaux's collect call from the Birmingham Jail just before midnight. He was devastated not as much about Amanda's accidental death as he was that the news stations reported that the bodyguard of Philip Lucci was arrested for Amanda's murder and that he was currently being held without bond. Philip panicked when he wondered what Boudreaux told the police.

Ron went home before lunch the day after his night in the hospital. His mom and dad both drove up to see him home. His mother cooked and cleaned for him. Ron was devastated, and completely effete as a result. Amanda was the true love of his life. She changed him by affirming the good within him and by loving him unconditionally. He knew he would never hold her again. The finality of it all caused him to recoil. He had little to say and wanted only to sleep as much as he could. He knew Lucci was behind all of his pain and trouble, but he didn't want to cloud his grief for Amanda with hate for his nemesis. He assured himself he would not allow Lucci to also claim his grief for his departed wife.

Amanda's funeral was particularly difficult for Ron. Not only did he have to bury Amanda and endure the army of well-wishers and friends and family offering condolences, he also had to worry about Lucci. Philip called and sent flowers to the funeral home. He also asked to pay his final respects to Amanda. He wanted to visit the body. Ron went ballistic. He saw it as the lowest of all the moves Lucci had ever pulled. The murderer wanted to view the body. It was typical Philip. Ron lamented and figured it would be easier to allow him time than not, so he arranged for Philip to view the body alone, two hours before Ron's family arrived. He and his family never saw him, but the funeral home director said Philip indeed came, wearing an expensive suit and carrying a small bouquet. He told Ron that he knelt before Amanda for about ten minutes, placed the bouquet, and left.

According to her close girl friends, Amanda hated turtlenecks. However, one was unavoidable for her casket viewing. The gunshot wound blew a huge hole in the middle of her neck. She looked beautiful, nonetheless. Her hair was tastefully done, curled and brushed to perfection. She wore a light white cardigan sweater over the crimson turtleneck.

Amanda's wake was well attended. Everyone who was anyone in the medical community went. Nearly all of the doctors who Amanda once called on paid their respects, as did all of Ron's colleagues and many of his patients and friends. Of course, Ron's parents were there with him throughout the ordeal. The wake was from 6:00 to 9:00 p.m. on a Wednesday. Several of Amanda's former fellow Alabama cheerleaders showed, as did her old cheerleading coach.

Shortly after 8:00 p.m. Dr. Leah Thompson entered the parlor after signing the guest register. She wore light makeup, a neat gray suit and matching heels.

Ron was talking to one of the doctors that bought pharmaceuticals from Amanda when he saw Leah. He immediately told the doctor that he appreciated him coming, but that he had to see someone. He excused himself and made his way over to Leah.

Leah was talking to one of the many visiting doctors she knew when Ron approached her. She saw him coming and moved to him, her arms open. Ron embraced her. They both got emotional. Leah fought off tears. They held each other's hands, hugged and separated, still holding hands.

"Ron, I'm so, so sorry."

"Thanks."

"I cannot imagine how you feel."

"I'll be okay," he said, fighting off tears.

Leah felt so bad for him. She hugged him again.

"You poor thing."

They hugged for a while.

Ron didn't want to let her go.

Amanda's funeral service was at her burial site. It was relatively short by design. Ron asked for it. Her parents had long been deceased and she was an only child. None of her family that she knew survived, as her uncle had died three years earlier. She and Ron had talked and she said she felt alone in the world after her daddy died. When her uncle passed it only compounded the lonesome feeling.

Ron took an entire week off from seeing patients. He performed two planned surgeries during the middle of the week, but that was it. He mainly just slept.

# 34

On Friday of that week the headline of the *Birmingham News* read, "Lucci, Siegel, Indicted on Bribery Charges."

Lucci was used to buying influence. It was his principal modus operandi. Nevertheless, when he bankrolled republican Fob Smiley's gubernatorial run he pissed off big-time the sitting democratic governor, Dan Siegel, the man who eventually won the race.

When he took office, Siegel's first big initiative was to try and pass a statewide lottery. Siegel's office and state leaders in the house and senate pushed the idea as a way to help education by improving teacher pay, facilities and supplies. His detractors tagged it big government in the making, and they effectively made their case with the help of a clever television advertisement campaign painting the endeavor as a classic back-room, fat-cat maneuver to get more spending cash for the democrats. Not to be outdone, Siegel found his own high-priced advertising consultants to come up with their own promotional campaign to pass the lottery. The problem was in doing so he overspent his advertising budget by nearly one million dollars. The head of the Democratic Party in the State of Alabama told him to pay the bill from his own money, that the party wasn't picking up the tab for his baby. He was in a pinch. Siegel badly needed cash.

Siegel called Lucci and told him that if he wanted to stay on the Certificate of Need Board he needed to cough up $500,000. Lucci was incensed at first, but he realized that he had to pay to play, especially after he backed Smiley, Siegel's opponent in the election. Lucci may have no longer been the CEO and Chairman of the Board of Dixie, but he was still an equity investor or principal in nearly a dozen or more health care firms. He needed to stay on the C.O.N. Board. He had too much to lose.

Shortly after the phone call Lucci wrote through one of his other companies out of Massachusetts a check for $500,000 to a political action committee called Alabama Democrats for Tomorrow, per the advisement of the sitting governor, Dan Siegel. It was Lucci's understanding that this would allow him to maintain his appointment to the Certificate of Need Board.

When Lucci pulled off the improbable acquittal in the securities fraud trial he simultaneously amazed and infuriated Federal prosecutors. None of them saw it coming. They'd been had. In the painful, embarrassing aftermath, they vowed to get him. Thereafter, they used their vast resources and might to do just that. This time the charge was bribing a public official.

Before the first trial, no one gave Lucci a chance of being acquitted. In the second, it was the exact opposite--no one gave him a chance of being convicted. Legal experts said that what Siegel did—accepting campaign money in exchange for an appointment--was done by governors across the United States, and was not an illegal practice. Governor Siegel's legal team fought hard to point out this fact, but to no avail. He and Lucci would stand trial in three short months for conspiracy to commit bribery and bribery.

On Friday after lunch Philip Lucci made his way into the jail to visit Jim Boudreaux. Under the advisement of his attorney he arranged to see Jim in person to discover what he told the police.

Philip was led to a row of glass-partitioned cubicles with a voice hole for conversation with the convict on the other side. A smiling Jim Boudreaux waited behind the glass in the third cubicle. Philip was allowed by the accompanying guard to approach the chair alone. The guard closed the door to the area behind him and left the two men alone.

Philip sat and looked at Jim.

"Hey Philip."

"Jim."

Boudreaux looked over his shoulder and to his right, to see if anyone was paying attention.

"I didn't say anything Philip. I'm taking the rap. It's all mine. Just take care of my family is all I want, Philip. Keep all this off my brother. I don't have kids. If you could set me up some kind of long-term insurance plan for when I get out—if I get out—that would be great, too. But I just want you to know that I'm going down for both raps. They're mine, and I'm gonna do the time."

Philip doubted if Jim would ever get out of jail. He figured two murders would certainly keep him in for life. He was nevertheless thankful to hear that Jim had not said anything, and was willing to take the proverbial big one of big ones for the Dixie Rehab team.

"I appreciate what you're doing Jim. I promise you I'll take care of your brother and you when you get out. I recently started a bank in the Bahamas with Ronald Dawkins. There are ways that I can get money to you and your family, trust me."

Jim Boudreaux liked the way this sounded. It was all he wanted to hear. He would never turn on Lucci now. All he needed was to see Philip and hear the words—even if they were hollow. He just wanted to see King Philip one more time, to have him acknowledge him for his years of service.

In the end, Boudreaux was another of the many whom Philip successfully used in his conquest. Like a Jim Jones character, Lucci pulled many into his tangled web of power and deceit, and each was in the end, dispensable. Unfortunately for Boudreaux, he, much like the former Dixie CFO's, would do the time while Lucci walked Scott free.

***

On his first day back at work Ron received a call from Detective Swansen.

"Yes Detective. This is Dr. Barton."

"Dr. Barton," I want you to know that I'm talking to the district attorney about prosecuting Mr. Lucci for conspiracy to commit the murders of Dr. Palifax and Amanda."

"He wasn't shooting for Amanda, Detective. They wanted me."

There was silence.

"Well, I'm still charging Lucci with conspiracy to murder Palifax."

"Please do and thanks."

"How's it going?"

"I'm hanging in there, you know?"

Swansen knew he was still all banged up inside.

"Well, look, I think I may be able to convince the D.A. to go after Lucci. Let's wait and see."

"Detective, I appreciate everything you do—thanks."

"Doc, you are welcome. I'll let you know how my meeting goes with the D.A. I'm supposed to see him tomorrow."

"Good enough, Detective."

***

On Tuesday Ron resumed his surgery schedule, which was hectic as a result of delaying four surgeries from the previous week because of Amanda's death and funeral. On his way in to the hospital to get cleaned up for surgery he ran into Leah Thompson, as her office was nearby. They made eye contact and smiled. Ron walked to where she was near the central work area that was like the hub of a wheel, its spokes the connecting hallways.

"Hey Leah."

"Hey, Ron! How are you?"

"I'm okay. Back to work, you know?"

She could tell he was coming around. He looked rested.

"That's great."

Ron was glad to see her. She looked pretty, as usual.

"I've got to get to surgery, but you want to have lunch some time?" He asked, blushing.

Leah blushed. She was thrilled, but it was a bit awkward.

"Sure," she said. "How about Thursday?"

"Surin West?"

"Sounds great. Noon?"

"You're on!" He said.

***

On Wednesday Ron got an early call from Detective Swansen.
"Yes Detective?"
"Good morning Doc."
"Morning."
"I talked to the District Attorney. Apparently Lucci gave him a bunch of cash for his campaigns. He's not going to do anything to him. He's only going to prosecute Boudreaux. I'm sorry, Dr. Barton."

Ron was hurt, but used to it. It was the way things were in Birmingham. It was part of the deal. It was the system; the Alabama way--the pervasive good ole' boy network.

"Detective, I appreciate the call. Thanks for all you've done."
"You're welcome, Doc," said the detective, sounding as defeated as Ron.

***

Ron was beaten down pretty good. Philip Lucci had gotten the best of him for the most part. He was just too rich and powerful to deny. Lucci had threatened his practice, taken the love of his life, an unborn child, cost him a shot at family life and surely in ways he'd not yet fully realized. He felt conquered, as he had little hope for a conviction in Lucci's second trial.

Ron arrived at Surin West at 11:50 a.m. With the help of a greeter he found a window seat with two chairs. Leah arrived seven minutes later. She was all smiles. Ron stood and they embraced. He pulled her chair for her and they were seated.

"Hungry?" Ron asked.
"I am." Leah answered.
"Good. My treat. Get what you want."
"Thanks!"

They got their drinks and ordered.

"What do you think about Lucci's second indictment?" Leah asked.

Ron's blood pressure rose. He took a deep breath.

"I think he'll walk." Ron answered.

"You don't think they have a chance? I read that the trial will be in Montgomery. I doubt if Philip will be able to taint the jury there the way he did in Birmingham. He can't have any ties there like he did here."

"Don't be so sure," Ron quipped. "The guy is resourceful."

"Well, all I know is that they're still the Federal Government. Their success rate is really high. I know the legal experts are saying they don't have a chance to get Lucci and Siegel, but I don't know. Greta Van Sustern on *CNN* said that she thinks Lucci's defense team needs to be careful and take the charges seriously—that anything can happen in Federal court."

"If they couldn't get Lucci on securities fraud I doubt if they get him on bribery. All he did was contribute to Siegel's campaign in return for an appointment. That's done in every state in the union! I want to see Lucci go down as much as anyone, but I just don't think they're going to be able to beat him. He has all that money and legal power."

Leah felt he was so jaded—but with good reason.

"Well, let's just wait and see. Maybe his luck will run out?"

"Yeah, maybe so." Ron said, thinking it would never happen.

Ron stared at Leah.

She noticed.

"Yeah?" She asked.

"Dinner Saturday night?" He asked with a smile.

She grinned and made eyes at him.

He had butterflies.

"Come on, we'll grab a burger and fries somewhere—we'll keep it low key."

He smiled.

She laughed. As sorry as she felt for Amanda, her death was certainly an ill wind that blew well for her.

"Okay, as long as we keep it *low key*," she winked. Her face remained red.

On his way back to work from lunch with Leah Ron felt he'd made Leah feel uneasy by asking her out. Amanda hadn't been gone a week and he was already dating. Trying to avoid guilt, Ron told himself that he and Leah were also good friends, and that he was just lonely and needed her company during what was certainly a difficult time. In reality, he was, but he and Leah were more than friends—they were former lovers.

# 35

Confident that Jim Boudreaux was the consummate team player, Philip Lucci focused on once again reinventing himself. He purchased a local Montgomery television station and a small, 1000-watt AM radio station and began broadcasting his program Perspectives live from Birmingham. Moreover, he began to network with black preachers in Montgomery, hoping to forge relationships that could prove to be helpful when the trial finally occurred. He flew several of them to Birmingham to participate in the program and more importantly—to get a hefty donation check. It was just like before. However, this time Lucci had different legal assistance.

Jim Darkman, the "aw shucks" country bumpkin attorney who had successfully portrayed the Dixie Rehab accounting team as "dirty rats," was no longer around. He took a job with Johnnie Cochran's law firm and was supposedly marrying for the fourth time. He was asked by Lucci to again defend him, but Darkman thanked him and said he wasn't interested.

Ronald Dawkins also received an invitation from Philip to represent him, but Dawkins too declined. He told Philip he was retiring to spend some of the money he'd made clearing Philip's name in the securities fraud trial. Philip begged him, offering more money, but he refused. Dawkins recommended a famous civil rights attorney—the same guy who represented Rosa Parks during the 1960's in Selma, Alabama, Arthur Gray, a man now in his late sixties, and years removed from a successful big case defense. Heading into the trial, Philip was doing so with a much less formidable legal team than he had before. Nonetheless, he was as arrogant as ever when questioned about his chances two weeks out from the trial. In a *Birmingham News* article about the trial through his attorney he gave the following statement:

"As a man of God and a child of God I can only do so much, but what I can do is preach for the truth and to the truth and the truth is the only thing that can truly set you free. This trial will serve as my final vindication. I will be set completely free from the binds of tyranny. God's will shall be done!"

***

Ron and Leah began seeing each other regularly after their first "date" subsequent to Amanda's murder. Ron tried to be disciplined, and to exercise control, but he and Leah began sleeping together after their third date. The two were both lonely, and the way Ron looked at it was that Amanda was gone—she was never coming back. He had to move on. He had to keep living. Furthermore, having Leah in his life again wasn't bad, as their sex life was better than it ever was.

Ron practically moved in with Leah, as he did not want to bring Leah back into the house they once shared and the bed he recently shared with Amanda. He just didn't want to go there. He ordered a new king-sized bed and had he and Amanda's bed moved into the bedroom he used for storage. He was slowly transitioning to the idea of having Leah move in with him again. It was all a slow process for both of them.

***

About a week before Lucci's second trial began Ron got a call from Dr. Troutman of the Alabama Medical Association, the same gentleman who had notified him of his nomination for the award of Outstanding Orthopedist for the State of Alabama. He returned it forthwith.

"Dr. Troutman?"

"Dr. Barton! How are you?"

"Fine, Sir. How can I help you? I understand you called…"

"Yes, yes. I have someone I want you to talk to. He's a successful enterpriser."

Ron wondered where the conversation was going. He said nothing. Troutman continued.

"His name is Dr. Ted Bonner. He is the head of the Alabama State Teacher's Retirement Fund. He is known as a progressive investor of these funds. He's bankrolled a number of business enterprises—like the Robert Trent Jones Golf Trail--that have produced more than handsome returns for the state's retired educators."

Ron had heard of him. Although controversial, he was liked because he got positive results for his investors.

"He wants to buy the digital hospital and he wants you to run the Orthopedic/Sports Medicine Clinic, which was and still is the principal focus of the hospital. He came to me with the idea. He has read your medical articles and he believes strongly in your approach to Orthopedic care—in aggressively prehabbing patients before surgery. He says you fit entirely into his proactive medicine ideal. This is a great opportunity for you Dr. Barton."

Ron was as surprised as he was excited. The concept was his—they wanted to build a digital hospital—toward the end of proactive medicine, which was his approach. Not only would Lucci's dream of a rehab monopoly never be realized, Birmingham health care truly would be revolutionized as a result of Bonner's idea—because he, Ron Barton, would be running it! He had to call him.

"What's his number Dr. Troutman?"

"I'll have him call you, Dr. Barton."

***

Theodore "Ted" Bonner was quite the character among Alabama political circles. As head of the Alabama State Teacher's Retirement System he'd caused quite a stir when early in his tenure he chose the unorthodox route of investing State Teacher's retirement funds outside of the traditional realm of stocks and bonds. The teachers deplored the move, until he returned twenty percent on their principal in two short years. After gaining the teachers as an ally, Bonner cultivated the success into a growing enterprise that spanned three governors, as he was always looking for emerging opportunities. In the Birmingham Digital Hospital he saw just that.

Dr. Bonner called Ron the next day and they talked on the phone for two hours. Ron was amazed at how clever and progressive Dr. Bonner was. Not only did he see the value in promoting proactive wellness, he knew a deal when he saw it.

The investment bankers who had financed the construction of the digital hospital under Lucci filed for bankruptcy on the project, so the unfinished structure was up for grabs at pennies on the dollar. Bonner knew if he could take control of the property with a new, even more cutting-edge plan in place, he'd succeed. It was brilliant because it capitalized on Lucci's idea while adding his own mark in terms of the type of health care that would be delivered. It melded two powerfully progressive ideas into an even greater business model. Ron had never been more excited. However, there was a concern, according to Dr. Bonner.

Philip Lucci was also interested in buying the unfinished digital hospital. No longer affiliated with Dixie Rehab, he was free to engage in the forthcoming bidding process for the property, which was abandoned and dormant for many months in the interim. Bonner felt that if he was soon acquitted in the second trial that Lucci might have the political and media momentum necessary to get back into some form of legitimate business, which was an oxymoron by his standards, but nevertheless a possibility. Moreover, if Lucci was allowed to bid on the property he would be difficult to outbid, as his wealth was staggering. But, if he was convicted, he'd be out of the picture and they'd likely have free reign. Ron could only hope for a conviction.

***

Philip's bribery trial started in Montgomery as scheduled and predictably amidst great media scrutiny. Footage of he and Clara manipulating the steps of the courthouse appeared almost daily on television. Clara wore loose-fitting clothing for the first day of the trial and it was reported shortly after that she was pregnant. It was a ploy by Philip to sway the jury. He shamelessly figured no decent person would want to send the father of a future infant to jail.

From the beginning Philip's second trial was different from the first. The amen corner he successfully created for the first trial—that cadre of supportive black preachers and reverends—factored largely into his acquittal. Philip got through to Birmingham's black religious leaders and their far-reaching influence undoubtedly helped him pull through. In Montgomery, Philip didn't have the necessary time to peddle and buy the genuine influence and power he needed for an acquittal. Furthermore, in Montgomery, some of the black leaders weren't as easily bought as their Birmingham counterparts.

One such Montgomery pastor was Margenius Moore. Margenius was the pastor of the Earthly Bounds Church. He received a call from Lucci's television production team. They wanted him to fly to Birmingham to be on the television program and to accept in a photo opportunity a donation to his church. Moore was incensed. He had watched with great pain Lucci use the black Birmingham pastors like *Kleenex*. He was intent on making sure Montgomery's black community wouldn't be similarly abused for the political gain of what he deemed a "white devil."

Three days into the trial Moore called a press conference and openly deplored Lucci's overt efforts to taint the Montgomery jury pool with what he said were "slave wages tantamount to bribes." The backlash was harsh, spawning a fiery debate in the Montgomery newspapers and radio talk shows.

The general consensus by the state capital community was that Lucci was a clever opportunist that had duped a city in Birmingham that did not want to believe their favorite son was a charlatan. The tenor was that they didn't want to be similarly fooled and subsequently ridiculed. Much was at stake for their community. Lucci's defense team was rightfully concerned heading into trial.

The prosecution was clear in their portrayal of Lucci and Siegel. According to the U.S. Government, both men broke the law when they arranged for the sale of the appointment to the Certificate of Need Board, because it comprised an illegal bribe—a clear-cut quid pro quo arrangement.

Siegel's counsel insisted that the arrangement was a normal political practice—honored even by the office of the President of the United States. They argued that former Republican Governor Rob James was also guilty of it, as many of his former supporters were still holding their purchased positions. In the end they creatively called the entire case a "vast, right-wing conspiracy" in a weak attempt to link Siegel's real troubles to politics.

Apparently Lucci's attorneys did not want to argue the bribery charges against their client. They instead painted him to be a Civil Rights activist, playing to the majority black jury of seven blacks and five whites, the identical racial composition of the first jury trial.

During the months leading to the trial Lucci made numerous church appearances throughout the Montgomery area, each time talking to the congregations about how when he was a young boy his father took him to the Edmund Pettus Bridge in Selma, Alabama and explained to him that racism was bad, and that he should mature to make a difference for black people. It was at that point that he would present a huge check to the pastor. This ploy was repeated often two and three times each Sunday morning and afternoon.

Before Lucci's two black attorneys addressed the jury for the first time, two black assistants—young ladies in their early twenties, dressed in pretty dresses, placed a portrait of Martin Luther King on an easel before the jury gallery. Each of the men in their repeated presentations to the jury played the race card heavier than in the first trial. It seemed they strangely made the entire case about race.

Lucci's lead attorney, the legendary Civil Rights lawyer, Arthur Gray, distilled his entire defense to the imploring line, "Fulfill Martin Luther King's unfinished business—acquit Mr. Lucci, his disciple, and allow his great humanitarian works to continue. Make him free and we will all be free—free at last, free at last, God almighty we'll be free at last!"

In the end, it was overkill, and the jury didn't take the bait like the Birmingham jury did the first time. They deliberated for only two hours before rendering a verdict. The foreman, an Auburn graduate, read the group's decision.

"Guilty, your Honor."

Ultimately Lucci and Siegel were found guilty on bribery, conspiracy and fraud, fortunately evading conviction on many other charges. However, they would definitely do time. The two stunned men left the courtroom with Federal Guilty Judgments against them. For the meantime, they were free to go. Their lawyers explained to them that their prison sentencing would occur at a later-determined date.

# 36

Ron and Leah were ecstatic, as were the rest of Birmingham and Dixie Rehab employees and shareholders everywhere. The judgment day they and countless others had long-waited for had finally come. Philip Lucci was going to jail. It was surreal. Ron heard the news when Amelia screamed at the top of her lungs the verdict to everyone in the office. Ron was between patients. He ran to his office and viewed breaking news on his television. He picked up the phone and called Leah and set a dinner date for the *Highlands*.

At the restaurant that night Ron and Leah celebrated not only Lucci's conviction, but also the fact that Leah was pregnant. Ron couldn't believe it. He was ecstatic, although he realized he needed to plan another shotgun wedding. He was truly happy, as was Leah. They talked about marriage and Ron decided that they should marry in Fairhope, in a church—pregnant and all.

A few weeks later the couple was married by a minister in a small ceremony at the Fairhope Unitarian Fellowship, before their parents and a few close friends. Seven months later, a baby girl, Eliza Meredith Barton, was born at UAB Hospital. Mom and dad were proud and happy, as were Ron's parents, who had waited so long to experience the joy of being grandparents. Ron and Leah moved into his house and made a home for Eliza.

Two weeks before Philip Lucci's sentencing hearing before a Federal Judge in Montgomery, Dr. Bonner closed on the purchase of the digital hospital where Dr. Ron Barton would eventually work. Ron couldn't believe it. In spite of all that had happened everything seemed to be working out fine for him after all. He was excited about his future at what Dr. Bonner told him would be called "The Professional Bone Clinic of Birmingham."

The day after Dr. Bonner bought the unfinished hospital Flo Thompson appeared on the cover of the *USA Today* Sports Page. The title above a picture of him soloing over left field read, "Flo Knew He'd Be Back." The article told about Flo's unlikely comeback and how his miracle medical tandem in Birmingham gave him a fighting chance to compete again in the show. Ron's phone rang off of the hook for speaking and radio appearances. *The Sporting News* was also doing a Flo piece, and needed quotes. It was fabulous publicity. Ron's name and associated expertise had never been bigger, and the national recognition was equally fantastic for his badly damaged psyche and heavy heart. He had been through so much, but like always, he'd fought back and had never given up. Now, he was on top, and it was Philip Lucci who was instead facing great difficulty.

***

In the months following his conviction, Philip's whereabouts were strictly monitored by the Feds. Everywhere he went out of the city or state had to be pre-approved by the Federal agents assigned to monitor his location.

During this time Philip planned a family vacation to *Disney World* in Orlando. The trip was approved. However, once in Orlando at his pre-approved resort, Philip took his family and drove to Miami, where they boarded his yacht, "Chez Partay" and cruised around the tip of Florida instead. This recalcitrance by Philip was not taken lightly. Federal agents reported to the judge that Philip had violated his travel agreement and he was thereafter considered a serious flight risk. Agents arrived at Philip's house immediately following the judge's order and fitted him with an irremovable GPS ankle bracelet.

Following the day he was fixed with an ankle bracelet, Philip read in the news that the Alabama Supreme Court ordered him to repay

$65 million in bonuses he wrongly received while Dixie Rehab was actually losing money. Nevertheless, it was just a precursor of what was to come.

On the day before his sentencing, Philip Lucci met with Clara, his young wife, and the mother of his youngest child. They sat in their massive backyard, amidst Italian fountain works, lush landscaping and an ever-changing assortment of concrete ponds stocked with Japanese goldfish. Their four-month old, Zachariah, napped on a nearby blanket.

"Clara, I'm going to be going away for a while. You need to know some things about our finances."

Clara perked up.

"Alright."

"You have access to our checking account. You have enough there to take care of all you will need while I am away. I will remain in control of all of my business assets, as well as my overseas holdings and investments, from prison. I don't know how long I'll get, but I'll soon be out and we'll pick up again at that time. Until then, take care of the kids and the house. Don't worry about everything else. Forget about all the other properties. I'll manage that. Just take care of the house and kids, okay?"

"How much is in our checking account?"

Philip twitched.

"As of this morning?"

She nodded.

"Ten million."

\*\*\*

Former Alabama Governor, Democrat Don Siegel, and Philip Lucci stood side-by-side before the Federal sentencing judge. Each man wore an expensive suit. Each had family members present. Each was given a chance to speak.

The Judge prompted Philip.

"Mr. Lucci, you have the floor."

Philip cleared his throat and injected the kind of enthusiasm he'd used to become a multi-millionaire salesman and pitchman.

"Your Honor, as a civic leader and CEO of the company, I felt it was Dixie Rehab's responsibility—our civic duty—to donate to the Alabama Lottery Campaign. We want Alabama to have the best education system money can buy."

Philip paused, then continued. His tone changed.

"I'm a man who loves God, who loves his country, who loves his family. God is my life."

Philip started to become emotional. He seemed off-track.

"If I am truly guilty of this, then every other person in public office had better look out! This is all a right-wing conspiracy!" He yelled.

The judge admonished Philip.

"Mr. Lucci! That is unacceptable! No more outbursts! Please use a civil tone!"

"Yes, your Honor. I apologize."

Philip straightened up. He lowered his tone.

"There is no evidence to tie me to these charges. It is sad this could happen in the United States of America!"

Siegel followed Philip with a diatribe of how the entire ordeal was politically-driven and that he would be vindicated in the Alabama Court of Appeals.

After each man spoke the presiding judge read each man's sentence.

Philip, who was 54, was ordered to pay a $250,000 fine and received seven years in the Federal penitentiary. Dan Siegel, who was 51, was also given a stiff fine of $200,000 and received eight years. Furthermore, both men were forced to make restitution payments of $100,000 to the United Way and to pay for their entire incarceration—which totaled $2,156 monthly.

While it was not a full measure of justice—the CEO's of Worldcom and Tyco had received sentences many times longer than Philip—it was nonetheless a measure. King Philip was headed to prison.

When the judge finished rendering the sentences Clara screamed and began crying. Dan Siegel's family loudly wept. Armed guards descended on Lucci and placed leg irons on his ankles. Two tall, husky men led him and Siegel away. Siegel went silently. Philip began crying.

"I am innocent!" Philip screamed as he was led into the detention area behind the courtroom. "This is not right! I am an innocent man!"

Neither man was allowed to talk to or see loved ones. Convicted and sentenced by the United States Government, they were no longer free.

***

Baron Screem ended up serving a total of 180 days in prison. After his release he returned to his wife, who found a home in Silver Hill, Alabama after selling all of their assets to pay legal bills and fines. He started a lawn care service called "Baron Landscape & Garden," and became an avid arborist.

Will Bowen was given a surprising five years in the same prison as Philip. Weston White, the other testifying CFO, got 18 months in a separate facility.

Multiple class-action lawsuits totaling in the billions of dollars were filed by disgruntled employees and stockholders of Dixie Rehab against Philip Lucci for the massive fraud he perpetuated. All suing parties made it clear that they wanted Philip Lucci's assets, both movable and immovable. Attorneys representing the multiple plaintiffs made it clear that all ill-gotten gains were being sought. "We will seek to find and confiscate every last penny," said one lawyer representing the action.

Jim Boudreaux got life for the murders of Dr. Jim Palifax and Amanda Barton. When he was sentenced the judge told him he'd be eligible for parole in 2038.

Mack Dawkins ran off to the Bahamas with Chastity Jones where he opened a small jet ski business on the beach. Chastity worked with him, attracting potential customers for Jim while also selling hair-braiding services to tourists.

***

When it was finally over, after the image of Philip Lucci being led away in leg irons, kicking and screaming, faded from his short-term memory banks, Ron Barton thought about all that had happened. He thought about how he and his life had changed immeasurably as a result of Philip Lucci.

He had waged war with a narcissistic, sociopathic maniac and somehow survived. However, had he won? Amanda certainly had not. His career had taken a hit, and then taken off; but so much had happened. He felt older. The last two years seemed like ten.

Ron thought ahead and how as long as Lucci was behind bars things would be fine. Nevertheless, he knew that Lucci, barring any further indictments and subsequent convictions, would soon be free. Seven years wasn't that much time. Ron could only wonder what Lucci was capable of doing when his release came, if he would still have money left, if he would still hold a grudge.

For now, Ron Barton was going to enjoy his infant daughter and wife, and a challenging, ever-changing medical career. All that he ever wanted he'd somehow found, by the hardest. Life for now was good.

Nevertheless, for Dr. Ron Barton, the not-too-distant future remained a disturbing mystery; one altogether concerning as Philip Lucci's already far-reaching impact on confidence in American free enterprise capitalism.

## The End.

# About the Author

Chris Warner is the author of thirteen books, including "The Tiger Among Us," an international terrorism novel set at Louisiana State University in 1990. He holds a doctorate from the University of New Orleans and lives in Fairhope, Alabama.

If you enjoyed Professional Bone by Chris Warner, you may also enjoy, "The Wagon to Disaster," by Aaron Beam, former HealthSouth CFO, with Chris Warner.

## The Wagon to Disaster
*Wagon Publishing*
*Copyright 2009*

It was the quintessential American success story: Identify a niche; form a company to exploit it; raise millions in venture capital; take the concept public; meet stockholder expectations for 40 straight quarters, in the process becoming a darling of Wall Street; and of course make money—plenty of it—while the stock price steadily climbs and revenue projections increase. In a few short years you've gone from rags to riches...you're on a monster roll...

Until your boss, saddled with the realization that the Street expectations cannot realistically be met, asks you to creatively "fix the numbers." It's the toughest decision you've ever made, and one where the easiest way out could be the most difficult, given the circumstances.

Caught squarely between greed and fear, Aaron Beam did the unthinkable.

Corporate greed is the Black Plague of the modern financial world—threatening America's ability to maintain free market capitalism in an increasingly distrusting, changing, and socialistic world economy.

*The Wagon to Disaster*, told by former co-founder and CFO Aaron Beam, is the untold story of HealthSouth, one of America's most successful health care companies and consequently, the perpetrator of one of its biggest frauds in history. How big was the fraud? In 2003, just before news of the crime broke in the mainstream media, HealthSouth paid more money in taxes to the Federal Government than it legitimately earned the previous year.

Beam takes the reader from HealthSouth's humble beginnings, through its meteoric rise and to its disastrous revelation, subsequent trial and his three-month incarceration in a Federal prison. Moreover, he reveals the nature of the fraud and the true personality of the driving force behind HealthSouth—Richard Marin Scrushy, one of the most enigmatic and nefarious characters the State of Alabama has ever produced—a hard-charging, unscrupulous visionary whose caustic, Machiavellian approach ensured HealthSouth's success, and oddly, his predictable fall as the company's benevolent dictator.

***